A Desirable Energy Future

A National Perspective

Robert S. Livingston
Truman D. Anderson
Theodore M. Besmann
Mitchell Olszewski
Alfred M. Perry
Colin D. West

*of Oak Ridge National Laboratory,
Oak Ridge, Tennessee*

THE FRANKLIN INSTITUTE PRESS

© 1982
THE FRANKLIN INSTITUTE PRESS^{SM}
Philadelphia, Pennsylvania

Current printing (last digit):
5 4 3 2 1
ISBN Number: 0-89168-045-4
Library of Congress Catalog Card Number: 82-1525
Printed in the United States of America.

PREFACE

When we started the ORNL National Energy Perspective (ONEP) Project in the summer of 1979, we were not completely confident that anyone could benefit from another energy study. After all, the first "energy crisis" of 1973-74 had been followed by a very large number of energy studies by government, universities, and private groups. However, even with these studies—some say, because of them—there seemed to be no national consensus about our essential energy problems, about the appropriate policies and programs to deal with these problems, or about the role of energy research and development. The last point was of particular concern for a research-and-development institution like Oak Ridge National Laboratory. Thus our goal was to develop an independent perspective for the planning of energy research and development.

During the course of this work we examined many previous energy studies for their relevant data, analyses, and insights. These studies, which include the Dixy Lee Ray report* of 1973, ERDA-48** in 1975, the second National Energy Plan† (NEP-II), and the three energy studies†† published in the summer of 1979, provided a good starting point for the task.

---

*D. L. Ray, *The Nation's Energy Future*, WASH-1281, US Atomic Energy Commission (December 1973).

**R. C. Seamans, Jr., *A National Plan for Energy Research, Development and Demonstration: Creating Energy Choices for the Future. Volume I: The Plan*, ERDA-48, US Energy Research and Development Administration (June 1975).

†US Department of Energy, *National Energy Plan II*, Washington, DC (May 7, 1979).

††H. H. Landsberg, *Energy: The Next Twenty Years*, sponsored by the Ford Foundation, administered by Resources for the Future, Ballinger Publishing Co., Cambridge, MA, 1979.

S. H. Schurr et al, *Energy in America's Future: The Choices Before Us*, RFF National Energy Strategies Project, Johns Hopkins University, Baltimore, MD, 1979.

Roger Stobaugh and Daniel Yergin, editors, *Energy Future: Report of the Energy Project at the Harvard Business School*, Random House, Inc., New York, 1979.

In addition to the authors, many people within the Laboratory contributed by preparing background papers on more than 20 topics. This broad participation does not imply, however, that this study represents a consensus about energy within Oak Ridge National Laboratory. Neither does the study represent an institutional position on energy.

This book is a unique departure from previous studies which typically attempt to predict the future or bemoan the obstacles which prevent the continuation of the established trend of growth in the standard of living. The desirable future described in this book includes continued economic growth at a level similar to that experienced by the U.S. over the last seventy years. It involves the continuation of personal freedom as embodied in the automobile and it means a continuation of established trends in housing. Such a desirable future allows for fulfillment of economic aspirations and the maintenance of lifestyles as a matter of choice.

This study asserts that there is no energy *crisis*, but rather a set of energy *problems*. Many of the energy problems the U.S. faces are important, but all are not equally important. The acceptance of this point alone can do much to ease the great confusion which is evident in governmental attempts to deal with energy issues. The most urgent, and by far the most significant, of the problems is the vulnerability of the nation to foreign oil exporters. The threat of an oil cutoff has reduced the nation's ability and willingness to act independently in its own best interests in either the domestic or international arena. It continues to affect the economy significantly and, most importantly, threatens international peace and stability. With a focus on vulnerability as the most urgent short-term energy problem, the book clarifies energy policy needs and indicates the courses of action they implicitly dictate.

The study demonstrates that oil imports can be reduced to less than 20% of oil demand by the end of the century, and that this level is sufficiently low that a cutoff of supply from a significant oil-producing area of the world would not gravely affect the U.S. It also concludes that the cost of energy service need not be higher than the price the nation is paying at present. Further, the necessary tasks can be, and must be, accomplished with demonstrated technologies or reasonable extrapolations of them, since developing technologies will not become widely available within the necessary time frame. All this can be achieved with a modest increase in investment relative to that required if the nation continues on its present path.

In the next two decades major changes need to be made on both the demand and supply sides of energy. This will require a combination of oil production, conservation and substitution. The substitution of other fuels for oil is a particularly valuable and rapid means for decreasing oil demand. Direct coal burning or electricity generated by coal, uranium, or hydropower, can supplant oil and natural gas use in many areas. Natural gas thus freed would be available to substitute for oil in applications where other fuels are not practical. The combined potential for cost-effective substitution approximately equals our recent oil import levels.

The Oak Ridge study describes a number of necessary actions the nation must take by the turn of the century. The fuel efficiency of the automobile fleet must approximately double, and the thermal efficiency of homes must be improved by over one-third. Oil and gas use for base-and intermediate-load power generation must be phased out. This will require that certain utilities be almost completely rebuilt. Synfuel and oil shale industries will need to be developed with the capability to produce at least six million barrels (oil equivalent) per day of gas and oil. The electric power generating capacity of the country will need to be increased by a factor of two or three, and coal production will need to be increased by up to a factor of three, even with near maximum utilization of nuclear power.

The role of nuclear power, therefore, becomes clear. It is an economical means of generating electricity which can be inexhaustible with the widescale application of breeder reactors. Its use can decrease the pressure on coal mining for electrical generating plants and allow production to be devoted to synfuels. The various solar and geophysical sources will also play an important role, most often by decreasing demand for purchased energy through the use of passive solar techniques and the utilization of waste materials. Many of these actions are already economical at today's oil prices, and all are attractive if the expected trend in oil price increases is realized.

One of the major reasons for the increasingly poor position the U.S. has found itself in over the past few years lies in the difficulty it has experienced in making and implementing decisions of national significance. The traditional mechanisms are failing due to the ability of groups across the whole ideological spectrum to halt or indefinitely suspend needed projects. This study, therefore, outlines a range of methods for making effective decisions ranging from improving information credibility, to compensation for impacts or increased risks, to institutional changes.

Provided the U.S. solves its oil import problem by the end of the century, the longer-term problem emerges as one which is not new—that of supplying adequate energy supplies at the lowest economic, environmental, and social cost. The actions recommended for the short term are consistent with this goal; they too offer movement away from limited resources toward very long-term or inexhaustible resources. The urgent energy issues in this time frame, however, are global in nature. The developing nations have traditionally had to rely on oil for power because of the low capital required for its use. Continued growth in demand for oil, however, will cause a shortfall in supply around the turn of the century, and the extreme prices which will result could cripple these nations' development. Coupled with the steady increase in population in these countries, such a situation can only lead to catastrophe. Thus the course the U.S., and perhaps the rest of the developed world, takes to minimize its oil imports can be expected to forestall these events; it can allow the developing countries to use the available oil to strengthen their economies so that they too will be able to make the transition to energy sources other than conventional oil and natural gas. The development of a substantial industry in synfuels and shale oil in the developed world may allow these nations to export excess fuel, thus easing the energy market further.

Energy research and development can play an important supporting role, although not a central one, in solving the oil import problem over the next twenty years. Beyond that, research and development's role of producing cheaper, better, easier ways of providing energy will be of essential importance over the longer term.

The energy future of the United States is not bleak; it is whatever the country decides it should be. This nation has the resources, the technology, and the ability to become sufficiently independent of foreign oil by the end of the century, and it is in the national interest as well as in the interest of the entire world that it do so. This will require the commitment of substantial, but not unreasonable, amounts of the country's resources and an ability to make decisions and see them through. The ultimate goal is for the U.S. to become an exporter of energy goods and technologies, which will help maintain peace and stability in the world and will continue the tradition of the nation as a world leader in the marketplace.

CONTENTS

Preface i

Introduction 1

Chapter I. Overview 7

Chapter II. The Energy Problem 15

Chapter III. Elements of Future Strategies 47

Chapter IV. National Energy Issues—Energy Service And Supply .. 155

Chapter V. Broad National Energy Strategy 207

References 221

Appendix A. The Role of Research and Development 235

Appendix B. Overview Papers 249

Appendix C. Definitions, Standards, Abbreviations, and Units ... 251

INTRODUCTION

The Nature of the Study

Success in human endeavor, while sometimes the result of chance or improvisation, usually results from the determined pursuit of a specific goal. This should be the case with energy in the United States and the world. Although the energy future remains largely uncertain, we feel that should not deter us from describing the future that appears desirable and starting to work toward it. Our judgement is that the national focus should be not on forecasting or predicting the future, but rather on shaping it. Thus we define a desirable future and then determine what the nation needs to actualize that future.

National Goals. In providing a framework for assessing the nation's energy problem and potential solutions, we defined the following set of national aims:

- Maintain a relationship with the rest of the world that improves its well-being, contributes to international stability, and leaves the United States free to follow relatively independent policies;
- Provide for future U.S. energy needs so that economic aspirations can be fulfilled and lifestyles can remain a matter of choice;
- Maintain and evolve institutions that allow citizen participation in decision making; and
- Ensure that benefits and costs are distributed fairly in U.S. society.

These objectives are similar in scope and meaning to those contained in previous energy studies, particularly NEP-II and ERDA-48.

Desirable Future. In contemplating a desirable future, many people might think of a pleasant home; a good job; a beautiful countryside; a bustling economy; a vacation at an uncrowded beach or mountain resort; fresh air; convenient shopping; abundant pure water, all at affordable prices. Needless to say the desirable future in this energy re-

1

port is hardly defined in such romantic terms. The more quantitative and mundane definition used here could, however, include all of the above and much more. Our desirable future includes a per capita GNP growth rate in the range of 2% per year, which would maintain or increase our present level of amenities. Adequate energy is needed to make this future possible. In addition, our country must be strong, independent, and free to follow policies that contribute to international peace and security.

Health, Safety, and the Environment. We have carefully considered the health and safety impacts and the environmental consequences of all energy sources, especially those that have been a major concern to some individuals and groups, (e.g., coal, oil shale, and nuclear power). While preservation of the environment should not be an overriding objective in itself, it nevertheless should be one of the important requirements—in addition to resource sustainability and technology cost-effectiveness—that each energy activity must meet. In addition, we feel that more emphasis should be placed on protecting *human* health and safety as compared to the current emphasis on environmental protection.

Research and Development. This report deals primarily with analysis of the energy system and with energy policy. It does not deal with energy R&D except for a brief compilation of research opportunities (in Appendix A). The whole purpose of this report, however, is to lay a foundation that will enable Oak Ridge National Laboratory to establish sound priorities in research and development. Establishing such a network of research and development judgements will be the subject of a follow-up study based on the energy policy and analysis laid out in the following chapters. Although we found it necessary to separate these studies, we feel very strongly that the world's energy future beyond the turn of the century depends upon completing vigorous and successful research by the time it is needed.

Elements of an Energy Program. In the course of developing an energy perspective, we have analyzed both quantitatively and qualitatively the many aspects of energy demand and supply. In performing these analyses we attempted to assess objectively the potential of each energy option for solving specific aspects of the energy problem. We did not begin the analysis with a prejudice for either the ''hard'' or ''soft'' paths.* Rather, each option was examined for its cost-effectiveness (including, where possible, environmental and social costs) and for which

---

*The ''hard'' path is characterized by large, centralized supply facilities that use technological energy production (e.g., nuclear and coal energy systems); the ''soft'' path is

aspect of the energy problem it addressed. Then, based on our belief that the solution to today's energy problems begins with today's technologies, we developed an energy strategy. The strategy emphasizes options that we found to be cost-effective and that focus primarily on critical near-term aspects of the energy problem.

Fervor and Energy. Today's energy scene in the United States includes the promotion of many single issues. Energy activism has become the work of professionals** and is often pursued with a fervor—akin to religious zeal—that is based on the proposition that if a certain focus is adopted, the problems of the nation will be largely (and easily, and quickly) solved. This attitude is found in some of the most enthusiastic and least thoughtful supporters of, say, solar energy, breeder reactors, or even conservation. Such promotions exert significant leverage on public attitudes and political decision making. The analyses in this report are not based on such a simplistic view of energy problems.

Primary Energy. † It has become fashionable in recent times, especially among advocates of "low energy futures," to focus attention on primary energy. This approach tends to treat conservation as a social objective in and of itself and results in a unit of energy from uranium or coal being valued the same as a unit of energy from oil or gas. This preoccupation with primary energy can have unfortunate consequences, such as reducing primary energy demands by substituting imported energy (particularly refined petroleum products) for domestic resources that require conversion (e.g., electricity or oil from coal). Because of the shortcomings of this point of view, we examined conservation from the standpoint of the cost-effectiveness of energy service. Thus the goal of conservation in this report is to provide equilvalent energy service at a lower cost. Using this approach, primary energy demand is an outcome of the analysis, not a constrained input.

---

characterized by energy conservation and by small, dispersed energy generation (e.g., decentralized solar, wind, and wood fuel).

**The media identifies these professionals as public interest groups, special interest groups, concerned citizens, intervenors, consumerists, litigators, antinukes, pronukes, nukes, advocacy groups, militants, adversaries, activist lawyers, and public relations professionals.

†Primary energy is the source of energy used to change the form of energy (e.g., to generate electricity or to operate a refinery). End-use energy is the energy used by the consumer, (e.g., electricity to run a refrigerator or heat pump, gasoline to fuel an automobile, or natural gas to operate a furnace). (Note that natural gas or heating oil can be either a primary fuel or an end-use fuel depending on the specific application.)

Recent Energy Trends

The analyses detailed in this study are based primarily on 1978 energy production and consumption data. Statistics for 1979 and 1980, however, exhibited some noteworthy departures from recent historical trends in these areas. Therefore we examined this period in some detail to determine whether these sudden changes fundamentally affect any of the conclusions reached in the study. In 1979 total energy consumption in the U.S. was 83.3 EJ (79.0 quad).* In 1980 it declined by 3.5% to 80.4 EJ (76.2 quad). During the same period oil imports declined by almost 20%, falling from 18.7 EJ/year (8.5 million bbl/d) to 15.0 EJ/year (6.8 million bbl/d). Also, the energy consumption per GNP dollar fell to 54.3 MJ/dollar (51,500 Btu/dollar) in 1980, a drop of 3.2% from 1979. This decline was far greater than the average decline since 1973 of 2% per year (U.S. Department of Energy, 1981).

On the surface these statistics seem encouraging. The energy intensity of the U.S. economy is falling, total energy consumption is declining, and oil imports are rapidly decreasing. However, the underlying causes of these declines are not heartening. The prime cause of the decline in total energy consumption, for instance, was a stagnant economy. The GNP for 1979 was $1.483 trillion (1872 dollars). In 1980 it was $1.481 trillion (1972 dollars). During the same 1979–1980 period, the industrial production index fell by 3.5% (U.S. Council of Economic Advisors, 1981). If, for example, the GNP had grown at a healthy 3% per year, total energy consumption would have been 82.9 EJ (78.6 quad). An additional 2.4 EJ/year (1.1 million bbl/d) of imported oil would have been required to meet the increased demand, raising the total oil import figure to 17.4 EJ/year (7.9 million bbl/d.) Thus oil imports would have declined only 7% during this period, instead of 20%.

It is also evident that much of the decline in energy intensity is due not to energy efficiency improvements, but to curtailed consumer activity (e.g., fewer automobile miles driven, lower thermostats in homes). An analysis by Marlay (1981) indicates that "behavioral actions of a curtailment nature have dominated the residential sector's market response" and were responsible for as much as 80% of the energy intensity decreases realized since 1973. Similar trends are present in the industrial sector, as well. In the transportation sector, statistics indicate that average fuel economy increased only about 8% between 1978 and 1980, while the number of miles driven per vehicle decreased by almost

---

*Exajoule (EJ) is a metric system unit of energy approximately equivalent to a quad(10^{15} Btu): 1 EJ (10^{18} joules) equals 0.9479 quads.

9% (U.S. Department of Energy, 1981; Energy and Environmental Analysis, Inc., 1981). Once again, most of the energy saving has come from decreased activity rather than improved efficiency.

Indeed, oil imports, energy consumption, and the energy intensity of the U.S. economy are all diminishing. However, the major causes for these trends are a stagnant economy and a curtailment of consumer activity. Both of these factors defy this study's fundamental goals of sustained economic growth and continued freedom of choice of lifestyles. We therefore conclude that these recent energy trends, for the most part, reflect negative effects and do not alter the basic conclusion of our study: that obtaining a desirable energy future will require strong direction and a substantial commitment of resources to enhance energy supplies and efficiency.

The Book

As described, *A Desirable Energy Future* defines an attractive future and describes measures for reaching it. The first chapter presents a general qualitative overview of energy in the world, followed by a description of the findings of the study.

Chapter II, "The Energy Problem," contains analyses of the historical role of energy in the world and in the United States. It describes the recent enormous growth in oil use and relates this growth to national and global oil supplies and other energy resources. As the patterns of fuel usage and resource availability are made apparent, the immediate and longer-term energy problems of both the United States and the world become evident. Finally, the chapter describes the constraints to solving the problems due to the time lag in energy system changeovers, social and institutional difficulties, and the linkages between our energy economy and those of other nations.

With the energy problems defined, we begin to examine our options. This is the subject of Chapter III, "Elements of Future Energy Strategies," which initially describes a broad approach to solving the short-term oil import problem. Then technical choices for increasing oil production, conserving oil, and substituting other, domestic energy resources for oil are discussed in some detail.

Along with the technical measures, we outline a number of social and political actions that might prove effective in reducing U.S. vulnerability to foreign oil producers. Looking beyond the next few decades, this chapter describes approaches for resolving long-term and global energy issues. A final section recognizes the difficulties in making and implementing necessary national decisions, and a good deal of discussion is devoted to methods for resolving this problem.

With the energy problem and the available options clearly stated, the stage is set for defining both the levels of energy demand required to secure a desirable future and the means for providing that energy. These levels and means are explained in Chapter IV, "National Energy Issues—Energy Service and Supply." Projections of population growth and desirable levels of GNP, along with assumptions about how we will use energy, combine to yield energy demands from the various sectors of the economy. The potential supplies are then matched with the demand to obtain ranges of energy use over the period 1980 to 2020. Factored in, of course, is the aim of decreasing our oil imports to a level of no more than 20% of consumption. Concluding the chapter, we compare this work with two other recent and major energy studies, the CONAES study (Brooks, et al, 1979) and ORNL's *Rational Energy Use* study (Pine, et al, 1981), and emphasize the different underlying assumptions of the three.

The path we see for the United States is laid out in the final chapter, "A Broad National Energy Strategy." We first describe a framework for the strategy, including the twin goals of avoiding vulnerability and of achieving the necessary GNP growth rate. We then describe the specific actions required to reduce our vulnerability to cutoffs of imported oil. These include recommendations for emergency planning, fuel substitutions, increasing efficiency, and expanding the domestic production of liquid fuels. Also included are a summary of the policy implications and a description of what has been accomplished thus far. The second major theme of the chapter is meeting longer-term energy needs at acceptable costs (economic, social, and environmental). We emphasize the need for remaining flexible, so that unexpected constraints on one supply option do not create unduly negative impacts.

I. OVERVIEW

During the first half of the twentieth century, the United States had an abundant supply of energy at a reasonable price. Questions about the future were raised occasionally, but they generated no sustained national interest because ample supplies of inexpensive fossil fuels continued to be discovered. The development of a new source of power—nuclear energy—arose partly from a desire for a constructive use of the atom and for cheaper energy, as well as from long-term concerns about the availability of other energy resources.

During the 1950s and 1960s, however, the growing U.S. dependence on imported oil was already a matter of concern to some. The oil embargo of 1973–74 validated these fears and stunned Americans into believing, at least temporarily, that a major energy crisis was at hand. More recently, events in Iran and elsewhere have again aroused national concern and provoked confusion. This confusion is such that we feel it necessary to seek an answer to the question: What is our energy crisis? This study, as developed in Chapter II, leads to the following conclusion: our energy crisis consists of a set of energy problems that must be overcome.

All these problems are important, or potentially important, but all are not equally urgent. Acceptance of this point can do much to ease the confusion. The most immediate and pressing problem is the vulnerability of the United States to the interruption of foreign oil supplies. This vulnerability is recognized by the members of the Organization of Petroleum Exporting Countries (OPEC) and by the United States alike. Consequently, the threat of an oil shutoff reduces our ability to act independently in our own best interests, both in international and domestic affairs. The real strategic lesson of 1973–74 was the national disruption resulting from the oil embargo, not the economic stresses associated with the price increases.

Beyond this short-term, national situation lies a different problem. World energy use increased from just over 100 EJ in 1956 to almost 300 EJ in 1976. Three-quarters of this tremendous increase was provided by oil and natural gas. Contrary to the impression created by many energy spokesmen, almost all of the increase (80%) took place outside the

United States. This is a positive trend since it has allowed most of the developing countries to survive, without reductions in their standard of living and despite the huge increases in their populations over the same period. Some of these countries (especially those in Southeast Asia and South America) have been able to make real gains in national and personal prosperity.

An expanding population, which is characteristic of the developing countries, is heavily weighted with younger age groups and contains a high proportion of women who are or will be of childbearing age. As a result, even if population control programs are fairly successful and the number of births per family is considerably reduced in the future, the world population will continue to increase for some time. By the middle of the twenty-first century, there may well be 9 billion people in the world—about double the present number. This is a frightening figure, although it corresponds to an average growth rate of only 1% per year and would, if achieved, represent a major success for the population control efforts of the developing countries.

These people need adequate food, and we hope that they can achieve a better standard of living than is currently available in the developing countries. Efficient agriculture, crop storage, and food distribution, however, are all energy-intensive activities. Unlike the U.S., the developing countries cannot easily reduce their energy consumption. Although most American homes could, for instance, offer a high degree of comfort with a much reduced energy consumption, the same is most emphatically not true of the dwelling places of the world's poor—and these far outnumber U.S. homes. Similarly, energy consumption will have to increase as industrial activity increases: even efficient industrial processes use more energy than no industrial processes at all. Thus, if living standards are to be improved worldwide, energy use must grow even faster than population.

As long as oil and gas are readily available, their relatively low capital costs at the point of use will make them the fuels of choice for developing countries. The market for natural petroleum products will continue to grow. Not to use oil and gas for as long as they are readily available would be an act of irresponsibility and inhumanity on the part of those governments struggling to provide for poor, expanding populations. At the current rate of consumption, known world oil reserves will last for perhaps 40 years and gas reserves for about 150 years, but with consumption increasing by 6 to 7% each year, even the gas reserves would be consumed in less than 40 years.

The broad path of the world's energy future therefore becomes clear: Barring a catastrophe that reduces world population, the readily available, inexpensive supplies of natural gas and oil will be severely depleted well before the middle of the next century. By that time world energy demand will have increased severalfold, even with very extensive conservation measures. Much of that increase will come in the developing nations of the world.

Beyond the beginning of the twenty-first century, then, sufficient energy for the increasing world demand must be provided while reliance on natural gas and oil is sharply decreased. This should be accomplished at a minimum cost to society (including environmental and social costs), but it should be remembered that a substantial energy shortfall would itself cause great human suffering and misery.

We hope to see a greatly expanded world energy supply system so that this expanding population can be well fed and comfortable. However, the amount of energy needed cannot come from the same resource base as it has for the last few decades, and therefore we must make a transition from our present situation—in which growth in demand has been met largely by natural oil and gas—to one in which more plentiful, or even renewable, resources are used to provide most of the energy. These large, long-term resources include coal and uranium and may also include light elements, in fusion reactors, and solar power. Again, the choices between these resources should be made on the grounds of technical feasibility and at minimal cost to society. An additional factor to consider is the restraining influence of institutional or social structures. In some cases, these structures (e.g., litigious groups) can effectively act to prevent the adoption of a course of action that may benefit the great majority of an entire society. Presently such a phenomenon seems to be occurring in the United States and in a few other countries.

The picture painted so far appears foreboding and not unlike many of the energy futures depicted recently by various organizations or spokesmen who have, or would like to have, an influence on the formation of energy policy. However, this impression is misleading. Certainly bad choices could bring about a dismal future, but such a future is by no means inevitable or even likely. By focusing on the most substantial problems and on their real urgency, instead of trying to attack short-and long-term problems simultaneously and indiscriminately, we soon realize that our energy problems are not insurmountable. There are good solutions to all these problems; indeed, there is a range of solutions that can provide sufficient flexibility to meet the uncertainties inherent in each element of our energy strategy. Our image of a desirable future and our perception of the constraints involved in reaching that future are clear enough that we can plan a reasonable course.

The essential ingredients of our plan are as follows: We need an accelerated fuel substitution program, especially in the utility industry;

we should encourage improvements in end-use efficiency, placing emphasis on measures that will reduce oil imports; and we should accelerate domestic energy production. By the turn of the century, these measures can reduce oil imports to less than 20%,* and perhaps to as low as 5%, of oil consumption.

The most urgent problem, national vulnerability to oil suppliers, can be met by a combination of fuel switching, cost-effective efficiency improvements,** increased automobile efficiency, construction of coal-fired and nuclear electrical power plants, and the manufacture of synthetic liquid and gaseous fuels from coal and oil shale. At the same time, we must address a number of institutional and societal issues both in order to speed up these measures and to give greater weight to long-term considerations in energy decision making.

These are the elements of the strategy for reducing the nation's vulnerability before the turn of the century. Because no single one of them offers a solution, we need to begin on all of them. Other technologies, such as the breeder reactor, solar power, and fusion energy, are not a response to the short-term energy problem, but are necessary to the solution of the longer-term problems identified earlier. It is in these areas that research and development can be most useful, by lowering costs and reducing impacts. Our short-term proposals, in contrast, do not require any research and development breakthroughs for their success. If there are such breakthroughs, we are fortunate; if not, we can still overcome the problems and provide plentiful energy supplies at acceptable costs.

The response to the short-term problem effectively removes the United States from the world oil market, reducing the pressure on both prices and production capacity. The period over which the developing countries can rely upon natural liquid and gaseous hydrocarbons to meet their needs will be extended, and the more moderate prices will allow their economies to strengthen and begin the transition to long-term energy sources. Eventually, the world will make the shift to other energy sources, but by that time nuclear, synfuel, and perhaps solar

---

*We will demonstrate that this level of imports (20%) is likely to be the maximum that the nation could cope with satisfactorily under emergency (imported oil cutoff) conditions.

**The term "efficiency improvements" is used deliberately to indicate that the same or equivalent energy service is provided but with less energy expenditure. We do not call for a general reduction of energy service: we consider that such a reduction should ordinarily be called not "conservation," but "deprivation," and we believe it is, in most cases, unnecessary.

technologies—along with energy-efficient industrial processes—will be available from the United States and other developed countries. If the developing countries have used the intervening period wisely, their economies should be strong enough to participate in the changeover to long-term resources, which is certain to be capital intensive.

Improvements in transportation efficiency, industrial process efficiency and residential design, together with the increased use of coal and coal-derived fuels, renewable energy sources, and unconventional sources of gas can carry the United States beyond the middle of the next century. This can happen without loss of amenities, with an expanding economy and population, and with increased freedom of action for the nation and for its individual citizens. We can, by the end of this century, reduce our oil imports to the acceptable level of less than 20% of demand. Neither availability nor cost of energy need be a significant constraint in economic growth or choice of lifestyle. For example, as a nation we could, in the year 2020, use less energy per unit of GNP than today while spending only the same proportion of our GNP on energy. Individuals could drive their automobiles the same distance as today for half the fuel cost.

In later chapters we will examine and document more fully, these and other problems. We will explore the range of responses and give estimates of the contribution and cost of each. We will provide substance to the statement, made earlier, that a range of options is available with sufficient flexibility to respond both to unexpected problems and unanticipated opportunities.

FINDINGS OF THE STUDY

The following is a recapitulation of the major conclusions of our study:

- The U.S. energy policies should create a desirable future for our nation.
- This future should include healthy economic growth (an annual per capita GNP growth rate of 2%), the opportunity to maintain our present lifestyles, and sufficient energy independence to avoid the economic and national security hazards of unexpected interruptions in imported energy supplies.
- The United States is not running out of energy; we have very large domestic resources of coal, oil shale, and uranium. Conventional natural gas and crude oil resources are limited, however. Their production will decline over the next several dec-

ades. Unconventional sources of liquid and gaseous fuels will be required to offset this decline and to replace imports.

- The urgent energy problem is our vulnerability connected to imported oil. Importing huge quantities of oil from sometimes unfriendly, sometimes unstable countries subjects us to insecurity and economic penalities, and the problem could become a crisis if the oil-exporting countries so desire.

- We can deal with the problem of imported oil by increasing domestic oil production, substituting other domestic sources for oil, and increasing the efficiency of our use of the remaining oil.

- The total substitution potential for the electric utility industry is 6.7 EJ/year (3.0 million bble/d) of oil and gas. The four options for this fuel substitution are 1. transferring power from utilities that have surplus power generated by coal, nuclear, or hydroelectric sources to utilities using oil as a power source; 2. converting boilers designed to burn coal, but now using other fuel, back to coal; 3. converting boilers designed to burn oil and gas to intermediate-Btu gas (from coal); and 4. constructing new nuclear or coal units to replace existing oil- and gas-fired units.

- Coal and intermediate-Btu gas from coal could function effectively in industrial steam and process-heat applications. About 7 EJ/year (3.1 million bble/d) of gas and oil could be displaced in this way.

- Electricity and gas can displace the oil used for space and water heating in buildings. This switch could take place without an overall increase in electricity and gas use by implementing cost-effective energy efficiency options.

- Conservation initiatives should be sharply focused on saving oil. Conserving gas should receive high priority as well because it can then serve as a ready substitute for oil in many other applications.

- Since automobiles consume 11.4 EJ/year (5.1 million bbl/d) of oil, increasing their fuel efficiency would be a very effective way to save a large amount of oil.

- Implementing massive conservation efforts can result in end-use demand growing at only 0.6 to 0.9% per year through the year 2020. To achieve this, automobile efficiencies must be increased by a factor of 3, and the rate of energy use in buildings and industry must be decreased in the next 40 years to half their current levels.

- Even with extensive energy efficiency improvements, considerable expansion of supply will be required. Greater dependence on manufactured fuels will result in primary energy demand growing at about twice the rate of end-use demand.

- Burning fossil fuels will increase the level of CO_2 in the earth's atmosphere. This could become a problem a half century from now, but present scientific knowledge does not allow us to predict accurately the exact timing or extent of the problem. Intensive research is needed to increase our knowledge about the factors that affect accumulation of CO_2.
- The federal government should focus on the following actions:
    1. Eliminate all price controls, including those on natural gas, as quickly as it is practicable.
    2. Overhaul the licensing process for nuclear power plants to eliminate excessive delays.
    3. Take steps to improve the financial health of the electric utility industry.
    4. Speed up the work of the U.S. Synthetic Fuels Corporation to establish quickly a synthetic fuels industry.
- The total funding for new electric plants and for establishing a synfuels industry is substantial but not unreasonable.
- In future years energy will increase in real price, but improvements in efficiency of energy service can more than compensate for this. The real cost of fuel for a mile of automobile travel in 2020 can be less than it is today, and the total cost of energy in the United States in 2020 will be about the same fraction of the GNP as it is today (about 10%).
- We should avoid listening too much to the doomsayers. The energy crisis has spawned more creativity in identifying and characterizing constraints than it has in solving problems.

II. THE ENERGY PROBLEM

INTRODUCTION

In this chapter we examine U.S. and world energy issues and realities, and we identify the essential nature of the U.S. energy problem. We consider *1.* the important role of energy in the evolution of human culture; *2.* U.S. and world energy resources; and *3.* recent trends in energy supply, the current energy supply profile, and the bearing these have on the U.S. energy situation in particular. We focus on those issues that are now urgent and on those that will assume special importance later. The former are related primarily to the current U.S. energy situation, and the latter are linked closely to the interrelationship between U.S. and world energy demands and to the depletion of liquid and gaseous fossil fuels. Facets of the U.S. energy problem related to the social, institutional, and international constraints on energy options are also studied.

ENERGY REALITIES

The Role of Energy

Historically, energy has been one of the fundamental components of human progress, and human cultural development has gone hand in hand with the ability to obtain and use energy (Fig. 1). Even today, in the developing nations, energy is used chiefly to satisfy the basic needs of food and warmth. In many developing countries, a reduction in marketed energy would pose a threat of death from starvation or exposure. In all of these countries, lack of an adequate energy supply would make any improvement in the standard of living unobtainable. Thus, these countries generally are compelled to pay almost any monetary price for fuel or pay a price in human suffering that includes privation and even death.

In the United States the role of energy differs somewhat because of our substantially higher standard of living. Since our energy is increasingly used to make life more comfortable and to enhance mobility, en-

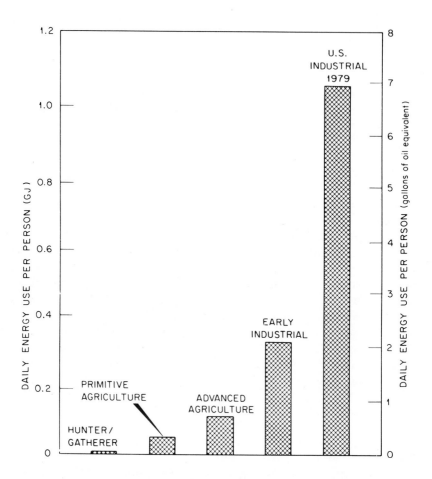

Fig. 1. Energy use is closely related to human cultural development. As the standard of living increases in a society, so does energy consumption. Thus, energy use in a highly industrialized nation such as the United States is dramatically greater than in developing countries. Data for this figure are from J. Bronowski, *The Ascent of Man*, Little, Brown and Co., Boston, MA, 1974.

ergy shortages do not threaten mass starvation as they can in the developing countries. Shortages here would result in a lower general standard of living. But since much of the energy we use is not needed for basic survival, the losses deal more with "necessary" conveniences. For example, higher fuel costs can be absorbed by giving up some conveniences (e.g., driving fewer miles) or by increasing energy-use efficiency (e.g., using more efficient automobiles).

World Energy Demand Patterns

Because of the close ties between the United States and other nations with respect to the energy market, a global perspective of energy demand and resource patterns is needed to understand fully our domestic energy problem. Between 1950 and 1976, energy use in the U.S. increased at an average rate of only 3.5% per year. During that same period, energy use in the rest of the world grew almost twice as fast, at an average rate of about 6.4% per year [increasing from about 42 EJ* (40 quads) per year to about 209 EJ (198 quads) per year (Fig. 2)]. Three factors were responsible for this sharp increase: rapid population growth, particularly in the developing countries; a general increase in standard of living throughout the world; and a decline in real prices of most forms of energy, including oil, over most of the period.

World population has increased dramatically from 2.7 billion in 1945 to 4.4 billion in 1980 and now has a doubling time of less than 40 years. During this same period, developing nations raised their per capita production and consumption. Consequently, energy use in these countries increased markedly—by factors of 8 in Latin America, 11 in southern and southeast Asia, and 14 in China. Increases in the developed nations, in contrast, were relatively much smaller:** a factor of 3.2 in Western Europe and only 2.5 in the United States, which showed the smallest growth factor of all (Fig. 2).

Since much of the world's population is in the developing countries, the established trends imply that world energy demand will continue to increase, even if the developed countries stabilize their total energy demand and real energy prices continue to increase. The increase in the next 50 to 75 years could be rapid, especially if the developing countries achieve a high rate of economic growth and social progress. For example, if a hypothetical equilibrium world population of 10 billion (World Bank, 1980)† eats according to present-day U.S. standards, the

---

*Exajoule (EJ) is a metric system unit of energy approximately equivalent to a quad (10^{15} Btu): 1 EJ (10^{18} joules) equals 0.9479 quads.

**It should be noted, however, that the absolute energy growth in the developed countries (United States, Canada, Western Europe, Japan, and Australia) was slightly greater than that for the developing countries.

†An equilibrium world population is one in which the birth rate and death rate are equal. The 9 billion population estimate appearing elsewhere in this report does not refer to an equilibrium population.

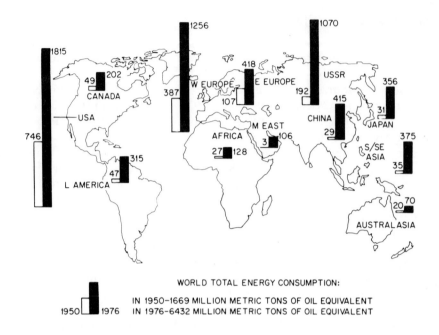

WORLD TOTAL ENERGY CONSUMPTION:

IN 1950–1669 MILLION METRIC TONS OF OIL EQUIVALENT
IN 1976–6432 MILLION METRIC TONS OF OIL EQUIVALENT

Fig. 2. During the past quarter century, the world total energy consumption has increased from 1.7×10^9 metric tons of oil equivalent in 1950 to 6.4×10^9 metric tons of oil equivalent in 1976. Much of this growth was caused by the striking increases in energy use by the developing countries. Adapted from David Crabbe and Richard McBride, *The World Energy Book*, The MIT Press, Cambridge, MA, 1979.

food system alone would require more energy than the current total world energy consumption. This would be true even if we assume that the world food system (production, distribution, and processing) was only half as energy intensive as the present U.S. system with its emphasis on distribution, packaging, and display (Pimentel, 1977). We must produce substantially more energy to better meet even the most basic needs of the world population in the future.

World Energy Resources

World energy reserves are sufficient to meet current annual world energy demands [290 EJ (275 quad)] for over a century (Tables 1 and 2).

Table 1. Recoverable reserves and resources of conventional fuels[a,b]

	Coal		Oil		Gas		Uranium	
	EJ	10^9 tons	EJ	10^9 bbl	EJ	10^{12} ft^3	EJ	10^6 kg
United States								
Reserves	4,300	178	177	29	221	205	264	643
Resources	43,300	1,800	671 1,130	110 185	788 1,107	730 1,030	697	1,700
World								
Reserves	15,400	636	3,920	642	2,710	2,510	780	1,890
Resources	122,000	5,060	8,850 12,810	1,405 2,160	9,410 10,200	8,710 9,500	1,760	4,290

[a] Resources refer to deposits that have been estimated with at least a small degree of certainty and might be recovered at some time in the future. Reserves refer to that portion of the resources that has been located with considerable certainty and can be recovered with current technical and economic means.

[b] Energy conversion factors: oil, 6.12×10^9 J/bbl; gas, 1.08×10^6 J/ft^3; coal, 24.2×10^9 J/ton; and uranium (based on existing light-water reactor technology), 411×10^{15} J/kg. Adapted from Schurr et al. (1979).

These reserves will be insufficient much sooner if energy demands continue to escalate. However, as fuels become scarcer, costs will rise and less conventional resources, more costly than current ones, will be added to the reserves. Thus, even for oil, which is least plentiful (relative to demand, not in absolute terms), world resources represent roughly a century's supply at current consumption levels and a 40-year supply even if world oil comsumption grows at 5% per year.

Table 2. Years of reserves and resources of conventional fuels at current consumption levels

	Coal	Oil	Gas	Uranium[a]
United States				
Reserves	285	4	11	33
Resources	2060	16 27	38 55	87
World				
Reserves	243	38	151	
Resources	1930	80 125	196 214	

[a] Domestic production in 1978 was 20,387 t with a net export of 880 t, thus giving a net domestic consumption of 19,507 t (U.S. Department of Energy 1979a). Uranium reserve and resource figures here show the available supply using conventional light-water reactor technology only; with breeder technology, uranium reserves would last at least 2000 years at the current rate of use.

If so, why then does the world experience periodic oil crises? A careful look at the world's energy demand and resource patterns reveals the answer. As noted earlier, world energy demand has risen dramatically since World War II, and much of this increased demand has been for oil (Fig. 3). By the late 1960s, the international oil market had become a sellers' market with OPEC assuming a powerful role in influencing price and production. The world's largest producer and consumer of oil, the United States, faced declining reserves. This led to reduced domestic production, while demand continued to rise. The consequent entry of the United States into the world oil market as a large-scale buyer placed additional pressure on international oil supplies and further increased the power of OPEC.

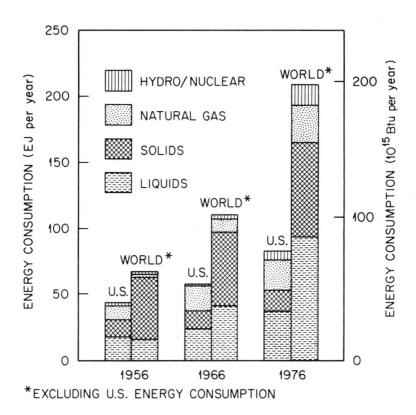

Fig. 3. Between 1956 and 1976, U.S. energy use increased 3.5% per year while energy use in the rest of the world grew much faster, at 6.4% per year. Large increases in the use of liquid (oil-derived) fuels have created a tight world market and a situation conducive to a supply-demand crises. Adapted from David Crabbe and Richard McBride, *The World Energy Book*, The MIT Press, Cambridge, MA, 1979.

By 1970, the world oil market was so tight that even small perturbations in supply could cause oil gluts or, more importantly, shortfalls for particular countries. For example, the production cutback of the Arab OPEC nations during the 1973–74 oil embargo caused less than a 10% drop in domestic consumption, but it was sufficient to cause an oil crisis in the major oil-consuming nations. Clearly, the decisions of OPEC, with its dominance over oil reserves and production (Figs. 4 and 5), can create world crises.

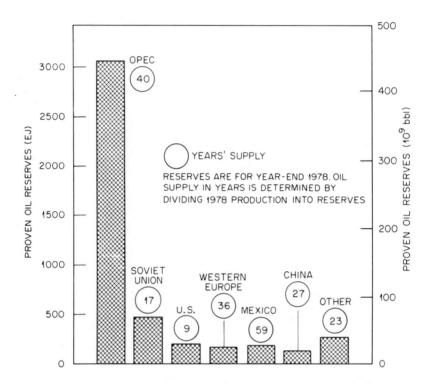

Fig. 4. The world has plentiful oil reserves, but most of them are controlled by the OPEC cartel. Adapted from "The Oil Crisis Is Real This Time," *Business Week* July 30, 1979, pp. 44-60.

Most of the developed world has no immediate control over much of its own energy supply. However, as we shall see, there are sufficient, and sufficiently varied, domestic energy resources to allow the U.S. to take back control of its own energy future.

U.S. Energy Resources

The availability of oil for the United States is not nearly as encouraging as it is for the world in general. At current U.S. consumption rates, domestic reserves represent only a 4-year supply, and the total resource base represents only a 20- to 30-year supply (Table 2). The natural gas situation, although similar, is less critical. Fortunately, these reserves

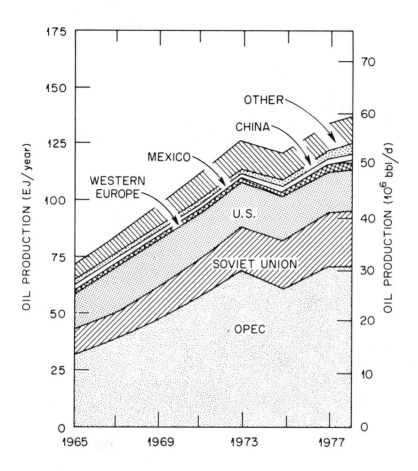

Fig. 5. The growth rate for world oil production has decreased in recent years. This results primarily from the OPEC decision to maintain an almost constant production rate. Adapted from "The Oil Crisis Is Real This Time," *Business Week*, July 30, 1979, pp. 44-60.

and resources of conventional fuels constitute just a small fraction of the energy resources indigenous to the United States. There exist unconventional sources of conventional fuels that formerly were not economically recoverable under the then-prevailing conditions of price and technology; unconventional sources usually represent a much larger supply than does the conventional resource base (Table 3).

    The notion that we are "running out" of energy is quite incorrect: Both the United States and the world have abundant fuel resources.

**Table 3. Recoverable U.S. conventional fuel resources
from unconventional sources[a]**

Source	Ultimately recoverable resources		Years of supply[b]
Oil, EJ (10^9 bbl)			
Enhanced oil recovery	128–700	(21–110)	3–17
Heavy crude	135–184	(22–30)	8
Shale oil	9,180–15,900	(1,500–2,600)	200–360
Natural gas, EJ (10^{12} ft^3)			
Tight sands	214	(198)	10
Devonian shale	77	(70)	4
Coal seams	92	(85)	4
Geopressure zones	325–6,820	(300–6,300)	15–315
Deep formations	650	(600)	30

[a]Data from *The Oil and Gas Journal* (1979a); Wilson (1979); Olszewski (1980); Pasini (1980); and Stobaugh and Yergin (1979).
[b]At 1978 levels of fuel consumption, assuming that each source alone supplies the total demand.

What we are running out of is cheap energy. We are depleting the hydrocarbon resources that are easy and inexpensive to use. The development of the additional resources will be much more costly.

From 1950 to 1970, real domestic energy prices decreased by almost 30% (Fig. 6). With such cheap and abundant domestic energy supplies

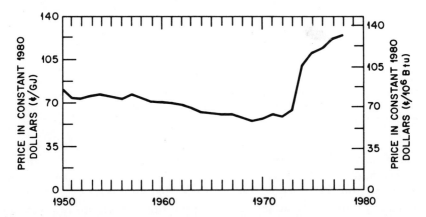

Fig. 6. The real aggregate price of domestic fossil fuels (in constant 1980 dollars) was actually about 30% lower in 1970 than in 1950. In the following decade the price doubled. Adapted from Energy Information Administration, *Annual Report to Congress 1978*, Vol. 2, DOE/EIA-0173/2, pp. 5 and 13.

the United States developed a highly productive and energy intensive economy. Today, U.S. energy consumption per unit of economic output, or gross national product, is slightly greater than the average for the rest of the world, and U.S. economic output per capita is far greater (Fig. 7).

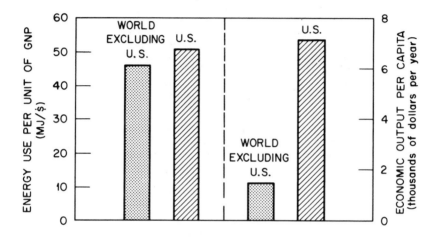

Fig. 7. The United States consumes slightly more energy per unit of gross national product, but produces much more economic output per capita, than the average for the rest of the world (excluding the U.S.).

A detailed examination of energy comsumption per unit of ecomonic output throughout the world yields some interesting facts. Table 4 compares the ratio of primary energy consumption to the value of gross domestic product (GDP) for selected countries and world economic groups. It is interesting to note that between 1960 and 1978 the industrialized countries were the only ones to reduce their energy consumption per unit of economic output. The decrease in the industrialized countries was coupled with an increase in the low- and middle-income countries. As a result, the average ratio of energy consumption per unit of economic output among the low-income, middle-income, and the industrial countries was almost identical in 1978. Another striking fact is the energy inefficiency of the countries having centrally planned economies (communist). These countries consume almost twice as much energy per unit of GDP as do the industrial nations.

Comparing the United States with other industrial countries indicates that further energy efficiency gains are possible.

Table 4. Trends in energy consumption per
unit of economic activity

Country or area	Primary energy consumption per dollar of GDP[a]		Change ($\%$ / year)
	kJ/$GDP (Btu/$GDP)		
	1960	1978	
United States	52,200 (49,500)	45,800 (43,400)	−0.7
West Germany	29,400 (27,900)	26,200 (24,800)	−0.7
Sweden	22,900 (21,700)	22,900 (21,700)	0
Japan	26,200 (24,800)	22,900 (21,700)	−0.7
United Kingdom	52,200 (49,500)	39,200 (37,200)	−1.0
Canada	42,500 (40,300)	42,500 (40,300)	0
Low income[b]	26,200 (24,800)	32,700 (31,000)	+1.2
Middle income[c]	22,900 (21,700)	36,000 (34,100)	+2.5
Industrialized[d]	39,200 (37,200)	36,000 (34,100)	−0.5
Capital surplus oil exporting	13,100 (12,400)	16,400 (15,500)	+1.2
Centrally planned economies[e]	62,000 (58,800)	68,600 (65,000)	+0.6

[a]Gross domestic product (GDP) measures the total final output
of goods and services produced by an economy (i.e., within a
country's territory by residents, regardless of its allocation to
domestic and foreign claims). Gross national product (GNP)
measures the total domestic and foreign output claimed by
residents of a country. It comprises GDP and factor incomes (such
as investment receipts and worker's remittances) accruing to
residents from abroad, minus the income earned in the domestic
economy accruing to persons abroad. Data from the World Bank
(1980).
[b]Countries with a 1978 GNP per capita of less than $400.
[c]Countries with a 1978 GNP per capita of between $400 and
$3500.
[d]Countries with a 1978 GNP per capita of more than $3500.
[e]Communist countries.

Table 4 indicates that West Germany, Sweden, and Japan use only
about half as much energy per unit of GDP as the U.S. Our nation's
higher energy consumption rate can be attributed, in part, to geographic factors (particularly differences in climate and population den-
sity) and to the heavy U.S. dependence on automobiles (train and bus
systems are more popular in the other countries). The energy price structure, unique to each country, also affects the reported energy use.
Germany and Japan supply over half their energy requirements by

importing oil, resulting in relatively high energy prices, which are aug-
mented by high taxes. These high prices tend to keep their energy consumption figures low. The reliance of these countries on directly used
imported oil, rather than electricity with its associated conversion
losses, also tends to keep their primary energy consumption figures
low. However, Canada, which is similar to the U.S. in its population
distribution and its energy prices, has an energy consumption ratio very
near that of the U.S.

The increased energy demands of the post-World War II period
were met primarily with petroleum and natural gas (Fig. 8). In 1945,
the United States depended on liquid and gaseous hydrocarbon fuels for
45% of its energy supplies. By 1970 this figure had risen to over 75%.

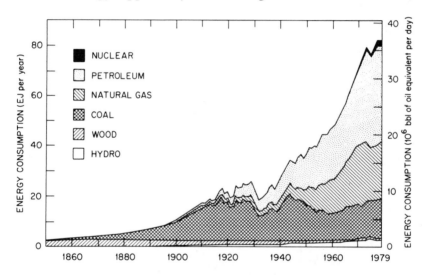

Fig. 8. The increased United States energy demands of the post-World War II
period have been met essentially with petroleum and natural gas. Adapted
from Energy Information Administration, *Annual Report to Congress 1979*,
Vol. 2, DOE/EIA-0173(79)/2, p. 9.

Initially, this expansion in the use of petroleum and natural gas was met
primarily by increases in U.S. reserves and production capacity (Figs. 9
and 10). Proven reserves increased steadily from 1945 to about 1959,
remained constant until about 1967, and decreased sharply after that.
The Alaskan oil reserves, first reported in 1970, are the only net reserves
added between 1967 and today.

In the United States, standard oil production practice is to maintain a reserve-to-production ratio of between 8 and 12 (the exact ratio

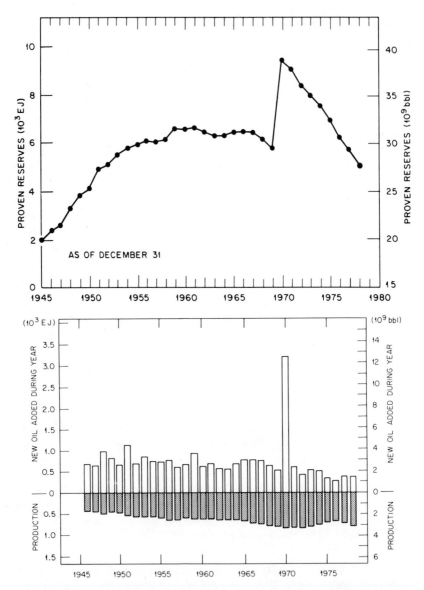

Figs. 9 and 10. Since 1970, the proven oil reserves of the United States have steadily declined, with no significant additions of new oil since the Alaskan oil reserves of 1970. Oil production in the United States has also declined during this period. Adapted from S. H. Schurr, J. Darmstadler, H. Perry, W. Ramsey, and M. Russell, *Energy in America's Future: The Choices Before Us*, Johns Hopkins University Press, Baltimore, MD, 1979 and Energy Information Administration *Annual Report to Congress, 1979*, DOE/EIA-0173(79)/2.

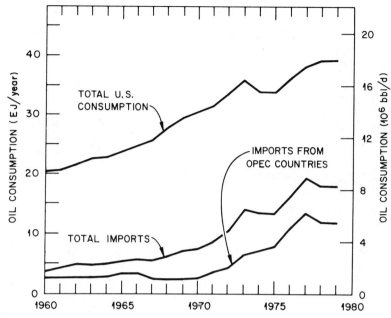

Fig. 11. Increasing demand for petroleum products coupled with declining domestic oil production has caused large increases in petroleum imports, especially from the OPEC countries. Adapted from Energy Information Administration, *Annual Report to Congress 1978*, Vol. 2, DOE/EIA-0173/2, pp. 40 and 42, and *Monthly Energy Review, August 1980*, DOE/EIA-0035 (80/08).

depending on geologic and economic conditions). As reserves decline, the rate of production similarly declines. Thus, as proven U.S. oil reserves declined 23% between 1970 and 1975, oil production fell by 16% (Figs. 9 and 10).

To meet rising energy demands in spite of sharply declining domestic production, the United States began importing large quantities of foreign oil after 1967 (Fig. 11). In 1973, for instance, the United States imported 35% of its oil requirements; by 1979, it imported 46%. Because more than two-thirds of these imports came, and still come,*

---

*Preliminary data for 1980 from U.S. Department of Energy (1980g) indicate that net imports will average about 14.5 EJ/year (6.5 million bbl/d), a decline of almost 20% compared to 1979 levels. Much of this decline is due to sagging industrial output and consumers doing without because of rising fuel prices and a decline in real purchasing power. It is doubtful that a major fraction of this consumption decline will persist if vigorous economic activity resumes. It is interesting to note that while the fraction of oil consumption that is imported has declined slightly (41% in 1980 compared to 46% in 1979), the fraction of total consumption that comes from Arab OPEC countries has remained virtually constant at the 1979 levels (17% of total consumption).

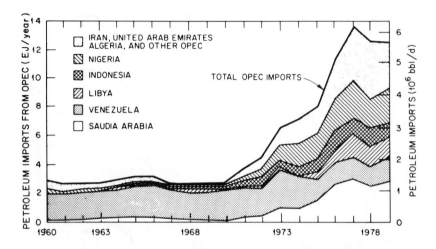

Fig. 12. Imports of crude oil and petroleum products from OPEC countries have increased dramatically since 1970, at a rate of nearly 20% per year. In 1979, almost one-third of total U.S. oil consumption was imported from OPEC countries. The largest fraction of these imports is supplied by the Arab nations. Adapted from Energy Information Administration, *Annual Report to Congress 1978*, Vol. 2, DOE/EIA-0173/2, p. 42, and *Monthly Energy Review*, August 1980, DOE/EIA-0035 (80/08).

from OPEC countries, the United States now finds itself in a situation where almost one-third of its oil is supplied by the OPEC cartel, and primarily by its Arab members (Fig. 12). The impact of this dependence on imported oil is a critical element of the U.S. energy problem.

IMMEDIATE AND NEAR-TERM ENERGY ISSUES

When examined within the framework of our national objectives, the current U.S. dependence on imported oil is unacceptable for several reasons. The most important is the political and economic vulnerability that results from the importation of oil from politically unstable and unpredictable sources. Significant disruption of this supply could be devastating. Another effect, although less critical, is the adverse influence this heavy reliance on imported oil has on the U.S. economy.

Political and Economic Vulnerability

The vulnerability of the United States is our most pressing energy issue. A significant oil import disruption could force basic changes in our lifestyle. In the case of a permanent disruption, an equilibrium would be reached eventually in which domestic resources would be reallocated; this would lead to a significantly lower standard of living. Our most significant vulnerability, however, is not the potential need for long-run reallocation of resources in the U.S. economy, but rather that of quick adjustment to that long-run equilibrium. Unless some sort of measures are available to assist the economy in this transition process, the short-run adjustment costs could be huge. In such a case, severe economic dislocations would increase greatly the probabilities of armed conflict. Past actions of the oil-exporting nations (particularly the Arab members of OPEC) have demonstrated, not unexpectedly, that they feel no obligation to act in the U.S. national interest. If they were responsible for a major oil supply shortfall, the United States would probably consider military action to ensure adequate energy supplies.

This vulnerability also threatens to limit U.S. freedom of action both at home and abroad. Without doubt, the 1973–74 Arab oil embargo and the 1979–80 Iranian oil supply disruption demonstrated that oil can and will be used as a weapon against the United States. This situation has already weakened the position of the United States as a world power and has also impeded domestic actions (e.g., filling the strategic petroleum reserve) necessary for pursuing the country's best interests.

Economic Impacts

A second, and lesser, issue related to U.S. dependence on imported oil is its negative economic impact.

Oil supply interruptions (whether unplanned or deliberate) and increased prices result in short-term dislocations in the economy that exacerbate inflation and unemployment and reduce real economic growth. The value of the dollar declines.

Recently, the President's Council of Economic Advisers estimated that the December 1979 OPEC price increases will add 1% to the 1980 inflation rate, increase the number of unemployed by 250,000, and reduce U.S. economic output by almost 1% (i.e., $25 billion). As long as oil price increases continue to outpace the domestic inflation rate (in 1979, the U.S. inflation rate was about 13% as measured by the Consumer Price Index and 9% as measured by the GNP deflator, while OPEC oil prices doubled), they will be an important factor in raising that inflation rate. That these effects may not be just momentary is also important. Some analysts have suggested that the adverse economic effects persisted for several years after the 1973–74 oil embargo and the subsequent fourfold price increase (Table 5).

Table 5. Effects of the 1973-1974 oil price increases on the
U.S. economy

	1973	1974	1975	1976	1977
Loss of economic output (GNP),[a] billions of 1972 dollars		38	63	41	40
Increased inflation rate, % change in consumer price		0.3	2.5	1.7	0.2
Increased unemployment rate, %		0.1	0.7	1.7	0.5
Loss of employment, thousands of jobs		84	600	1450	500

[a]The differences between actual performance of the economy and simulations of how the economy would have performed if world oil prices had not increased. The simulations were performed using the Data Resources, Inc., econometric model and the Interindustry Transactions Model developed by Edward Hudson and Dale Jorgenson. Adapted from U.S. Department of Energy (1979g).

The rapid price increase for imported oil has also been a major factor in the large U.S. trade deficits since 1976 (Fig. 13). With the recent oil increases, the U.S. oil import bill rose from about $60 billion in 1979 to almost $80 billion in 1980. This will further aggravate the balance-of-trade position, and has already contributed to a general malaise in the U.S. economy, a weakening of the dollar abroad, and a decreasing level of material standards for some sections of U.S. society.

Economists disagree as they attempt to estimate the external costs to society from the purchases of imported oil. External costs are those incurred by society in addition to the direct cost of the oil purchase. The external costs of oil imports are the result of three factors:

1. Oil Price. A change in demand for oil will influence its price. If, for example, the U.S. were to reduce imports, the world price of oil would decline. Thus, the remaining U.S. imports would cost less per barrel. Uncertainties about the price effect relate to how oil producers actually react to changes in demand.

2. National Economy. The outflow of money to pay for imported oil can result in a loss in national income. The size of this loss depends upon the extent and speed with which dollars sent abroad return through increased purchases by other countries of U.S. goods and

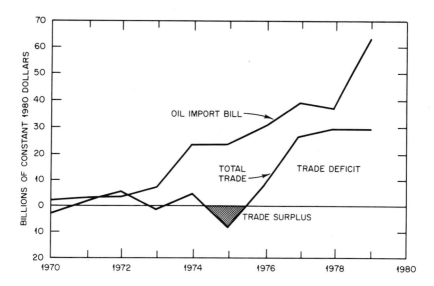

Fig. 13. The increasing cost of oil imports has been reflected in large trade defi-
cits, resulting in a weakened U.S. economy. Adapted from U.S. Department of
Energy, *National Energy Plan II*, Washington, DC (May 7, 1979) and Energy
Information Administration, *Monthly Energy Review*, November 1980,
DOE/EIA-0035(80/11), p. 10.

services. Another external cost to the U.S. economy is an increase
in the inflation rate caused by currency depreciation and other
factors.
3. *Supply Disruption Costs.* Either an actual oil embargo or the
threat of an embargo results in costs to society not covered by the
market price of imported oil. In case of an actual oil cutoff, the
cost consists of unemployment, lost production, and altered lifestyles. Even the threat alone is costly: It causes increased government spending for such items as the military and for the preparation of a strategic petroleum reserve.

As noted, economists differ on the actual figure for the external
costs, though most economists recognize their existence. Some (Hogan,
1979 and Landsberg, 1979) believe the external costs are small, perhaps
$13 to $31 per cubic meter ($2 to $5 per barrel). Others believe the cost
may be large. Stobaugh and Yergin (1979) indicate the external costs
are in the range of $63 to $625 per cubic meter ($10 to $100 per barrel).
Nordhaus (1980) suggests that the external costs may be comparable to
the direct cost. Lemon (1980) estimates a range of $270 to $438 per
cubic meter ($43 to $70 per barrel). A breakdown of Lemon's estimate

of the benefits (both external and direct) of reducing U.S. oil imports by
500,000 bbl/d is as follows:

| | Benefits [$/m³ ($/bbl)] | | |
	Year 1	Year 2	Year 3
Direct benefit of reduced oil imports	233 (37.00)	237 (37.74)	242 (38.49)
External benefits			
Lower oil prices	77 (12.32)	112 (17.71)	119 (18.98)
Improved trade, currency appreciation, lower inflation	70 (11.19)	128 (20.41)	133 (21.18)
Added real output	42 (6.60)	80 (12.70)	108 (17.13)
Decreased supply disruption costs	85 (13.50)	85 (13.50)	85 (13.50)
Total	274 (43.61)	405 (64.32)	445 (70.79)
Total benefits	507 (80.61)	642 (102.06)	687 (109.28)

Policy Implications

Our present political and economic vulnerability, and the attend-
ant threats to world peace, mean that the reduction of oil imports
should be the cornerstone of U.S. energy policy in the near- and mid-
term.* By the end of that period, we should have achieved this
objective.

In principle we could achieve this goal by several approaches. However, some of these are unacceptable (e.g., military takeover of a major
oil-producing nation) because they are not consistent with our other national goals. Other approaches are impossible because of the realities of
the world oil situation. Replacing OPEC oil with new world sources, for
example, is not feasible because we already import oil from almost every
major world oil reserve (Russia, China, and the North Sea being the
only exceptions). Attempting to import substantially more oil from
non-OPEC, or at least non-Arab OPEC, sources is also impossible because the existing OPEC producers (notably Saudi Arabia and Iran) are
the only countries capable of meeting the large-scale U.S. require-

---

*In this energy study, "near-term" is defined as 1980 to 1990, "mid-term" as 1990 to
2010, and "long-term" as 2010 to 2050.

ments. In addition such a strategy, even if it could be implemented, would not eliminate our vulnerability unless we had enough influence over the new exporter to ensure that this supply would be reasonably stable.

Strategic storage of oil is a very important way to reduce vulnerability and generally is accepted as the least costly measure to respond to import disruptions of short to medium duration. If, however, import disruptions are expected to be very large or long-term, strategic storage is not practical as the only answer to the problem because of the sheer quantity of oil involved. In addressing this issue, the domestic economy must begin to adjust its energy production and use in order to reduce the impact of that disruption. By doing so, the transition costs will be much smaller if such a disruption occurs. Thus, the reduction of U.S. oil imports should be the focal point of our near- and mid-term energy policy, even though other steps designed to reduce vulnerability should also be taken (e.g., establishing a strategic reserve).

LONGER-TERM ENERGY ISSUES

Assuming that we resolve the problem of our political and economic vulnerability before the end of this century, as we can and should, the longer-term energy issues—which are both global and domestic—will then be dominated by the challenge of providing adequate energy supplies at the lowest possible economic, social, and environmental costs. (The dominance of this and other longer-term issues may, of course, be changed by unforeseen events.) Within this time frame, resource depletion will limit world oil production from conventional sources, which in turn will make world oil supplies scarcer. Some environmental impacts may also be of an international scope.

Global concerns are expected to become increasingly important in evaluating domestic energy policy. World energy demands will continue to rise, especially if needed economic and social progress occurs in the developing countries. The impact of U.S. energy policy on the availability and cost of international energy supplies will remain significant, even though U.S. energy consumption will become a smaller fraction of the world total. The developing nations will be particularly dependent upon oil as an energy source, having little capital available for the major alternatives (synfuels, nuclear power, and solar energy). The continued upward pressure on oil prices resulting from resource depletion, together with a stable or growing world oil demand, will be a particular challenge to developing countries and could be a threat to world stability.

Table 6. Assumptions used in projecting world energy demands

	Developed nations	Communist nations[a]	Developing nations[b]
1975 gross domestic product, 10^{1} 1972 dollars	2.60	1.00	0.56
Future per capita GDP growth,[c] % year	2.0	2.5	4.0
1975 population (10^6)	797	1262	1907
Population growth rate,[d] % year			
1975 1985	2.0	1.3	2.7
1985 2000	1.6	1.3 ·	2.0
2000 2015	1.0	0.7	1.3
2015 2030	0.8	0.6	1.0
2030 2050	0.6	0.5	0.7
End-use energy demand per dollar of GDP,[e] watt-year $			
1975	1.41	1.91	1.09
1985	1.25	1.71	1.27
2000	1.08	1.51	1.39
2015	0.94	1.35	1.41
2030	0.81	1.18	1.38
2050	0.66	0.99	1.26
Ratio of primary to end-use energy demand[e]			
1975	1.37	1.18	1.26
1985	1.37	1.27	1.29
2000	1.44	1.32	1.32
2015	1.50	1.37	1.36
2030	1.58	1.46	1.39
2050	1.68	1.55	1.42

[a] Centrally planned economies.

[b] "Developing nations" refers to low- and middle-income countries defined in Table 4.

[c] Projections are based on a desirable future in which the currently developing nations can raise their standard of living to nearly that of the developed nations. Once this occurs (after 2050), future per capita GDP growth in the developing nations is expected to lessen and become equal to that of the developed nations.

[d] Population projections to 2030 are from Keyfitz (1977). Projections from 2030 to 2050 are our projections based on the assumption that population control and increased standard of living will accelerate the move toward replacement-level fertility rate.

[e] Based on International Institute for Applied Systems Analysis (1981). Projections after 2030 reflect our judgment that energy efficiency improvements will continue to make possible dramatic decreases in end-use demand per dollar of GNP and that greater use of manufactured fuels will increase the primary to end-use demand ratio.

Global Issues

It is hoped that during the next several decades much more attention will be devoted to improving the standard of living in the developing nations. If this hope is fulfilled, the impact on the world energy situation will be dramatic. Consider, for example, the case outlined in Table 6 in which the average annual per capita growth rate of the gross domestic product (GDP) is 4.0% for the developing nations, 2.5% for the centrally planned economies, and only 2.0% for the developed nations. The resulting average per capita GDP of $4400 (1980 dollars) for the developing countries in 2030, if achieved, would be equivalent to the standard of living enjoyed by the developed nations in the mid-1960s. The world energy consumption profile associated with this economic growth scenario is based on two major assumptions: *1.* The energy demands per unit of GDP (shown in Table 6) for the developed nations and the communist nations decline as a result of an increase in energy conservation efforts; and *2.* the ratio of primary to end-use energy consumption increases to reflect a growing dependence on electricity and synthetic fuels.

According to this projection of world energy demand (Fig. 14), the energy consumption of the currently industrialized nations will become less significant as their fraction of world consumption drops from its current level of 63% to only 28% in 2030. By that time, the nations now classified as developing will account for almost 50% of world energy consumption and will thus play an increasingly important role in the world energy situation. It is most important to appreciate that these broad observations are not dependent on the detailed assumptions given in Table 6 and are valid even though the detailed projections are open to debate.

More significantly, the cumulative world energy consumption in this case equals only 25% of the world's conventional fossil and uranium fuel resources (only 3% if uranium is used in a breeder). Thus, no overall energy shortage need occur. However, a serious oil and gas supply problem could develop during the latter part of this century. For example, assume that oil use by the developed nations does not increase any further and that although the developing countries continue to use more energy, they do not increase the proportion of their demand that is met by oil. In that case, world oil demand (corresponding to the energy consumption figures in Fig. 14) would rise at about 2.8% per year (Fig. 15). If world oil production matches demand until the maximum technical limit of production is reached, world oil supplies should be sufficient to meet demand until about the year 2000. If world oil production is held to its current level because of government actions in the

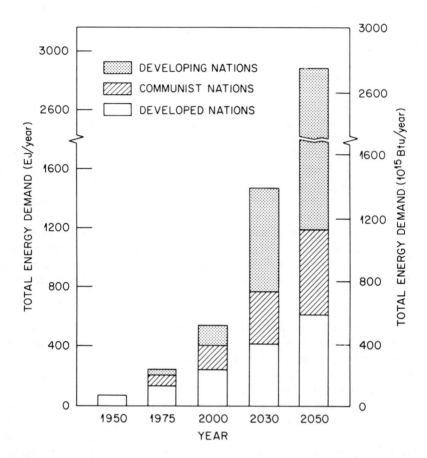

Fig. 14. By the year 2030, the energy consumed by developed countries will represent a much smaller fraction of the total world energy consumption than at present. In 1950 total energy demand for developed nations was 54.4 EJ; for communist nations, 14.7 EJ; and for developing nations, 4.8 EJ. Sources for data include *BP Statistical Review of the World Oil Industry, 1978*, the British Petroleum Co., Ltd., 1978; and *Energy in a Finite World: A Global Energy Systems Analysis*, Report by the Energy Systems Program Group, International Institute for Applied Systems Analysis (February 1981).

producing nations (and this possibility seems more realistic given the current world political climate), world oil shortages would begin to appear before the end of the 1980s.

An analysis of the natural gas situation reveals a similar, although not so critical, picture. World production limits would not be reached until sometime between 2010 and 2020. Large-scale fuel switching from

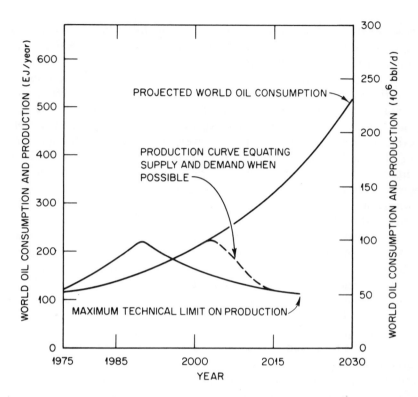

Fig. 15. Projected world oil consumption and production figures indicate that world oil shortages could begin before the year 2000. Adapted from *World Energy Resources 1985–2020*, executive summaries of reports on resources, conservation, and demand for the Conservation commission of the World Energy Conference 1978, published by IPC Science and Technology Press.

oil to natural gas, however, would result in gas shortages occurring sooner.

For the developed countries who can afford to use more capital intensive energy sources (such as uranium, low-grade hydrocarbon resources, solar energy and efficiency improvements to meet increased energy demands and to replace oil and gas), the outlook is relatively bright. In contrast, the outlook for the developing countries who will need oil to meet their growing energy demands is much less hopeful because their demand for oil is increasing at a time when shortages of oil production capacity will probably occur. This places the developing countries in a very serious dilemma. If they continue to meet their growing energy demands with oil, the pressure on the world oil supply will result in price increases that would have severe impacts on their economies and cripple further development. Meanwhile, their heavy borrowing to meet current oil bills is draining away the capital needed to exploit alternative energy resources.

A major way for developed countries to support the developing countries in this situation is to relieve the pressure on the international oil market and thus help stabilize both the price and the supply. The United States could easily undertake such an endeavor. Alternatively, developed countries could support developing countries through some sort of subsidy (e.g., grants could be made to developing countries to purchase oil or to develop other energy sources). The preferable action, however, is our withdrawal, as a large-scale buyer, from the international oil market. This action would not only establish a relationship with the rest of the world that would improve its well-being and contribute to international stability, it would also be an essential step toward alleviating our own political and economic vulnerability. Even if the U.S. isolates itself from the world oil market, our allies will still be subject to politically motivated supply disruptions that could affect the U.S. because of international agreements related to such disruptions. Thus, they too must begin to alleviate their vulnerability in this area.

Although world fossil fuel resources are sufficient to satisfy world needs for the time frame considered here, the costs, environmental impacts, and other concerns, all uncertain at present, could significantly limit their use. One such possible constraint, currently receiving much attention, is the projected effect the escalated use of fossil fuels would have on world climate due to the higher levels of atmospheric CO_2.

To better understand the potential role CO_2 could play in curtailing fossil fuel use, we anlayzed the energy demand projections given in Fig. 14 to determine potential future levels of atmospheric CO_2. We analyzed two limiting cases. In the high CO_2 case, we assumed that all of the world's energy needs would be met by coal combustion. Thus, we assumed that oil and gas use would decline substantially and synfuels would counterbalance the use of non-CO_2 producing energy options. In the low CO_2 case, we assumed that carbon release throughout the time period would be the same as that associated with the actual world composite fuel mix in 1975. The basic assumption here is that increases in nuclear and solar energy are sufficient to counterbalance increased reliance on coal. In both cases we assumed the airborne fraction (the fraction of carbon in the fuel that remains in the atmosphere, hence increasing the CO_2 concentration) was 0.40.* The results (shown in Fig.

---

*This value of the airborne fraction allows for a significant carbon release from the biosphere during recent years of precise CO_2 measurements. It could prove to be too low; if so, the CO_2 concentration would rise somewhat more steeply than shown in Figure 16

16) indicate that it is unlikely that atmospheric CO_2 will reach 500 ppm before 2030. And even in the high CO_2 case, a level of 700 ppm (which may prove to be acceptable) is not exceeded in 2050.

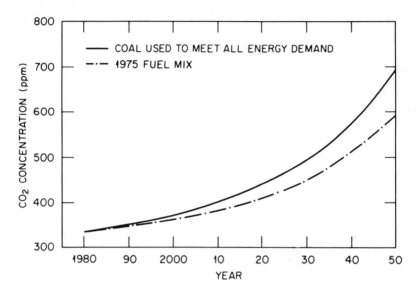

Fig. 16. It is very improbable that atmospheric CO_2 will reach 500 ppm before 2030.

Not enough is known about the mechanisms of CO_2 transport and storage to determine an ultimate policy regarding it. It is fairly clear that no serious climatic changes will result from fossil energy use in this century. For the present, fossil fuels will continue to be used while the potential consequences of the CO_2 problem are investigated. Should CO_2 prove to be a major problem, an eventual worldwide shift to energy sources that do not produce CO_2 (solar, wind, geothermal, nuclear, etc.) would be necessary. In either case, the trend indicated by Fig. 14 implies that the U.S. portion of fossil fuel consumption will be less than 15% of the world's total. This suggests that the solution to a CO_2 problem would require an international effort. Action by the U.S. alone would have only a minor impact, although perhaps it would be important as a symbol.

Domestic Issues

If the United States successfully reduces its import vulnerability, the salient energy issues will focus on the costs and environmental impacts of long-run transitions from oil imports to other energy sources. Some of the alternative sources being considered—including the major ones currently available, such as coal and nuclear fission using light-water reactor technology—face serious constraints (e.g., economic, environmental impacts or because they entail risks judged by some to be unacceptable). Because of these possible constraints, several alternative resource options should be available.

During the next three decades, high capital-investment technologies such as coal liquefaction and breeders will probably be implemented in the United States, and lower-grade resources such as oil shales and gas from tight formations will probably assume greater prominence. One result may be higher energy costs. The real and projected environmental and health costs associated with energy technologies will continue to be internalized to a greater extent than in the past. The challenge in the future will be tó provide U.S. energy needs at the lowest cost to society (i.e., including costs of production, distribution, and environmental and health effects).

CONSTRAINTS TO A SOLUTION OF THE U.S. ENERGY PROBLEMS

The United States possesses resources and technologies that can solve these energy problems, if we are willing to accept the costs. Success, however, requires formulation and implementation of a carefully crafted national energy policy. Unfortunately, several institutional, societal, and international factors impair our ability to deal rationally with the energy problem. Thus they become an integral part of it. The three most important factors are the difficulty society and its institutions have in acting swiftly and resolutely, the long lead time associated with energy system changeovers, and the linkage of our economy with the international community.

Energy System Changeover

Historically, the lead time before a new energy system gains a substantial share of the market (25 %) has been about 30 years (Fig. 17). In addition, new energy sources traditionally meet an increase in energy demand, while existing sources tend to decline slowly or not at all (Fig. 8). Although not completely applicable today, these precedents indicate that energy systems change slowly. Given this fact, and the urgent need to reduce our vulnerability, we must seek and, more importantly, implement new systems and policies to accelerate the transition to new technologies.

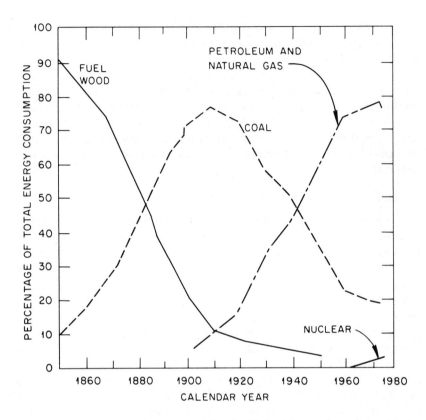

Fig. 17. Energy consumption patterns for the United States show that a 30-year lead time is needed for substantial market development of a new energy source. This fact emphasizes the need for immediate action in developing new sources to meet U.S. energy needs. Adapted from Energy Research and Development Administration, *A National Plan for Research, Energy Development, and Demonstration: Creating Energy Choices for the Future, Vol. 1: The Plan*, ERDA 76-1, 1976, p. 2.

Most major energy supply options require facilities that take 5 to 15 years to build; thus new supply installations cannot make a significant contribution for a decade. Similarly, because existing energy-consuming equipment and buildings have lifespans of several years, the current capital stock will not be replaced immediately by more efficient units (e.g., conservatively, the lifespan of existing automobiles is 7 to 10 years; of industrial process equipment, 5 to 20 years; and of homes, 30 to 40 years). Thus, many energy efficiency improvements will not make more than a small difference for a decade or more. Although some of these changes could be accomplished faster in a lively economy, the U.S. economy appears to be less vigorous than some others (for reasons we do not fully understand.

Our energy policies may not actually reduce oil imports to an acceptable level in the near term, but they can demonstrate our firm intention to reduce oil imports and thereby serve to spur other industrial nations to do the same. The U.S. can serve notice to the oil exporters that we will not always remain vulnerable to them. Such a demonstration could reduce the likelihood of a major supply interruption in the near term.

Societal and Institutional Difficulties

Although we must begin implementing some of our energy options at once, the United States has thus far been unable to act resolutely. A political agreement on major energy policies and actions has been elusive, and agreements that have been reached have often been changed later (although there have been exceptions to this, such as oil price decontrol). Several factors have caused this indecisiveness. The most important factor is the adversarial nature of our new pluralistic policy-making system. It does not lead often enough to positive decisions (i.e., decisions that outline specific, direct action to handle problems); more often it leads to indecision, which results in no action being taken at all. This is especially true when the benefits of the decisions appear to be more diffuse than the costs. These processes also make it difficult to arrive at, and to sustain, decisions about long-term needs, partly because the special interest groups who participate in the decision-making process by definition tend to look only at their special interests. This narrow approach does not provide for the long-term needs of the nation.

Clearly, solutions to these problems will be difficult to implement, but progress in this direction would help the country to reduce not only its vulnerability in the short- and mid-term, but also to make a smooth energy transition to the long-term. Reducing uncertainties, developing approaches for reaching consensus, and creating incentives for considering long-term needs should therefore be part of the strategy designed to solve our national energy problem.

International Linkage

The economic and political linkage between the United States and other nations also complicates our handling of the energy situation because it makes a purely national solution to our energy problems—especially a long-term one—impossible. Through international trade agreements and the international monetary system, the U.S. economy ties in with the economies of other trading nations. Thus, the prospects and progress of developing countries, whose demands for economic equality will increase, will have an effect on our economy as well as on world peace and stability. Similarly, energy policy decisions that make sense in terms of U.S. energy objectives may adversely affect our trading partners and the entire international community. Because of their widespread impact, these decisions clearly should be made with thoughtful attention to the wider U.S. interests.

III. ELEMENTS OF FUTURE STRATEGIES

INTRODUCTION

In this chapter we examine a range of options for dealing with the energy issues discussed in Chapter II. The options considered include individual supply and demand technologies, combinations of technologies, and nontechnical approaches.

This chapter responds to the short-term oil import problem with a broad outline of possible approaches to its solution: increased production of oil; the conservation of oil and its substitutes; and the substitution of other, domestic, energy resources for oil. We explore in some detail the most promising elements of these approaches and the chapter culminates in a comparative assessment. The chapter highlights the environmental and social impacts of the various courses of action because they can be equally important in assessing the technical and economic feasibility of an option. In conjunction with the technical measures, a number of social and political actions can prove effective in reducing U.S. vulnerability, and we outline them too. Looking beyond the next twenty or thirty years, this chapter describes approaches for dealing with long-term energy issues.

Providing technical options alone would not address the entire problem, for it would neglect the social means for making and implementing decisions. A good deal of the nation's present difficulty can be attributed to a failure of traditional social mechanisms. Therefore, we give substantial consideration to the means of increasing the effectiveness of energy decisions. This includes a discussion of possible approaches to domestic decisions that affect energy. Finally, we bring selected options face to face with the national energy issues they address.

THE OIL IMPORT PROBLEM

Summary Statement of the Issue

The U.S. dependence on foreign sources of oil is an extremely undesirable situation, as was demonstrated in the previous chapter. The present position of the nation is one of great vulnerability.

- World peace and stability are threatened because no major power like the United States is likely to accede to the loss of a large fraction of its oil supply.
- The nation's freedom of action at home and abroad is threatened by the need to bend to the wishes of oil-controlling forces.
- The health of our economy is threatened by potential oil cutoffs and large balance-of-trade deficits.

The only effective means for reducing this vulnerability is through a considerable reduction of oil imports.

Other Views of the Issue

The last decade has seen a number of major studies that describe other views and possible solutions for the U.S. energy problem. It is instructive to compare several of these briefly.

The Federal Energy Administration in 1974 issued a report requested by the President, entitled *Project Independence* (Zausner, et al, 1974). The report was a response to the Arab oil embargo of 1973, and it accurately identified the near-term energy problem as one of vulnerability to disruptions in oil imports. Many of the policy recommendations* made then seem reasonable today, and indeed, had they been carried out, our present position would be much less precarious.

The recently completed project by the Committee on Nuclear and Alternative Energy Systems (CONAES) recognized that the United States' vulnerability to oil-supplying nations is a significant problem, but it failed to focus on the urgency of the situation. The report of the CONAES Demand and Conservation Panel did not focus on the objective of limiting oil imports as it could have, and instead treated all energy sources equally. Consequently, one is astonished to see that in every single scenario (including those assuming aggressive energy conservation), oil is expected to supply 10% of the primary energy to produce

---

*Some of the policy recommendations included: accelerated development of Alaskan and Outer Continental Shelf oil and gas; standardization and expedited licensing of nuclear power plants; greater use of enhanced recovery techniques for oil; stimulated oil shale production; additional oil and gas pipelines from Alaska to the lower 48; major new domestic pipelines; increased federal leasing and actions to deal with possible environmental and water constraints to allow additional oil shale production; the need to deal directly with fuel mix by sector when implementing conservation policy; substitution of coal for oil and gas in both utility and large industrial use; and stimulation of electric use rather than oil and gas in the building sector. [The recommendations are contained on pages 46-55 of the *Project Independence* document (Zausner, et al, 1974).]

electricity in 2010. Further, oil imports as a percentage of total oil consumption remained at about 40% through 2010, and in the high conservation case imports actually increased to over 50% of consumption.

The style of this CONAES study carries over to the full CONAES report, *Energy in Transition 1985–2010* (H. Brooks, et al, 1979), where moderating demand growth, regardless of the resources affected, is considered the essential response. It is clear that this work misses attacking the most fundamental issue within the planning horizon, the United States' vulnerability to foreign, oil-controlling forces.

The recent update of the National Energy Plan II (NEP-II) in November of 1979 contains the first serious attempt to deal with the problem of vulnerability. Under the proposed program, oil imports are projected as decreasing to zero by 2010, whereas earlier NEP-II strategies projected a *minimum* level of imports equal to 40% of total demand in the year 2000.

The Reagan administration's views are embodied in the *National Energy Policy Plan* (NEPP) of July, 1981. Although NEPP recognizes that reducing oil imports is an important objective, it expresses the view that this problem can be solved by normal market forces. According to NEPP, the primary role of government in reducing oil imports is in deregulation and in expanded leasing of federal lands. The NEPP cautions against subsidies for substitutes for imported oil lest market forces by distorted; no recognition is given to external costs. In essence, the report recognizes imported oil as a problem, but seems not to consider it to be of high national priority requiring major actions by the federal government.

The CONAES report and the National Energy Plans, except for the November 1979 update, are typical of previous attempts to address the energy problem. They superficially recognize the problem of vulnerability, yet they do not deal with it. The following section of this report accepts that neglected challenge.

Broad Outline of Possible Approaches to Solving the Oil Import Problem

Present Uses of Oil

During 1978 the U.S. consumption of petroleum equaled 40 EJ (18 million bbl/d). Imports during this period were 18 EJ (8 million bbl/d), or about 45% of consumption. Developing approaches to reduce the level of imports requires a knowledge of where and how oil is consumed in the U.S.

The use of oil by four end-use sectors in 1978 is shown in Table 7. It is apparent that the transportation sector is by far the largest consumer

Table 7. Oil consumption in 1978 by end-use sector[a]

End-use sector	Consumption		
	EJ/year (10[6] bbl/d[b])	Percentage of total U.S. oil use	Percentage of U.S. oil imports
Transportation	21.16 (9.49)	52.8	117.6
Industrial	7.57 (3.39)	18.9	42.15
Residential/ commercial	7.30 (3.27)	18.2	40.05
Electric utility boilers	3.55 (1.59)	8.9	19.6
Electric utility, peaking	0.47 (0.21)	1.2	2.7
Total	40.05 (17.95)	100.0	222.1

[a]U.S. Department of Energy (1980*d*).

[b]Throughout this report, energy consumption or demand figures will be converted to equivalent oil quantities to provide uniformity and to conform to standard, adopted practices in analyzing energy-related matters. To convert from EJ/year to million bbl/d, divide by 2.23. This calculation is based on a conversion factor of approximately 6.12 GJ/bbl (5.8 × 10[6] Btu/bbl). It should be noted, however, that, based on actual refined product mix (all petroleum products) in 1978 for total U.S. oil consumption, the conversion factor was 5.82 GJ/bbl (5.519 × 10[6] Btu/bbl). Other actual conversion factors were 5.83 GJ/bbl (5.530 × 10[6] Btu/bbl) for the buildings sector; 5.79 GJ/bbl (5.487 × 10[6] Btu/bbl) for the industrial sector; and 5.71 GJ/bbl (5.410 × 10[6] Btu/bbl) for the transportation sector. For the electric utility sector, the fuel mix resulted in an average energy content of 6.56 GJ/bbl (6.225 × 10[6] Btu/bbl).

of petroleum. Nevertheless, none of the end-use sectors is so insignificant relative to oil use that a major change could not cause a significant reduction in oil imports. For example, elimination of use in the utility sector, the smallest user, would be equivalent to reducing imports by over 22%.

Tables 8, 9, and 10 give more detailed information on the end-uses of oil in the transportation, industrial, and residential/commercial sectors, respectively. Oil use in the transportation sector is dominated by automobiles, 11.4 EJ/year (5.13 million bbl/d), and trucks, 5.50 EJ/year (2.47 million bbl/d).

Table 8. Oil consumption by end use in the transportation sector, 1978

End use	Oil consumption [EJ year (10^6 bbl d)]	Percentage of sector oil consumption[a]
Automobile	11.43 (5.13)	54
Truck	5.50 (2.47)	26
Trains, ships, and buses	2.12 (0.95)	10
Aircraft	1.69 (0.76)	8
Miscellaneous	0.42 (0.18)	2
Total	21.16 (9.49)	100

[a]From Samuels (1981).

Table 9. Oil consumption by end use in the industrial sector

End use	Oil consumption[a] [EJ/year (10^6 bbl/d)]	Percentage of sector oil consumption
Process heat	1.12 2.50 (0.50 1.12)	15 33
Process steam	1.06 2.20 (0.48 0.99)	14 29
Nonfuel uses[b]	1.97 2.35 (0.88 1.05)	26 31
Other	0.90 3.04 (0.40 1.36)	12 40
Total	7.57 7.57 (3.39 3.39)	100 100

[a]The numbers on the left side of each column were obtained by using the 1974 disaggregated oil use information in Maloney et al. (1978) and multiplying that information by the total 1978 industrial oil consumption from U.S. Department of Energy (1980d). The numbers on the right side of each column were obtained by using the industrial disaggregations from two studies (Roberson 1979 and Schurr et al. 1979), which are based on interpretations of the data in Maloney et al. (1978).

[b]Primarily for feedstocks.

For industry, there are no reliable energy consumption data. However, the oil use in process heating is at least 1.12 EJ/year (0.50 million bbl/d), and could be as high as 2.50 EJ/year (1.12 million bbl/d). Similarly, oil use for steam-raising applications is at least 1.06 EJ/year

Table 10. Oil consumption by end use in
the residential/commercial sector[a]

End use	Approximate 1978 oil consumption [EJ/year (10^6 bbl/d)]	Percentage of sector oil consumption
Space heating	5.74 (2.57)	79
Road surfacing	1.22 (0.55)	17
Water heating	0.34 (0.15)	4
Total	7.30 (3.27)	100

[a]Data for 1977 (Blue et al. 1979) adjusted to 1978 oil consumption in the residential commercial sector (U.S. Department of Energy 1980d). The difference between 1977 and 1978 is less than 1%.

(0.48 million bbl/d), and could be as high as 2.20 EJ/year (0.99 million bbl/d). Nonfuel uses (primarily feedstocks) are in the range of 1.97 to 2.35 EJ/year (0.88 to 1.05 million bbl/d). All other uses equal between 0.90 and 3.04 EJ/year (0.40 to 1.36 million bbl/d). Data from Barnes, et al, (1976) indicate that as much as 75% of industrial non-feedstock energy is used for process heat and steam-raising applications. Therefore it appears that industrial of oil use are closer to the Roberson-Schurr figures in Table 9 than the DOE/EIA numbers. Consequently, we will use the Roberson-Schurr industrial breakdown in this chapter.

Space and water heating consumes 6.08 EJ/year (2.72 million bbl/d) and accounts for over 80% of the oil used in the residential and commercial sectors. The electric utility sector uses approximately 88% of its oil for boiler fuel, and uses the remainder for peaking operations. Therefore, about 3.55 EJ/year (1.59 million bbl/d) are used for steam-raising.

About 80% of our oil is used in the six devices listed in Table 11. In order of oil use, they are: *1.* automobiles, *2.* space and water heaters, *3.* trucks, *4.* electric utility boilers, *5.* process heaters, and *6.* industrial boilers. These are the end uses that should be given primary attention in any program to reduce oil imports.

Methods of Reducing Oil Imports

There are three general means by which oil imports could be reduced: *1.* produce more oil from domestic resources; *2.* increase the efficiency of oil use (oil conservation); and *3.* substitute other, preferably domestic, energy resources for oil.

Oil Production. The five methods by which the U.S. could increase domestic oil production are shown in Fig. 18, along with a rough measure of the amount of oil associated with each approach. All five approaches are potentially important, but the two with the largest resource bases are coal liquefaction and oil from shale. In both cases, the resource base could supply our 1978 level of oil demand for several hundred years.

Oil Conservation/Efficiency. There are many opportunities to reduce consumption through improvements in efficiency. The efficiency of oil-consuming devices, such as those shown in Table 11, can be improved, or the efficiency of the processes served by these devices can be improved. Improvements in "processes" range from better building envelopes to more efficient manufacturing methods. These have the secondary benefit of decreasing potential environmental and social impacts by lowering the growth rate of energy demand.

Table 11. The six major oil-using devices[a]

Device	Oil consumption (1978)	
	EJ/year (10^6 bbl/d)	Percentage of total U.S. oil consumption
Automobiles	11.43 (5.13)	29
Space and hot water heaters	6.08 (2.73)	16
Trucks	5.50 (2.47)	14
Electric utility boilers	3.55 (1.59)	9
Process heaters	2.50 (1.12)	6
Industrial boilers	2.20 (0.98)	5
Total	31.26 (14.02)	79

[a]Data in this table extracted from Tables 7, 8, and 9.

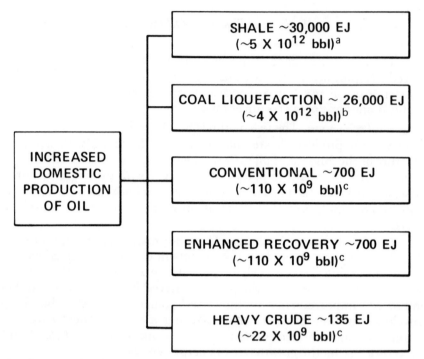

[a]In-place resources [Pasini, J., "Unconventional Sources of Oil," ONEP Overview Paper Number 15 (May 1980)].
[b]Based on converting recoverable resource from Table 1 to oil at 60% efficiency.
[c]Estimated recoverable (Pasini, 1980).

Fig. 18. There are five methods which can substantially contribute to the domestic production of oil. Although one can now only take advantage of the conventional oil resource, they are all potentially important. The two with the largest resource bases are coal liquefaction and oil from shale, which are each sufficient to supply our present oil demand for 500 years.

Even though there are many possibilities for oil conservation, the most effective approach concentrates on the transportation sector, with emphasis on automobiles and trucks. Transportation appears to hold the least promise of being effectively dealt with through the direct substitution of other fuels* for liquid hydrocarbons.

---

*Electricity, natural gas, and hydrogen have been examined as fuels for the transportation sector. Analyses of the electric car concept (Graves, et al, 1980; Samuels, 1980) have indicated that without significant improvements in battery lifetimes and costs electric vehicles are not competitive with internal combustion engines for 1980 gasoline prices below $1.06/L ($4.00/gal). Analysis of hydrogen fuels (Carpenter, 1980) has also indicated that hydrogen will probably not be competitive with hydrocarbon fuels in the transportation sector. While gaseous fuels could function with vehicle and distribution modifications, these fuels could function in the industrial and buildings sector with far fewer modifications to the end-use device and the distribution system.

Substitution. Of the six major oil-using devices shown in Table 11, four are prime candidates for substitute fuels (Table 12). The total substitution potential amounts to about 14 EJ/year or over 6 million barrels of oil per day.

Table 12. Candidates for fuel substitution

Device	1978 oil consumption [EJ/year (10^6 bbl/d)]	Possible substitutes for oil
Space and hot water heaters	6.08 (2.73)	Natural gas Substitute natural gas Electricity (nuclear and coal)
Electric utility boilers[a]	3.55 (1.59)	Coal Nuclear
Industrial process heaters	2.50 (1.13)	Natural gas SNG Intermediate-Btu gas Electricity (nuclear and coal)
Industrial boilers	2.20 (0.99)	Natural gas SNG Intermediate-Btu gas Coal
Total	14.33 (6.44)	

[a] This excludes distillate fuel oil used for peaking operations. In 1978, utilities used 0.47 EJ of distillate fuel oil and jet fuel for peaking (U.S. Department of Energy 1980a).

Of the three general approaches to reducing oil imports, substitution is potentially the most effective in the near-term, although in some ways it is the most complex. This is because it involves both the production and conservation of the substitutes for oil and can involve secondary substitution (i.e., substitution of a third fuel for a second, freeing it to substitute for oil). Methane is a good example of a substitute for oil. Methane can be produced from conventional sources (natural gas), from coal, from Devonian shale, etc., in exact parallel to the production of more oil. Methane can be conserved in one place so that the savings can be used to displace oil elsewhere. And finally, another fuel can be substituted for some present use of methane (e.g., in the production of electricity) so that the displaced methane can be used to substitute for oil in another application.

Approaches Selected for Detailed Analysis. Based on the above considerations, the approaches selected for more detailed analysis are:

Production

Enhanced Oil Recovery

Heavy Crudes

Oil From Shales

Oil From Coal

Substitutes for oil

Coal For Industrial Boilers

Coal and Nuclear For Electricity Production

Electricity and Gas For Space and Hot Water Heating

Conservation

Automobiles and Trucks

Conservation of Oil and Oil Substitutes (Gas and Electricity) in Buildings and Industries

Many energy source and saving options have been omitted from this list, and their absence does not necessarily indicate that they are not worthwhile. However, those selected have the potential for making a rapid and significant impact and, in all cases, are technologies that are both available and economical at the present time. For example, these selection criteria eliminate various solar-based technologies because they either cannot provide major oil-replacement energy within the near- to mid-term or because they are not economically competitive (although with additional development they may become so).

In the subsections that follow, the various energy technologies are discussed with an emphasis on how much oil they can produce or displace. Note that the ranges indicated are maximum capabilities and are not necessarily either suggested or desirable strategies. These figures give the reader an understanding of the upper limits to which the technologies might be pressed.

Production of Oil or Oil Substitutes

Oil

Enhanced Oil Recovery. Conventional and unconventional production of oil in the United States could maintain oil supplies at a fairly constant level, with the possibility of a small decline, over the next two decades. Much of this oil would be produced using enhanced recovery techniques or be obtained from less conventional sources. Enhanced oil recovery (EOR) processes can include thermal processes (steam injection or partial combustion to decrease viscosity and to drive oil), chemical processes (injection of petroleum sulfonates or other surfactants to decrease the tension between oil and water phases, polyacrylamide and polysaccharide use to increase viscosity and control mobility of the aqueous drive phase), and gas miscible displacement (by injection of gases such as carbon dioxide or nitrogen, which also provide oil drive) (Pasini, 1980).

Estimates of ultimate recovery and daily production from EOR have been made by the Office of Technology Assessment (OTA) (Robel, et al, 1978) and are shown in Table 13. This table displays both a high performance and a low performance set of figures that depend on the eventual efficiencies of the technologies employed. According to the OTA study, EOR could add from 155 EJ to 254 EJ (25.3 to 41.6 billion bbl) to the estimated domestic oil resource, with oil priced at $4.58/GJ ($28/bbl). Higher oil prices would result in an increase in the recoverable resource base.

Pasini (1980) estimates that 1400 EJ (230 billion bbl) of oil will remain in place following primary production and thus will be a target for EOR. He judges that about half of this, 700 EJ (115 billion bbl), will be potentially recoverable. However, he believes that EOR will ultimately yield only 1.1 EJ/year (500,000 bbl/d) from 1990 through 2010. The general lack of understanding about potential EOR formations, the need for further development of EOR techniques, and the uncertain economics of the more costly processes will combine to limit yields severely.

Heavy Crudes. Heavy crude oils, found mainly in California, represent a smaller potential resource estimated to equal 450 EJ (74 billion bbl) (Pasini, 1980). Recoverable resources, assuming 30% recovery, are estimated to be 135 EJ (22 billion bbl) or about 20% of the conventional resources. Current production is about 0.55 EJ/year (0.25 million

Table 13. Estimate of ultimate recovery and daily
production rates from enhanced oil recovery
at $4.58/GJ ($28/bbl)[a,b]

Ultimate recovery [EJ (10^9 bbl)]	Production rates [EJ/year (10^6 bbl/d)]		
	1985	1990	2000
High process performance 254 (41.6)	2.9 (1.3)	6.2 (2.8)	18 (8.2)
Low process performance 155 (25.3)	2.0 (0.9)	4.0 (1.8)	11 (5.1)

[a]Robel et al. (1978).
[b]Price adjusted to 1980 basis.

bbl/d). Federal legislation in 1979 exempted heavy crude from price controls and excise taxes and was designed to raise production by 0.44 EJ/year (0.2 million bbl/d) in 1985 and 1.1 EJ/year (0.5 million bbl/d) in 1990 (Olszewski, 1980). Pasini (1980) estimates that heavy oils can be produced at levels of 0.9 EJ/year (400,000 bbl/d) in 1990, increasing to 2.2 EJ/year (1 million bbl/d) after 2000.

Oil From Shale. The production of oil from shale has attracted considerable interest in the U.S. because of the enormous resource of the Eastern and Western shales, totaling 30,000 EJ (4,900 billion bbl) between them. The major oil shale deposits in the United States are the Green River Formation in the west and the Devonian Formations in the east.

The Green River Formation underlies parts of northern Colorado, eastern Utah, and southern Wyoming. The oil contained in the formation exceeds 12,000 EJ or two trillion barrels (in-place resources), but the oil content and formation thickness are highly variable. The Piceance Creek Basin of northern Colorado is the area of greatest commercial interest for the foreseeable future. This area contains approximately 3700 EJ (600 billion bbl) of oil (in-place) in shale greater than 400 feet in thickness and containing greater than 4 MJ/kg (25 gallons of oil/ton) (Pasini, 1980).

The Piceance Creek Basin resource, over 80% of which is owned by the federal government, covers an area of only about 600 square miles. Since the stripping ratio (overburden to shale thickness ratio) generally ranges from 0.3 to 0.5, open-pit mining would be the appropriate ore recovery technique. Using open-pit mining and surface retorting, the recoverable oil from the Piceance Creek Basin alone could provide nearly a century of oil at the 1978 U.S. consumption rate ($\sim$40 EJ/year or 18 million bbl/d)—this from an area that could be contained in a circle with a 24-km (15-mile) radius (Lewis, 1979).

The eastern Devonian black marine shale was laid down by a shallow inland sea, the Chattanooga Sea, which covered much of the eastern U.S. until about 350 million years ago. The shale is a potential source of several strategic resources including natural gas, oil, and uranium. The Institute of Gas Technology (IGT) conducted a survey of the kerogen (oil) content of Devonian shale in 1977. The IGT conclusion was that the best commercial possibilities are in Ohio, Kentucky, Tennessee, and Indiana. Oil content of the shale is generally around 1.6 MJ/kg (10 gal/ton) as determined by the Fischer assay. IGT claims, however, that by using hydrogen retorting, rather than conventional thermal retorting, the total hydrocarbon yield was up to 2.5 times that indicated by the Fischer assay. This difference in hydrogen retort behavior between the eastern and western shales is probably due to the lower hydrogen content of the Devonian shales.

Based on their survey results, IGT estimates that the recoverable resource of surface-minable eastern shales is 2590 EJ (423 billion bbl), if oil is recovered by their HYTORT process. Table 14 shows the geographic distribution of the surface-minable resource.

Table 14. Recoverable resources of eastern shale[a]

State	EJ	10^9 bbl	GJ m^2	bbl acre
Ohio	860	140	333	220,000
Kentucky	1,160	190	169	112,000
Tennessee	270	44	67	44,000
Indiana	240	40	157	104,000
Michigan	31	5	74	49,000
Alabama	24	4	32	21,000
Total or average	2,585	423	160	106,000

[a]Weil et al. (1978).

The basic approach in most shale processing is to heat (retort) the rock to above $\sim$400°C ($\sim$750°F), thermally decomposing the kerogen to shale oil and gaseous products. However, the oil produced is not suitable for feedstock to an oil refinery without further hydrotreating (increasing the hydrogen-to-carbon ratio). Two general methods of shale retorting are under consideration: *1.* mining and surface retorting and *2. in situ* retorting.

Mining and surface retorting is the more conventional approach and is considered ready for near-term commercialization. In addition, various *in situ* retorting concepts are being developed. The basic approach is to recover the oil directly from the shale in the ground. A modified *in situ* (MIS) process has near-term possibilities. It involves creating a cavity by mining a portion of the shale, rubblizing the surrounding shale with explosives, and retorting by establishing a flame front within the rubble. Expected advantages of *in situ* processes include reduced shale disposal problems, reduced water requirements, access to deep shale resources, and lower cost. Oil recovery does, however, tend to be low. Commercial applications of *in situ* processing are not expected before 1990.

Generally, economic data on shale oil production are not well established. Two example cost estimates for producing a refining feed from western shale via surface mining and retorting are shown in Table 15. A similar example for oil from eastern shale is given in Table 16.

Table 15. **Examples of cost estimates for oil production from western shale (includes hydrotreating)**

	Source of data	
	Lawrence Livermore Laboratory[a]	Office of Technology Assessment[b]
Capital cost, $ GJ d ($ bbl d)[c]	2,160 (13,230)	6,100 (37,400)
Operating and maintenance cost, $ GJ ($ bbl)[c]	1.59 (9.73)	2.16 (13.20)
Levelized costs, $ GJ ($ bbl)[d]		
Capital	1.36 (8.30)	3.83 (23.45)
O&M	2.40 (14.69)	3.27 (20.00)
Total	3.76 (22.99)	7.10 (43.45)

[a]Lewis (1979).
[b]Sladek et al. (1980).
[c]These data were adjusted to 1980 basis using the standards in Appendix C.
[d]Levelized costs based on this study's ground rules for 20-year industrial financing.

Table 16. Cost estimate for oil production from eastern shale
using the HYTORT process (includes hydrotreating)[a]

	$ GJ	$ bbl	$ GJ d	$ bbl d
Capital cost[b]			4,590	28,100
Operating and maintenance cost[b]	1.23	7.50		
Levelized costs[c]				
Capital	2.89	17.60		
O&M	1.85	11.30		
Total	4.74	28.90		

[a]Weil et al. (1978).
[b]These data were adjusted to 1980 basis using the standards in Appendix C.
[c]Levelized costs based on this study's ground rules for 20-year industrial financing.

The estimated investments range from $2,160/GJ/d ($13,200 per daily barrel) to $6,100/GJ/d ($37,400 per daily barrel) of capacity. The levelized production costs range from $3.76/GJ ($22.99/bbl) to $7.10/GJ ($43.45/bbl), and they compare favorably with a levelized price of $9/GJ ($55/bbl) for conventional oil based on a 1980 price of $4.90/GJ ($30/bbl).

The environmental and health considerations in developing a shale oil industry have been reviewed by Walsh, et al (1980) and by Craig and Salk (1980). These concerns include *1.* the possibility of toxic and/or carcinogenic constituents being released in the environment; *2.* solid waste disposal; *3.* air pollution problems; *4.* water requirements in a water poor area; and 5. socioeconomic impacts.

Issues of water quality encompass the wastewater produced by retorting, the effect of discharge water on the total dissolved salt content in the Colorado and White Rivers (for the western shales), and the leaching of trace elements and other contaminants from stockpiled oil shale and from processed oil shale. For the *in situ* processes the water quality problem is more uncertain. Water is available, even in the semiarid west, to support a 2 EJ/year ($\sim$1 million bbl/d) industry. Moreover, with the high-value product of such an undertaking, many options for water aquisition become economic (importation, distillation, etc.), and further study should tend to dispel the "water short-age" myth.*

There is little question that a 2 EJ/year ($\sim$1 million bbl/d) shale oil operation would have an impact on the land surface due to the solid waste that would accumulate, but this impact should not be exaggerated. If half the plants are surface retorts, the total land used for disposal by the year 2000 would be only 2000 *hectares* (5000 acres) and, with successful reclamation and proper siting, should not cause a major impact. Longer-term use of such techniques would, naturally, involve considerably more land, although the total disturbed area would probably never become great.

Air quality problems are most likely to arise in using the oil shale resources underlying the Piceance Basin. Inversions are common, and while there are, as yet, few industrial activities in the basin, ambient levels of ozone, non-methane hydrocarbons, and particulates occasionally exceed the National Ambient Air Quality Standard. It is therefore likely that increased oil shale development will increase the number of times the standard is exceeded.

Standards may also be violated for sulfur dioxide. In addition to the usual pollutants, mercury, cadmium, and selenium are volatilized in some processes and would escape unless controlled. EPA models suggest that present air quality standards for the prevention of significant deterioration will limit Piceance Basin production to 0.9 EJ/year (400,000 bbl/d) (Sladek, et al, 1980†), although product value is likely to be great enough to allow considerable application of control technology.

A 2 EJ/year ($\sim$1 million bbl/d) industry would employ about 40,000 workers in steady-state operation. This would rapidly bring some

---

*Consider, for example, the economic implications of hauling water 1600km (1000 miles) by rail from the Mississippi River to oil shale processing plants in northwest Colorado. Assuming a rail tariff of 1.4¢/Mg-km(2¢/ton-mile), the cost of transporting 200L (1bbl) of water would be approximately $3.40. Since a barrel of water would process at least a half barrel of oil, the water would contribute a cost of less than $1.15/GJ($7/bbl) of oil. Even though the rail transport of Mississippi River water thus seems to be economically feasible, it is not proposed because there are many better ways of providing water (e.g., pipeline transport, choice of closer sources of water, redesign of plants for improved water-use efficiency, etc.). But the water supply "problem" is clearly amenable to practical solutions.

---

†The application of gas-cooled reactors to this problem has been suggested. High-temperature nonpolluting heat of the HTGR could have significant advantages (Kasten, 1981).

200,000 people into a previously rural area. It is clear that this population increase would be one of the major impacts. The socioeconomic issues are the usual ones: First, increases in employment and other economic activity, followed by increases in crime, divorce, alcoholism, and mental illness; and strains on schools, wastewater treatment plants, housing, and public facilities of various kinds. Many of these factors have always (inevitably perhaps) been part of the cost of economic growth and progress. These costs should be covered by revenues from the industry as much as possible. The rise in product price necessary to accomplish this should be regarded as a desirable internalization of the total social costs of production (Schuller, 1981). Good planning and mitigation strategies can reduce or eliminate some of the problems and turn others into opportunities.

Assuming that the limitations imposed by various environmental standards are removed or that ways are found to mitigate the impacts of a major shale oil industry, Pasini (1980) projects production levels of 0.9 EJ/year (400,000 bbl/d) in 1990 and 2.2 EJ/year (1 million bbl/d) in 2000. Lewis (1979) believes that production can reach 2.2 to 4.4 EJ/year (1 to 2 million bbl/d) in 1995 and that 11 EJ/year (5 million bbl/d) is possible. Present projects should yield 0.18 to 0.29 EJ/year (80,000 to 130,000 bbl/d) in 1985, with further growth dependent on environmental regulations and the logistics of development.

Oil From Coal

The production of liquid fuels from coal is a particularly attractive option because of the enormous recoverable coal resources possessed by the U.S. (43,300 EJ or 1,800 billion tons), which are relatively inexpensive to recover (Olszewski, 1980). Furthermore, the technology to produce liquids from coal has been demonstrated on a large scale with the South African SASOL plant.

About two-thirds of the oil used in the U.S. is in the form of gasoline, distillate fuel oil, or jet fuel. Only 17% is in the form of heavy (residual) fuel oil (US Department of Energy, 1980d). The market for this product, however, has an uncertain future because most residual oil is used in utility and large industrial boilers. No new oil-fired boilers should be planned. Therefore, coal liquefaction plants need to produce a product mix biased toward the light to middle hydrocarbons.

Processes. Over 70 coal liquefaction processes have been proposed. These generally fall into one of three classes: *1.* indirect liquefaction, *2.* direct liquefaction, and *3.* pyrolysis.

There are three major indirect liquefaction processes: methanol synthesis, Fischer-Tropsch (SASOL), and Mobil-MTG. The first two are commercially available, and the Mobil process appears to be ready for commercialization. All of the indirect processes start with intermediate-Btu gas produced from coal, followed by catalytic synthesis to liquids. Generally, indirect processes tend to produce product mixes biased toward the light to medium hydrocarbons (Cochran, 1980).

Direct liquefaction processes involve reacting coal with hydrogen at elevated temperature and pressure. There are no direct liquefaction processes commercially available today. Because of the potential for lower cost with direct liquefaction (relative to indirect), the DOE has put most of its research and development resources into direct processes. The DOE program focuses on four processes: *1.* two solvent refined coal processes (SRC-I and SRC-II), *2.* the Exxon Donor Solvent (EDS) Process, and *3.* the H-Coal process. It is possible that one or all of these processes will be commercial within 5 to 10 years. Generally, the product mix from direct processes has a high fraction of heavy hydrocarbons and, as noted previously, the future market for heavy fuel oil is likely to decline. Further hydrotreating (at additional cost) will probably be necessary to obtain more marketable products. Table 17 shows a representative set of products from each of the processes discussed above.

Pyrolysis processes convert coal to a wide variety of liquid, gaseous, and solid products through the application of heat in a gas-solid contactor with or without the application of hydrogen overpressure. A small commercial pyrolysis plant has been in operation in Kemmerer, Wyoming for more than a decade. Pyrolysis is at or near commercial readiness for western non-caking coals and is about ready for demonstration on eastern caking coal (Cochran, 1980). Neither the U.S. government nor industry is enthusiastic about pyrolysis. Nevertheless, if applied in conjunction with the supply of coal for electric power plants, pyrolysis could be used to skim the cream, so to speak, from coal prior to combustion.

Economics. Cost estimates for coal liquefaction plants show wide variations because many of the processes are highly conceptual. Industrial experience in the United States is lacking even for those that are near-commercial. Capital cost estimates for coal liquefaction plants range from $4,000 to $11,000/GJ/d ($25,000 to $70,000 per daily barrel) of capacity. Product cost estimates generally range from $3 to $10/GJ ($20 to $60/bbl).

A recent study by Gilbert Associates for ORNL, discussed by Cochran (1980), probably contains some of the best capital cost as well as operations and maintenance (O&M) cost information presently available. Two liquefaction processes were evaluated: EDS, representing di-

Table 17. Typical product states from
coal liquefaction processes[a,b]

Process	Product	Percentage of fuel output
Direct processes		
SRC-I	SRC solid	88
	Heavy fuel oil	12
SRC-II	Liquid petroleum gas	6
	Naphtha	14
	Heavy fuel oil	73
	Gas	7
Exxon Donor Solvent	Propane	3
	Butane	3
	Naphtha	29
	Heavy fuel oil	50
	Gas	15
H-Coal (fuel oil)	Naphtha	26
	Heavy fuel oil	69
	Gas	5
H-Coal (syncrude)	Naphtha	44
	Heavy fuel oil	40
	Gas	16
Indirect processes		
Fischer-Tropsch	Gasoline	33
	LPG	28
	No. 2 fuel oil	2
	Heavy fuel oil	5
	Gas	32
Mobil-MTG	Gasoline	90
	LPG	10
Methanol	Methyl fuel	93
	Methanol	7

[a]Product states are illustrative only, and significant shifts of a product state for each process are possible by adjustments to plant design.
[b]Cochran (1980).

rect processes, and Mobil-MTG, representing indirect processes,. Cost data based on the Gilbert study are shown in Table 18. For the EDS process, the estimated capital cost is $5,770/GJ/d ($35,300/bbl/d). The estimated capital cost for Mobil-MTG is $6,980/GJ/d ($42,700/bbl/d). Levelized product costs are $6.60-8.00/GJ ($40-49/bbl) for EDS and $7.70/GJ ($47/bbl) for Mobil-MTG. In comparison, the levelized cost of natural crude, based on the analogous economic ground rules of this study, would be $9/GJ ($55/bbl) if the 1980 price is taken to be $4.90/GJ ($30/bbl).

There are two general observations that can be made if the cost estimates can be taken at face value. First, the Mobil-MTG process is clearly worth early commercialization because it produces a very marketable product (gasoline) at a cost not much different from the mix of products from EDS, 50% of which is heavy fuel oil. Second, both of the processes are a good buy relative to imported oil.

Environmental and Health Issues. In reviewing the implications of accelerated mining and coal conversion, Walsh, et al (1980) conclude that the number of deaths and disabling injuries per year could equal 100 to 330 and 6,900 to 23,000, respectively, by the year 2000, extrapolating from current rates. Underground accident rates (the larger number given above) are about three to four times surface accident rates, and therefore the rate of death and injury might be slowed by greater reliance on the surface mining of western coals. The source of disease in coal miners is related to dust concentrations (coal worker's pneumoconiosis). It is also expected that mining deaths and injuries per unit of production will continue their historic decline as safety technology continues to improve.

The public health and safety are also affected by the transportation of coal to energy demand centers. This could amount to 10-15% of the fatalities associated with mining. Potential health hazards from coal storage and preparation are related to methods of controlling wind erosion of coal piles, coal pile runoff, and sulfur reduction. Trace elements are also a concern in developing methods for coal preparation.

While concern about the effects of coal combustion on health centers on the general population, the major concern about coal conversion processes is for the work force. The principal concern is lung cancer although cardiovascular, pulmonary, and metabolic toxins are also important. There are indications that increased coal conversion could result in increased cancer among workers. The use of direct processes in particular could cause a higher incidence of cancer among workers. Indirect conversion processes appear to pose considerably less of a carcinogenic problem than do the direct processes.

Potential for Displacing Imported Oil. An early construction program for coal liquefaction plants would probably be based on an indirect process, either Fischer-Tropsch (SASOL) or Mobil-MTG or both, because: *1.* indirect processes are technically and commercially better established, *2.* the products fit the market needs, and *3.* the public health effects are a lesser issue for indirect than for direct liquefaction. Using the cost data for Mobil-MTG (Table 18) and making allowances for mine development, it appears that \$8,170/GJ/d (\$50,000 per daily barrel) of capacity is a representative investment for indirect liquefaction plants.

Table 18. Representative[a] cost data for coal liquefaction[b]

	EDS	Mobil-MTG
Capital investment, \$ GJ d (\$ bbl d)	5,770 (35,300)	6,980 (42,700)
Conversion efficiency, c_i	63.3	62.0
Levelized product cost, \$ GJ (\$ bbl)		
Capital	3.61 (22.12)	4.28 (26.21)
Coal	3.05 (18.69)	1.68 (10.30)
Operating and maintenance	1.33 (8.12)	1.66 (10.17)
Total	8.00 (48.93)[d]	7.63 (46.68)

[a] These estimates are for plants that might reasonably be designed, built, and operated beginning immediately. It is reasonable to assume that an Exxon Donor Solvent plant (or other direct liquefaction plant) designed, built, and operated beginning in 1990 would have improved efficiency by 5 to 15 percentage points, resulting in substantial improvements in cost. The Mobil-MTG process (and other indirect liquefaction processes) appears to be less·amenable to such substantial improvement.

[b] Cochran (1980).

[c] The cost for the eastern coal used in the EDS process is \$1.25/GJ (\$28.90/ton), and its energy value is 25.6 MJ/kg (22.0 million Btu/ton). The cost for the western coal used in the Mobil-MTG process is \$0.67/GJ (\$13.90 ton), and its energy value is 22.8 MJ/kg (19.6 million Btu/ton).

[d] Eastern coal is much more expensive, but has a slightly higher energy content, than western coal. If coal with the same price per unit of energy as western coal could be used in the EDS process, the product price would fall to \$6.59/GJ (\$40.33 bbl).

If, within 20 years, the U.S. could develop a new source of domestic oil equal to our 1978 level of imports (18 EJ/year or 8 million bbl/d), the oil import problem would be under control. Doing this with coal liquefaction alone probably is not the best solution, but to understand better the magnitude of such an undertaking, we developed an example which included a construction schedule, capital needs, and mining requirements. These data comprise Tables 19 and 20, merely as an example of the capability of coal conversion and not as a suggested strategy. The example schedule (Table 19) shows two construction starts (0.134 EJ/year or 60,000 bbl/d each) in 1981. By the early 1990's, a steady-state is established with 12 plants being completed each year. The approximate oil production rates are: 2.4EJ/year ($\sim$1 million bbl/d) in 1990, 9 EJ/year (4 million bbl/d) in 1995, and 18 EJ/year (8 million

Table 19. **Example of a building schedule that could provide 18 EJ/year (8 × 10⁶ bbl/d) of liquids from coal in 20 years**

Calendar year end	Number of plant starts	Number of plant completions[a]		Capacity [EJ/year (10⁶ bbl/d)]		Total oil production[b] [EJ year (10⁶ bbl/d)]
		Per year	Cumulative	Per year	Cumulative	
1980	0					
1981	2					
1982	4					
1983	6					
1984	8					
1985	10					
1986	12	2	2	0.27 (0.12)	0.27 (0.12)	
1987	12	4	6	0.54 (0.24)	0.80 (0.36)	0.241 (0.108)
1988	12	6	12	0.80 (0.36)	1.61 (0.72)	0.723 (0.324)
1989	12	8	20	1.10 (0.48)	2.67 (1.20)	1.445 (0.648)
1990	12	10	30	1.34 (0.60)	4.01 (1.80)	2.408 (1.080)
1991	12	12	42	1.61 (0.72)	5.62 (2.52)	3.613 (1.620)
1992	12	12	54	1.61 (0.72)	7.23 (3.24)	5.058 (2.268)
1993	12	12	66	1.61 (0.72)	8.83 (3.96)	6.503 (2.916)
1994	12	12	78	1.61 (0.72)	10.4 (4.68)	7.948 (3.564)
1995	12	12	90	1.61 (0.72)	12.0 (5.40)	9.393 (4.212)
1996		12	102	1.61 (0.72)	13.6 (6.12)	10.84 (4.860)
1997		12	114	1.61 (0.72)	15.3 (6.84)	12.28 (5.508)
1998		12	126	1.61 (0.72)	16.9 (7.56)	13.73 (6.156)
1999		12	138	1.61 (0.72)	18.5 (8.28)	15.17 (6.804)
2000		12	150	1.61 (0.72)	20.1 (9.00)	16.62 (7.452)
2001			150		20.1 (9.00)	18.06 (8.100)

[a]Five-year design and construction period for each 0.134 EJ/year (60,000 bbl/d) plant.
[b]Plants operated at 90% of their capacity.

Table 20. Capital and coal-mining requirements related
to a hypothetical 20-year program to produce
18 EJ/year (8 × 10⁶ bbl/d) of liquids from coal

Calendar year	Capital requirements (10⁹ 1980 dollars)	Coal mining requirements[a] [10⁶ t/year (10⁶ tons/year)]	
1980	0		
1981	0		
1982	1.2		
1983	3.6		
1984	7.2		
1985	12.0		
1986	18.0		
1987	24.0	15	(17)
1988	28.8	46	(51)
1989	32.4	92	(101)
1990	34.8	153	(169)
1991	36.0	230	(253)
1992	36.0	322	(355)
1993	36.0	414	(456)
1994	36.0	505	(557)
1995	36.0	598	(659)
1996	36.0	689	(760)
1997	28.8	781	(861)
1998	21.6	873	(963)
1999	14.4	965	(1064)
2000	7.2	1057	(1165)
2001		1149	(1267)
Total	450.0		

[a]Assumes an equal mix of eastern and western coals.

bbl/d) in 2001. Annual capital requirements (Table 20) reach $36 billion in the 1990's. Coal requirements (Table 20) start at 15 million tonnes/year (17 million short tons/year) in 1987 and reach 1.1 billion tonnes/year (1.3 billion short tons/year) in 2001.

A program to replace all imported oil by liquids from coal would result in a major new energy industry, but certainly not one of unprecedented size. The peak investment of $36 billion per year for the coal liquefaction program in the example is approximately the same as the current rate of expenditure by the electric utility industry. Actually, the utility industry's rate reflects the current low level of new construction. By the mid-1990's, utilities will probably have an annual capital expenditure of greater than $80 billion (*Electrical World*, 1979) or more than twice the peak rates of investment for the example coal conversion industry. Furthermore, the average annual growth in capital expenditures for utilities is expected to be $3.3 billion per year from 1980 to 1995. The average annual increase during the growth period of the example coal liquefaction industry is $3.6 billion per year, a figure close to the expected annual increase for utilities. The average annual increase in investment is a good indication of the required expansion in engineering, construction, and manufacturing (heat exchangers, pumps, etc.) capability.

Whether or not the necessary rate of expansion and the magnitude of coal mining are feasible depends very much upon other demands for coal, especially by the utility industry. The demand for coal by utilities will depend, among other things, upon the extent to which nuclear power is used. Total U.S. demand for coal mining for domestic consumption is illustrated in Table 21 given three different assumptions about the use of nuclear power. The required growth rate in coal mining ranges from 5.2% per year for the maximum use of nuclear power to 7.5% per year for a nuclear power phaseout. Based on historical evidence, it is likely that either growth rate is achievable (see Figs. 8 and 17 for increased energy demand and energy consumption patterns).

Table 21. Total demand for coal in the year 2000 if coal liquefaction were proceeding at 18 EJ/year (8 × 10^6 bbl/d)

	Domestic coal demand in the year 2000[a] [10^6 t/year (10^6 tons/year)]		
	Nuclear phaseout	NEP-II nuclear 270 GW(e)	Maximum nuclear 450 GW(e)
Industrial	0.37 (0.41)	0.37 (0.41)	0.37 (0.41)
Oil production	1.15 (1.27)	1.15 (1.27)	1.15 (1.27)
Electricity	1.55 (1.71)	0.91 (1.00)	0.47 (0.52)
Total	3.08 (3.39)	2.43 (2.68)	2.00 (2.20)
Growth rate in mining capability from 1980, %/year	7.5	6.2	5.2

[a]Based on NEP-II electricity demand and industrial coal use (medium oil-price case) (U.S. Department of Energy 1979g).

Concluding Remarks. If industry and the federal government make a major commitment to coal liquefaction, it is likely that a production capability of 18 EJ/year (8 million bbl/d) *could* be achieved in the next 20 years. The total investment would amount to about $450 billion (1980 dollars), a modest figure considering that our imported oil bill over the 20-year period would be four times as great, based on current oil prices and import rate. Furthermore, the levelized product price would be less than the levelized import price of oil. The required investment would approximately equal

- About 1% of U.S. GNP over the 20-year period or
- 15% to 20% of the U.S. military budget and or
- An investment as a percentage of GNP similar to South Africa's SASOL program.

The required rate of coal mining expansion over the 20-year period seems well within our capabilities, especially if the electric utility industry makes maximum use of nuclear power; in this case the needed rate of coal expansion would be a little over 5% per year. The potential environmental effects from such levels of coal use are large, but can be kept to traditionally acceptable levels with care in site selection, careful use of control technology, and adequate reclamation (Craig and Salk, 1979).

A serious effort to reduce our oil imports through coal liquefaction must, by necessity, be based initially on indirect liquefaction. This is not to say that direct processes will not be useful, especially near the end of the century, as the technology develops with improved efficiency, and *if* they can create the products that are needed at a cost competitive with established indirect processes.

Substitution for Present Uses of Oil or Oil Substitutes

There are a number of significant consumers of oil or oil substitutes in several areas of the industrial, building, and utility sectors. Many of these users could improve both their own and the nation's energy position by using less precious fuels than they do now. In industry, coal and coal-derived fuels can potentially replace oil and natural gas. Coal and nuclear fuels are prime candidates for replacing oil and natural gas in the utility sector; federal legislation (Fuel Use Act) is now mandating use of these more abundant fuels for new plants. In the building sector, both electricity (that not generated by oil) and natural gas are good substitutes for oil.

The following section will discuss the potential of such substitutions as a partial solution to the oil import problem. Again, the magnitude of the substitutions show the maximum effect that is reasonable but it does not necessarily reflect an optimum strategy.

Coal and Coal-Derived Fuels in Industry

While there are many diverse industrial processes, the applications for coal and coal-derived fuels fall into two general categories: steam generation and nonsteam process heat. These account for approximately 70% of the non-transportation use of liquid fuel in the industrial sector. The Fuel Use Act of 1978, which requires a shift from oil and gas to coal, is aimed primarily at new installations. However, the immediate challenge is the replacement of existing oil and gas equipment, and therefore the major target of this analysis will be retrofit applications.

For much of industry, the switch to direct coal combustion involves consideration of environmental constraints, financing difficulties and economic feasibility. Unfortunately, the heavily industrialized regions of the country already reach or exceed the ambient limits for one or more air pollutants, and a switch to coal may result in the violation of air quality regulations. Areas that are not in compliance must offset a new source of pollution with an equal decrease in another source within that region.

Direct Coal Combustion for Steam Applications. Since present legislation does not require the industrial sector to convert existing equipment to coal, any decision to convert will be based on economic merit.

The capital requirements for coal systems are three to four times greater than those for equipment burning oil or gas. This is complicated by the need to replace steam generation facilities in large increments because of the economies of scale regarding coal handling facilities. And this conflicts with past practice of using packaged oil and gas units, which can be added as needed to accommodate growth and to replace obsolete units. Further, the inability to produce package coal units with capacities in excess of 6 kg/s (50,000 lb/h) of steam restricts coal use. Unlike oil and gas units, which can be produced in package form for generating up to 50 kg/s (400,000 lb/h) of steam, equivalent coal units would be too large to produce in a package form.

The scope of the project changes from an equipment purchase to a major construction project for those industries that choose a field-erected, coal-fired boiler. Adding to the complexity are environmental regulations that require coal-fired installations to include devices that remove sulfur and particulates. A packaged unit can be installed in less than a year; a field-erected, coal-fired system will take three to four times as long and will require greater amounts of management and technical support.

These difficulties are reflected in Fig. 19, which shows an estimate of the aggregate market for direct combustion in steam boilers. This represents the voluntary market for boiler installations that could economically justify shifting to coal. At oil prices of $4/GJ ($25/bbl), coal would be competitive for less than 20% of the market. This would displace about 0.44 EJ/year (197,000 bbl/d) of oil.

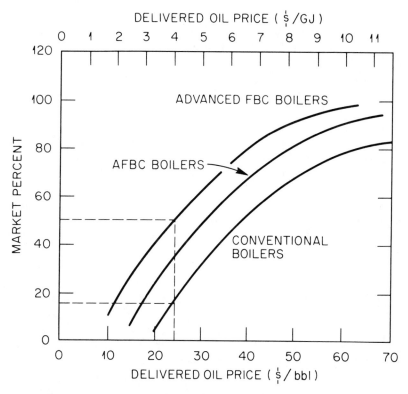

Fig. 19. The market for coal as an industrial boiler fuel is a strong function of the cost of oil. The large capital expense required for coal combustion and the lack of small, conventional packaged boilers has kept the market modest in size. The availability of larger capacity packaged boilers made possible by the use of fluidized bed combustion can significantly expand the potential for coal. [Fox, E. C. and Graves, R. L., "The Outlook for Coal Combustion," ONEP Overview Paper Number 11B (January 1980)].

Several technological improvements, however, could improve the economic feasibility of coal combustion and add to the potential market. The atmospheric fluidized bed combustor (AFBC) concept is one such technology. It allows the elimination of scrubbers, making the system somewhat cheaper (Fox and Graves, 1980). More importantly, however, the AFBC is compact and could be marketed as a packaged system with larger capacities than conventional coal-fired boilers. The decreases in capital cost result in a comparable market penetration of up to 30%. Thus the total oil displaced by using AFBCs is potentially 0.66 EJ/year (296,000 bble/d).

The supercharged or intermediate-pressure fluidized bed combustor (advanced FBC) could offer further improvements. Because these systems operate under a pressure of 0.3 to 0.5 MPa (3 to 5 atm), the boiler can be one-third to one-fifth the size of an AFBC. An advanced FBC would be somewhat cheaper, and a preliminary design estimate indicated that shop-fabricated, packaged boilers with a capacity as large as 25 kg/s (200,000 lb/h) could be built to fit on a rail car (Fox and Graves, 1980). Experience with conventional boiler systems shows that shop fabrication can provide a 30% to 40% savings in cost for the system. Figure 19 indicates that this technology could increase the market penetration of coal to 50% compared to oil at $4/GJ ($25/bbl), raising the potential oil and gas savings to 1.10 EJ/year (493,000 bble/d).

Direct Process Heat Applications. The conversion of industrial process heat sources to coal is quite different from the conversion of boilers. Some applications, such as kilns for cement production, are relatively easy to convert to coal. However, conventional coal equipment suitable for most direct process heat applications is not available. Even if suitable equipment were developed, it is unlikely that the conversion would be economical. Unlike boilers, which generally have an economic lifetime of 15 to 25 years, a direct process heater is often an integral part of a specific process and may be obsolete in 3 to 5 years. Thus, a high capital energy option will not be favored even if operating costs are much lower. In addition, process heaters are typically much smaller than boilers (Fig. 20). As demonstrated in previous sections, this does not lend itself to the use of coal. In view of these considerations, direct coal combustion is not likely to have a significant impact on process heat applications other than, perhaps, kilns.

Coal-Derived Gas. Gas derived from coal can be used directly in existing industrial facilities. Thus, the potential market includes all of the gas and most of the oil currently used by industry.

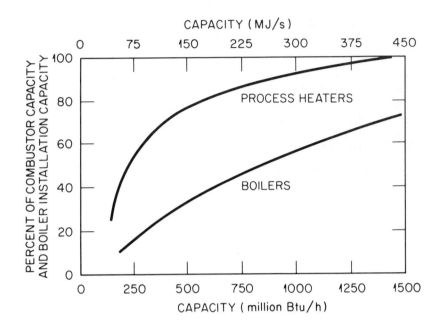

Fig. 20. A comparison of the distribution of direct process heater capacity with that of industrial boilers reveals that process heaters are biased towards substantially smaller sizes. They therefore do not usually lend themselves to coal combustion which requires greater capacity to be economical [Fox, E. C. and Graves, R. L., "The Outlook for Coal Combustion," ONEP Overview Paper Number 11B (January 1980)].

Cost estimates for coal gasification plants vary with the type of gas produced. Recent cost estimates (Klepper, et al, 1979) for substitute natural gas (SNG), intermediate-Btu gas (IBG) and low-Btu gas (LBG) are given in Table 22. We can draw two general observations from these estimates: First, all coal gasification options produce gas for far less than the levelized cost of imported oil ($9/GJ); and second, the product costs for IBG are not much different than for LBG. Therefore, IBG is a better buy because it can be economically transported longer distances due to its higher energy content.

At the turn of the century, low-Btu gas ($\sim$5,500 kJ/ m^3 or$\sim$150 Btu/ft^3) from coal was widely used in homes and industry, and as shown in Table 22 it is presently estimated to have a levelized cost of $5.03/GJ ($30.77/bble). There has been recent industrial experience with low-Btu gas produced as a byproduct from industrial processes (e.g., off-gas from blast furnaces). In applications where a boiler or process heater is

Table 22. Representative cost data for coal gasification[a]

	Substitute natural gas	Intermediate-Btu gas	Low-Btu gas
Capital investment,[b] 10^6 1980 dollars	1826	751	776
Conversion efficiency, %	67	69	70
Levelized annual cost,[c] 10^6 dollars/year			
Capital	376.0	155.0	160.0
Coal[d]	297.6	289.2	284.9
Operating and maintenance	137.4	60.4	49.8
Total	811.0	504.6	494.7
Product cost, $/GJ ($/bble)	8.25 (50.47)	5.13 (31.39)	5.03 (30.77)

[a]Using data from Klepper et al. (1979) and escalating their 1977 costs to 1980 dollars at 10% per year.

[b]For a plant producing 98.3×10^{15} J/year (93.2×10^{12} Btu/year).

[c]Assuming 90% plant capacity factor and 20-year industrial financing ground rules (Appendix C).

[d]Using eastern coal at 25.6 MJ/kg (22×10^6 Btu/ton) and a price of $1.25/GJ ($28.90/ton).

designed to use low-Btu gas, performance is quite acceptable. Low-Btu gas, however, cannot readily be substituted for natural gas or oil in existing boilers. The low-flame emissivity renders the radiant portion of the steam generator virtually useless, causing the superheat region to absorb too great a load. To convert steam generators to low-Btu gas would require extensive redesign.

The use of low-Btu gas in process heaters is usually not acceptable due to raw gas impurities (oil, tars, sulfur) that condense and prevent the transport of unheated gas more than a few hundred feet. Cleanup of the gas reduces the conversion efficiency by 20% (U S Department of Energy 1979e), and piping low-Btu gas any significant distance is uneconomical due to its low energy content (Cochran, 1980). This was not the case around 1900 when clean low-Btu gas, although costly, could compete with other fuels. Some applications (e.g., brick kilns) can tolerate impurities, especially if the heat demand is concentrated so that the gasifier can be located close to the point of use.

Intermediate-Btu gas ($\sim$11,000 kJ/m^3 or $\sim$300 Btu/ft^3) can be used for steam generation and process heat applications with only minor equipment modifications, and the estimate of its levelized cost of $5.13/GJ ($31.19/bble) makes it an extremely attractive option. The energy content of intermediate-Btu gas allows economical transmission up to distances of 250 km. A central intermediate-Btu gas plant feeding industries within this distance is a viable proposition. A survey of steam consumption by five major industries (paper, chemicals, petroleum, rubber, and primary metals) indicated that at least 3 EJ/year (2.9 × 10^{15} Btu/year) of their demand could be satisfied by central intermediate-Btu gas plants (Barnes, et al, 1976). Since this survey did not include relatively small users (<40 kg/s or <300,000 lb/h), it is a fairly conservative measure of the potential for central intermediate-Btu gas plants.

Assuming the market for process heat applications is roughly equivalent to the process steam market, central intermediate-Btu gas plants have the potential to displace about 6 EJ/year (5.8 × 10^{15} Btu/year or 2.7 million bble/d) of oil and natural gas used in the industrial sector. Additional natural gas could be released by using intermediate-Btu gas as a feedstock where appropriate.

Substitute natural gas (SNG) ($\sim$38,000 kJ/m^3 or 1020 Btu/ft^3) has a potential market encompassing the entire natural gas market plus the substitutional market now using oil for non-transportation applications. Because of its relatively high cost of $8.25 GJ ($50.74/bble), it may be more suitable to use intermediate-Btu gas and liquids from coal and shale rather than SNG.

It appears that on-site production and use of low- or intermediate-Btu gas from coal has only limited industrial application. A central intermediate-Btu gas plant supplying industries within a 150-250 km radius could, however, displace appreciable quantities of oil and natural gas. The widespread use of SNG should have a lower priority than intermediate-Btu gas because of the relatively high cost of SNG.

Coal and Nuclear for Electricity Production

Over the last two decades much of the U.S.'s electrical generating capacity was either constructed or converted to use oil or natural gas. This occurred because of the low price of generating power with these fuels and/or because of the need to meet environmental standards. In 1978 oil and natural gas were used for 30% of the electrical power generated in the U.S. (Table 23): 4.0 EJ (1.8 million bbl/d) of oil (including fuel for peaking) and 3.5 EJ (1.6 million bble/d) of gas (DOE/EIA–

Table 23. 1978 U.S. fuel distribution for generated electricity[a]

Energy source	Generation [EJ (10^9 kWh)][b]		Percentage
Coal	3.51	(976)	44
Petroleum	1.31	(365)	16
Natural gas	1.10	(305)	14
Hydro	1.01	(281)	13
Nuclear	0.99	(276)	13
Geothermal and others	0.01	(3)	
Total	7.93	(2,206)	100

[a]U.S. Department of Energy (1979f).
[b]Bus-bar power.

0035/10 [79]). Fortunately, there are other energy sources as important (or more so) in the production of electricity, which have not yet been fully utilized. This next section will focus on the replacement of oil and gas use in the electrical utility sector.

Only 12% of the oil used for power generation is light oil used in peaking operations; similarly only about 10% of the gas burned by utilities is used in gas turbines to meet peak requirements. Since peaking operations require relatively low capital investment (due to the low capacity factor inherent in this application), the use of oil and gas can perhaps be justified. This analysis will, therefore, focus on the 3.55 EJ/year (1.59 million bbl/d) of residual oil and 3.15 EJ/year (1.4 million bble/d) of gas that are used in baseload steam power plant applications. Replacing oil in the utility sector will have a direct impact on the oil problem, and replacing gas in this sector will allow the displaced gas to be used in place of oil in other sectors.

The capital and operating and maintenance costs of nuclear, oil, and several coal-fired generating options are given in Table 24. A comparison of the cost of electricity is shown in Figure 21. Some clear implications are immediately obvious. First, the development of advanced coal technologies for electrical generation will most likely have very little impact on the oil problem. The economics so strongly favor new nuclear or coal-fired plants over new oil-fired units that the former will be the economic choice for expansion, even in the absence of advanced coal technologies. Second, there are incentives for a utility to replace an

Table 24. Capital and operating and maintenance costs for electric generating plants, delivered

Plant	Capital cost		O&M cost, $/GJ ($/kWh)	
	$/GJ/d [$/kW(e)]		Fixed	Variable (includes fuel cost)
Oil-fired power plant[a]	6,260	(541)	0.42 (0.0015)	14.7 (0.053)[b]
Conventional coal with scrubbers[c]	9,300	(804)	0.53 (0.0019)	4.7 (0.017)
Combined cycle gasification[a]	10,700	(927)	0.53 (0.0019)	5.0 (0.018)
Atmospheric fluidized bed combustor[a]	7,040	(608)	0.36 (0.0013)	5.3 (0.019)
Light-water reactor	11,600 (1,000) 23,200 (2,000)[d]		0.72 (0.0026)[e]	1.6 (0.0058)[e]

[a]Fox and Graves (1980).
[b]Based on $4.90/GJ ($30/bbl) oil.
[c]E. C. Fox, personal communication.
[d]Spiewak and Cope (1980).
[e]J. G. Delene, personal communication.

existing oil-fired system *before the end of its economic life* with a new coal or nuclear plant. The same conclusions apply to the replacement of gas-fired plants under the assumption that gas prices will be deregulated.

The environmental effects of replacing oil with coal in utility steam-raising applications were analyzed by the Presidential Commission on Coal (1980). Their findings were that, "new coal-burning powerplants built under the Clean Air Act New Source Performance Standards will cause in most instances, no more, and generally fewer, sulfur dioxide, nitrogen oxide, and particulate emissions than most existing oil units. The replacement of older oil units with new, relatively clean coal units allows increased reliance on coal with no net increase in environmental and health-related emissions.''

If economics so heavily favor the construction of coal and nuclear power plants, and environmental concerns are not a serious problem, why is rapid changeover not taking place? There are several contributing factors, including air pollution in nonattainment areas, the nuclear debate, and the lack of capital available to utilities. The major reason has to do with the regional pattern of fuel uses.

Tables 25 and 26 list the utilities that consume almost half the oil and 60% of the gas used for electricity generation. The use of oil and gas is concentrated in specific power systems which depend on these fuels for generating a major proportion of their power. Therefore, a shift to coal or nuclear sources would require replacement of over half

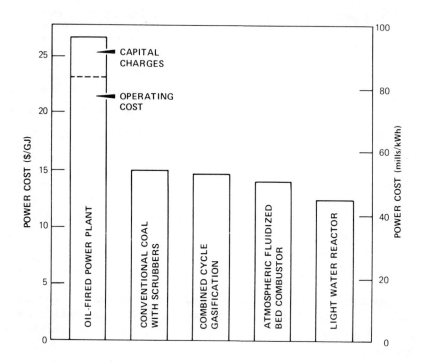

Fig. 21. Estimates of electric power costs (30-year leveled cost using utility financing) reveal that light water reactors and the various coal combustion systems produce electricity at a cost substantially less than just the operating cost (fuel cost) of an oil-fired plant. There are thus even incentives for a utility to replace an existing unit using oil before the end of its economic life, with a new coal or nuclear power plant. Note that the range for LWR capital costs of $1,000 to $2,000/kW(e) yields power costs $3/GJ either side of the indicated cost.

the entire generating capacity of a few utilities within a short period. Although economic analysis favors such a shift, the financing required in such a short time lies beyond the capabilities of any of the utilities that need to make the changeover.

As pointed out in *Recommendations for Restoration of Financial Health to the U.S. Electric Power Industry* (written by utility executives and financial analysts), public utility commissions are the primary cause of the utilities' financial problems. By refusing to give utilities access to funds, they prevent utilities from building needed plants or converting from oil use.

Table 25. Utilities highly dependent on oil[a]

Utility	Type of generation		Fossil fuel consumed		1978 oil consumption [EJ (10^6 bbl)]
	Fossil steam (%)	Combustion turbine (%)	Fraction that is oil (%)	Fraction that is gas (%)	
Southern California Edison	81	8	58	25	0.276 (45.2)
Consolidated Edison	70	21	100		0.240 (39.3)
Middle South Utilities	89	3	51	49	0.239 (39.1)
Florida Power & Light	63	18	69	31	0.223 (36.5)
Pacific Gas & Electric	74	4	57	43	0.174 (28.4)
Virginia Electric & Power	66	5	60		0.162 (26.5)
New England Electric System	67	3	100		0.130 (21.3)
Long Island Lighting	71	29	100		0.129 (21.0)
Public Service Electric & Gas (New Jersey)	54	30	63		0.126 (20.5)
Florida Power	55	30	69	15	0.100 (16.3)
Niagara Mohawk Power	67	7	56		0.087 (14.2)
Boston Edison	65	11	100		0.086 (14.1)
Total					1.972 (322)[b]

[a]Smock (1979).
[b]Or 0.883 × 10^6 bbl/d.

Table 26. Utilities highly dependent on natural gas[a]

| Utility | Type of generation | | Fraction of fossil fuel use | | 1978 gas consumption [EJ $(10^9$ ft^3)] |
	Fossil Steam (%)	Combustion turbine (%)	Oil (%)	Gas (%)	
Houston Lighting & Power	89	11	<1	97	0.545 (506)
Central & South West	100		5	86	0.415 (385)
Texas Utilities	100			45	0.378 (351)
Middle South Utilities	89	3	51	49	0.232 (215)
Gulf State Utilities	100		26	74	0.221 (205)
Oklahoma Gas & Electric	99	1		79	0.184 (171)
Pacific Gas & Electric	74	4	57	43	0.132 (123)
Southwestern Public Service	98	2		77	0.112 (104)
Total					2.219 (2060)[b]

[a]Smock (1979).
[b]Or 0.993 × 10^6 bble d.

There are two other reasons why substitution is not occurring faster. First, new investment causes an increase in present fuel rates. In effect, present rate payers are subsidizing future rate payers, and in the case of nuclear plants, which may take 15 years to license and build, the future rate payers may be a different group from the present rate payers. Due to such subsidies, considerable opposition to new construction is developing, and is reflected through the public utility commissions. Second, fuel adjustment clauses may be reducing the incentive to move away from oil (Kaserman and Tepel, 1979). If firms can pass along price increases to rate payers immediately, without the long, involved process of rate hearings, it may be more profitable to stay with oil than to switch.

Without a major federal program, the shift away from oil and gas in electricity production will require 15 to 20 years. This could not be considered a crash program to displace oil.

In the interim, utilities that are heavily dependent on oil are buying lower cost (i.e., non-oil-generated) power from other systems. These transfers are called powerwheeling (OUS/PSR 50). At present, utilities are reducing oil consumption by 0.44 to 0.66 EJ/year (200,000 to 300,000 bbl/d) through regional transfers of nuclear, coal-fired, and hydroelectric power. This is estimated to be about 80 to 90% of the potential oil savings that can be realized using the existing electrical intertie system.

To gain an understanding of what could be accomplished if all existing coal and nuclear stations operated at their maximum availability, we analyzed data concerning capacity factors (capacity factor is similar to availability factor but also accounts for partial outages) and equivalent availability factors (DOE/ERA–0007). The analysis indicated that existing coal and nuclear power plants operating at maximum capacity (corresponding to their availability) could displace 1.8 EJ/year (800,000 bbl/d) of oil—half of the replaceable oil used in the utility sector—provided sufficient interties existed. In addition, if current construction of coal and nuclear plants is accelerated, and if power from the plants is used to displace oil- and gas-fired capacity elsewhere, they could realize an additional saving of 2.4 EJ/year (1.1 million bble/d) of gas and oil used in 1986. We devised this estimate by using projected capacity additions (DOE/ERA–0020/1 Rev. 1) and assuming that given a national commitment, a 5-year construction schedule would be possible.

The analysis indicated that plants scheduled for completion prior to 1985 could not be accelerated. However, those scheduled for later start-up could be brought on line earlier. In order for this transfer to be effective, interties need further strengthening and there needs to be a greater integration of the eastern, western, and Texas electrical intertie systems. In later years, as these plans are needed to meet increased demands in their own service areas, the power available for transfer would naturally decrease (Table 27). The interim plan, however, provides time for importing utilities to replace their own oil- and gas-fired power-plants. Thus, accelerated construction of coal and nuclear capacity, coupled with strengthened interties could result in the displacement of 4.2 EJ/year (1.9 million bble/d) of oil and gas in 1986. This represents all of the nonpeaking oil and 14% of the nonpeaking gas now consumed by the electric utility sector.

Additional savings could be gained by adding units specifically constructed to displace oil and gas. Recent federal legislative initiatives requiring utilities to cut oil use by 50% in 1990 may result in the construction of some additional units for this purpose. Continued conservation efforts would allow new units to continue displacing oil and gas

Table 27. Summary of potential for displacing oil and gas use in the utility sector via regional transfer of power (assuming 70% plant availability)[a]

	Displacing potential [EJ/year (bble/d)]				
	Existing stations		Accelerated construction		
Year	Coal	Nuclear	Coal	Nuclear	Total
1980–85	1.54 (700,000)	0.177 (80,600)			1.72 (781,000)
1986	1.54 (700,000)	0.177 (80,600)	0.956 (435,000)	1.56 (707,000)	4.23 (1,922,000)
1987	1.54 (700,000)	0.177 (80,600)	0.672 (306,000)	1.37 (622,000)	3.76 (1,708,000)
1988	1.54 (700,000)	0.177 (80,600)	0.325 (148,000)	0.842 (383,000)	2.89 (1,311,000)
1989	1.54 (700,000)	0.177 (80,600)	b	0.489 (222,000)	2.20 (1,003,000)
1990	1.54 (700,000)	0.177 (80,600)	b	0.177 (80,600)	1.90 (861,000)

[a]U.S. Department of Energy (1978, 1979a).
[b]Planned coal capacity additions for 1989 and beyond not available.

rather than meeting increased demands within a utility's service area. This replacement will be driven primarily by economic factors favoring coal or nuclear. In the interim, oil can be displaced through regional transfers of power.

Electricity and Gas as a Substitute for Oil in Buildings

In the past forty years many space and water heating systems installed in the U.S. have used fuel oil. Again, the choice of oil as a fuel was due to low price and convenience (mainly in the northeast), but oil prices have now risen to the point where oil is often no longer a fuel of choice. Even the reliability of delivery has been questioned. We are left, however, with a considerable stock of oil-fired furnaces in place. In 1978 approximately 5.74 EJ/year (2.57 million bbl/d) of oil was used for heating residential and commercial buildings, and an additional 0.34 EJ/year (0.15 million bbl/d) was used for water heating (Table 28). These represent the only significant uses of oil by the residential sector and about 85% of the oil used by the commercial sector (most of the rest is asphalt for road surfacing, which, using DOE procedures, is sometimes included in the energy statistics for the commercial sector).

Table 28. Residential and commercial space and
water heating by oil, 1978[a]

Heating	EJ/year	10^6 bbl/d
Residential space	3.11	1.39
Commercial space	2.63	1.18
Residential water	0.19	0.08
Commercial water	0.15	0.07
Total	6.08	2.72

[a] 1977 proportions (Blue et al. 1979) applied to 1978
residential and commercial oil consumption (U.S.
Department of Energy 1980a).

All of the oil used in space and water heating could be replaced by
electric heating (with or without heat pumps) with advantage if the electricity is not generated from oil. Four of the federal regions (1, 2, 3, and
9 – see Fig. 22) do, in fact, use oil to generate 20% or more of their electricity, and these four between them account for about 70% of the oil

Fig. 22. Four of the federal regions shown here (numbers 1, 2, 3, and 9) use oil
to generate 20% or more of their electricity and these four between them account for about 70% of the oil used by utilities [DOE/EIA-0192, *Federal Energy Data System Statistical Summary Update,* the U.S. Department of Energy
(July 1979)].

used by utilities (DOE/EIA-0192). As a rough guide, suppose that these four regions switch from oil to gas for residential and commercial space and water heating. Of course it is necessary that gas service can be readily provided in these areas, and as we shall see, the necessary gas can be made available in a cost-effective way, mainly through conservation. In the other regions that do not use oil for electricity generation, oil space and water heating is switched to electricity; the extra electricity required can also be made available through conservation. The result, using 1978 figures, is a savings of 6.08 EJ/year (2.72 million bbl/d) by replacement with 3.25 EJ/year (0.573 Tcf/year) of gas and 1.46 EJ/year (4.0 TWh/year) of electricity (Table 29).

Table 30 compares the 1978 energy use, by fuel type, with the energy that would be used after substituting gas and electricity for oil. We see that 6.08 EJ/year (2.72 million bbl/d) of actual oil would be saved, in return for an expenditure of 8.1 EJ/year in other fuels (mainly gas and coal). The extra expenditure of energy in return for this 6.1 EJ/year (2.7 million bbl/d) of oil saved is therefore only 2.0 EJ/year, and none of it is oil.

Conservation

A mainstay of most recent energy strategies has been conservation, which in some cases can be viewed as efficiency improvement. This section examines both the potential for oil conservation within the various sectors and the conservation of oil substitutes so that they can replace oil in specialized applications. In the short term there is no shortage of fuels other than imported oil. This is not to imply that the conservation and efficient use of other fuels is not important; however, they should be conserved for strictly economic, environmental, and social reasons and do not have the added importance that clearly exists for imported oil.

Oil Conservation

As shown in Table 7 the transportation sector is by far the largest petroleum user: It is the only sector whose oil consumption exceeds total U.S. oil imports. Therefore, it is a primary target for conservation. For example, a 10% decrease in energy demand in the transportation sector would have a greater impact on U.S. oil consumption than a 25% decrease in any of the other sectors. A further consideration is is the difficulty of substituting directly for liquid fuels in many end uses in this sector. Continued dependence on liquids seems likely.

Table 29. Substitution of **gas** or **electricity** for oil by **federal region**, using 1978 oil consumption data[a]

	Regions I, II, III, IX (switch from oil to gas for space and water heating) [EJ/year (10⁶ bbl/d)]	Regions IV, V, VI, VII, VIII, X (switch from oil to electricity for space and water heating) [EJ/year (10⁶ bbl/d)]	All regions [EJ/year (10⁶ bbl/d)]
Oil savings			
Residential space heating	1.52 (0.68)	1.59 (0.71)	3.11 (1.39)
Residential water heating	0.09 (0.04)	0.10 (0.04)	0.19 (0.08)
Commercial space heating	1.55 (0.70)	1.08 (0.48)	2.63 (1.18)
Commercial water heating	0.09 (0.04)	0.06 (0.03)	0.15 (0.07)
Total savings	3.25 (1.46)	2.83 (1.26)	6.08 (2.72)
Additional gas and electricity used after switch			
Gas	3.25 (1.45)		3.25 (1.45)
Electricity[b]		1.46 (0.65)	1.46 (0.65)

[a] 1977 regional consumption data (U.S. Department of Energy 1979d) applied to the figures given in Table 29.
[b] Assuming that space heating is provided by a heat pump with an average efficiency of 150% and water heating is provided by resistive heating at 100% efficiency. In both cases, it is assumed that the oil heating had an average efficiency of 75%.
[c] At a conversion efficiency of 30%, including transmission losses, the primary energy needed to generate this electricity is 4.85 EJ (4.60 × 10¹⁵ Btu).

Table 30. Usage of various fuels in the residential and commercial sectors and proposed changes, 1978

[EJ/year (10^6 bble/d)]

	Oil	Gas	Electricity (end-use energy)	Electricity (primary energy)[a]	Total primary energy
Current usage[b]	7.30 (3.27)	8.04 (3.60)	4.33 (1.95)	14.43 (6.47)	29.77 (13.34)
After switching[c]	1.22[d] (0.55)	11.29 (5.06)	5.79 (2.60)	19.28 (8.64)	31.79 (14.25)
Change	−6.08 (−2.72)	+3.25 (+1.46)	+1.46 (+0.65)	+4.85 (+2.17)	+2.02 (+0.91)

[a]Assuming a 30% overall ratio between electricity sold and primary fuel usage for electricity generation. Remember that electricity was substituted for oil only in those federal regions where electricity is not generated from oil. Therefore, this additional primary energy will be in the form of coal, uranium, etc., and not oil.

[b]U.S. Department of Energy (1980g).

[c]Switch from oil to gas or electricity, as shown in Table 30.

[d]Mainly asphalt for road surfacing.

Since automobiles and trucks are the predominant energy users (Table 8), conservation efforts for these applications are primary. If the automobile fleet averaged 7.8–8.2 km/L or 18.3–19.3 mpg (corresponding to the EPA rating of 11.7 km/L or 27.5 mpg mandated for new cars in the 1985 model year) instead of the current 6 km/L (14 mpg) (McNutt, et al, 1979), U.S. oil consumption could be cut by 3.9–4.1 EJ/year (1.7–1.8 million bbl/d). This would reduce the 1978 level of oil imports by about 20%, assuming the distance traveled per year remained constant. The use of autos with higher mileage ratings could, of course, add to this saving.

Conservation efforts in the truck subsector (which includes light-duty pickups, recreation vehicles, and vans) could also provide significant savings. Many techniques for mileage improvement from the auto subsector could also apply to trucks.

Although aircraft presently consume a relatively small amount of oil, this end use is growing rapidly, increasing from 100 to 1200 passenger-km per year per capita between 1950 and 1975 (Gibbons, et al, 1979). Technical opportunities for increasing aircraft efficiency include: *1.* improving engine propulsion components, *2.* more efficient aerodynamics, *3.* composite primary aircraft structures, and *4.* improving systems and controls. Although these improvements would now yield only small oil savings, the potential future savings could be significant if air travel continues to grow as it has in the past.

Samuels (1980) projects that the maximum reasonable level of conservation in the transportation sector could reduce oil use to 17.5 EJ/year (7.84 million bbl/d) in 1985, 16.0 EJ/year (7.17 million bbl/d) in 1990, and 14.4 EJ/year (6.48 million bbl/d) in 2000, assuming an approximate annual growth rate of 2% in total travel distance. Because conservation brings with it less production of liquid fuel and related materials, there may be an added benefit to the environment as well.

The building, industrial, and electric utility sectors present a different situation. The total oil consumption of these three sectors is less than that of transportation. However it is possible to substitute completely for liquid fuels in these end uses, thus producing an oil saving that is higher than for the transportation sector. As shown in a previous section, four end uses account for 75% of the oil use in these sectors (Table 12), and each has several alternative energy sources. Together these represent a substitution potential of 14.3 EJ/year (6.4 million bbl/d) or almost 80% of the 1978 import level.

While cost-effective efficiency improvements will be important in reducing oil consumption, fuel substitution has an even greater potential for doing so. Conservation can only reduce the oil demand (perhaps by as much as 50% in some instances); however, fuel substitution has the ability to eliminate totally the demand for oil in these applications.

The fuel substitution strategy will require the application of significant energy conservation. Natural gas use, for instance, parallels oil use in these sectors (Table 31), and many oil burners (especially in utility and industrial applications) have the capability to burn gas. In the building sector gas and electricity could replace oil for space and water heating with some equipment changes. Supplying the needed gas to replace oil and providing gas service to oil-using areas thus become important considerations. Conservation and efficiency improvements for saving natural gas—to make it available for replacing oil—are therefore crucial. This section will present detailed examples of such a strategy.

Table 31. Gas and oil use in industrial, buildings, and utility sectors[a]

End-use sector	Consumption of oil and gas in 1978 [EJ/year (10^6 bble/d)]	
	Oil	Gas
Industrial	7.57 (3.40)	9.01 (4.03)
Residential and commercial	7.30 (3.27)	8.04 (3.61)
Electric utility	4.02 (1.80)	3.48 (1.56)
Total	18.89 (8.47)	20.53 (9.20)

[a]U.S. Department of Energy (1980g).

Substitution is also attractive because the amount of oil saved per dollar spent is generally greater than for conservation. A recent study (Maulhardt, 1979) examined conservation potentials for a typical residence currently using oil for space and water heating. It concluded that oil consumption could be reduced by about 50% by investing $2000 to $3000 for insulation, storm windows, and other conservation measures. For this same residence, oil use can be totally *eliminated* by investing about $3500 for an electric heat pump system.

Following consistent economic ground rules (see Appendix), the levelized costs of switching to a heat pump system are essentially equal to those for cutting oil use by half (see Table 32). This analysis did not

Table 32. Comparison of substitution of electric heat pumps for oil and conservation

	Output [GJ (10⁶ Btu)]	Efficiency (%)	Levelized fuel cost [$ GJ ($ 10⁶ Btu)]	Yearly fuel cost ($ year)	Capital charges ($ year)	Total cost ($ year)
Oil heat	63.3 (60.0)[a]	50[b]	18.75 (19.78)[c]	2374	0	2374
Heat pump	63.3 (60.0)	150	26.27 (27.72)[d]	1109	460[e]	1569
Conservation with oil	31.65 (30.0)	50	18.75 (19.78)	1187	262–393[e]	1449–1580
Conservation with heat pump	31.65 (30.0)	150	26.27 (27.72)	554	722–853[e]	1276–1407

[a]Total use from Table 38 is 120 × 10⁶ Btu; from Table 37, heating is 51% of the total electrical use.

[b]Although an efficiency of 75% is frequently used in the literature, this efficiency is generally unobtainable in actual operation. Actual efficiency levels for gas- and oil-fired furnace systems are closer to 45% (Burwell 1981 and Hise and Holman 1975). In constructing this table, a value of 50% was used.

[c]Assumes initial fuel cost of $0.26 L ($1 gal) and levelizing factor of 2.59 (corresponds to real resource, 30-year case in the standards in Appendix C).

[d]Average 1980 residential electricity cost is 5.5¢ kWh (U.S. Department of Energy 1980g); levelizing factor of 1.72 (Appendix C).

[e]Using a capital recovery factor of 13.1% (corresponds to a 10% discount rate over 15 years).

include the hidden cost of imported oil in the oil fuel price, and adding this cost would result in enhanced viability for the heat pump options. From the resident's point of view, some conservation measures, in addition to the conversion to the electric heating system, would provide an additional reduction in future utility bills and would be economically attractive. In fact, switching to a heat pump and investing $2000-3000 for conversation is clearly the economic choice (Table 32). Cost-effective efficiency and conservation measures should be encouraged, but these alone do not yield nearly the oil savings realized from fuel-switching.

A strategy that couples conservation efforts in the transportation sector with fuel substitution in the building, industrial, and utility sectors holds the greatest promise for near-term reductions in oil consumption. The potential oil savings from this strategy are nearly 16 EJ/year (7.2 million bbl/d) in 1990, which almost equals the 1978 import total of 18 EJ (8.1 million bbl/d) (DOE/EIA 0035/04[80]). The strategy is also attractive because it uses existing technology, and in many cases it can yield the greatest oil saving per dollar invested.

Conservation of Oil Substitutes in Buildings

As indicated earlier, the displacement by gas or electricity of oil used for residential and commercial heating would save approximately 6.08 EJ/year (2.72 million bbl/d) of oil. The residential and commercial use of gas would be increased by 3.25 EJ/year (in federal regions 1, 2, 3 and 9); electricity use would increase by 1.46 EJ/year (in all other federal regions), assuming that heat pumps are used for electric space heating (Table 29). These figures are only approximate, including as they do many assumptions about the availability of non-oil-fired peak electricity and the efficiency of oil heating.

This section examines conservation measures that would reduce the amount of gas and electricity used for space and water heating. The objective is to reduce direct gas and electricity consumption by 3.25 EJ/year and 1.46 EJ/year, respectively, in the specified regions. Such a conservation effort, if combined with the oil displacement program described earlier, would save the 6.08 EJ/year (2.72 million bbl/d) of oil without any net increase in the end-use consumption of other fuels, and without the need for any new power station construction. This amount of gas and electricity (and more) can be made available in a cost-effective way by conservation measures.

Maulhardt, et al (1979) have developed information about investment in energy savings in residential buildings from which incremental investment-vs-savings data can be derived. Some of these data were published by the American Council for an Energy Efficient Economy (ACEEE). A simplified version of their graphical representation of the results is shown in Figure 23; Table 33 is a numerical representation of this graph and forms the basis for the analysis in this section. Although the figures are for a small, single-family home in northern California, the general shape of the curve is consistent with data generated for residential and commercial applications in a number of other studies (Johnson and Pierce, 1980; Ross and Williams, 1979; OTA, 1979; Hirst, 1979; Hirst and O'Neal, 1979; Hirst, 1978; Hutchins and Hirst, 1978). The specific costs and benefits of any application depend on the location and thermal integrity of the existing structure. Since the Maulhardt data base was among the most extensive, we used it as the basis for further analysis.

Assuming that oil heating in houses and commercial buildings is largely eliminated by substituting gas or electricity, Table 33 can be used to estimate the cost of saving enough gas and electricity to substitute for the oil. (For the moment, we shall ignore the fact that some utilities use gas to generate electricity, because our primary objective is to switch away from oil).

In federal regions 1, 2, 3 and 9, we want to switch from oil to gas. In 1978 the domestic and commercial use of gas in these regions was approximately 2.6 EJ [1.8 EJ (houses) + 0.8 EJ (commercial buildings)] (DOE/EIA-0192). As we have already shown (Table 29), the switch, if carried out without additional conservation measures, would increase the gas usage by 3.25 EJ to approximately 5.85 EJ [3.4 EJ (houses) + 2.44 EJ (commercial buildings)]. Table 35 derived from Figure 23 and Table 33, ranks domestic gas conservation activities in order of the investment per unit of gas saved. Initial gas heat use for the house in this example is 161 GJ/year (153 million Btu/year); however, according to Table 34, the recommended conservation measures would reduce this to 53 GJ/year (50 million Btu/year)—33% of the initial usage. If all the houses that use gas were dealt with similarly, their gas consumption after the switch would fall to (3.41 × 53/161) = 1.1 EJ/year. Adding the commercial gas consumption after the switch (2.44 EJ/year) to this figure, the total amount of gas consumed in regions 1, 2, 3, and 9 would be (1.1 + 2.44) 3.54 EJ/year. This is only about 1.1 EJ/year more gas than is used at present, although oil use would be decreased, through the fuel switching, by 3.25 EJ/year. The conservation measures required would cost $35 billion, and $19 billion would be the price for converting from oil to gas ($900/conversion, excluding the cost of additional pipelines). Gas could be saved for an equivalent capital investment of $15/GJ/year ($34,000/bble/d).

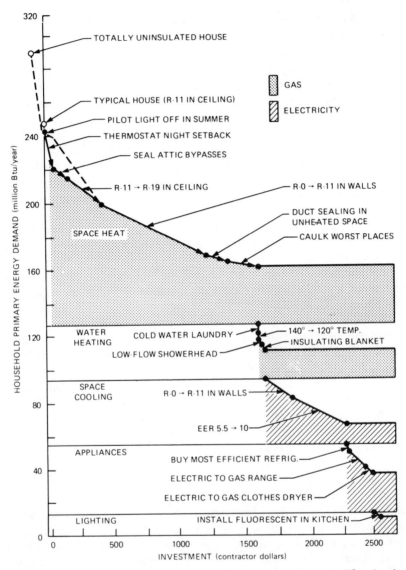

Fig. 23. The energy conservation potential in a northern California single-family home [110 m² (1200 ft.²), 1400°Cxd (3000°Fxd) degree days] is shown here versus the required investment. This information was developed by Maul-hardt, M., et al [*Some Potentials for Energy and Peak Power Conservation in California*, LBL-5926 revised (October 1979)], and the figure above was adapted from one used by the ACEEE in their proposals. There are a number of highly cost-effective conservation measures indicated, as well as some which are likely to be more costly than some reasonable supply options.

Table 33. Results of investment in conservation, as outlined in Fig. 23

Investment per household	Annual energy usage per household[a]		
	Electricity[b] [GJ (kWh)]	Space heating [GJ (10^6 Btu)]	Water heating [GJ (10^6 Btu)]
Initial usage	30.9 (8580)	126.6(120)	34.8 (33)
Housekeeping ($0)[c]	30.9 (8580)	112.9(107)	26.4 (25)
$ 40	30.9 (8580)	99.2 (94)	26.4 (25)
$ 150	30.9 (8580)	92.8 (88)	26.4 (25)
$ 420	30.9 (8580)	77.0 (73)	26.4 (25)
$1225	30.9 (8580)	45.4 (43)	26.4 (25)
$1400	30.9 (8580)	40.1 (38)	26.4 (25)
$1600	30.9 (8580)	36.9 (35)	26.4 (25)
$1620	30.9 (8580)	36.9 (35)	23.2 (22)
$1660	30.9 (8580)	36.9 (35)	15.8 (15)
$1850	27.3 (7580)	36.9 (35)	15.8 (15)
$2290	21.8 (6060)	36.9 (35)	15.8 (15)
$2310	20.5 (5690)	36.9 (35)	15.8 (15)
$2360	19.6 (5440)	36.9 (35)	15.8 (15)

[a]This table ignores the American Council for an Energy Efficient Economy suggestion of switching from electricity to gas for cooking and clothes drying for two reasons: first, we may not wish to exchange, say, nuclear electricity for gas anyway; and second, ACEEE does not give figures for the increase in gas usage that would result.

[b]These items are necessarily electric (space cooling, appliances, and lighting).

[c]Switching off pilot lights in summer, laundering with cold water, and lowering hot water temperature.

Actually, this greatly overstates the marginal cost of the last elements of a sensible conservation effort, because it seeks all the savings from the domestic sector and none from the commercial.

Unfortunately, it has not been possible to identify an exact analogue of Table 34 for the commercial sector.* In the absence of this information we shall assume that the level of investment required to save 50% of the gas used for heating is the same in the commercial as in the

---

*The American Council for an Energy Efficient Economy (ACEEE) (1979) argues that 28% of the energy used in the commercial sector can be saved with "virtually no" capital investment, and a total of 50% can be saved "cost effectively"; however, it is not clear what the ACEEE considers to be "cost effective." For example, the last items in Table 34, taken from their figures, account for almost half of the savings, but require an investment considerably in excess of that required to produce SNG.

Table 34. Domestic gas conservation actions in order of cost effectiveness[a,b]

	Investment per household ($)	Annual space and water heating energy saving per household [GJ (10^6 Btu)]	Percentage of total annual usage saved	Investment per unit of energy saved [$/GJ/year ($/bble/d)]
Initial usage		161 (153)		
Turn pilot light off, launder in cold water, lower hot water temperature, set back thermostat manually at night	0	22 (21)	13.7	0 (0)
Install automatic night setback on thermostat	40	14 (13)	8.7	2.9 (6,000)
Insulate water heater	40	7 (7)	4.3	5.7 (13,000)
Install low-flow shower	20	3 (3)	1.9	6.7 (15,000)
Insulate ceiling to R-19	270	16 (15)	9.9	16.9 (38,000)
Seal attic bypasses	110	6 (6)	3.7	18.3 (41,000)
Insulate walls to R-11	805	32 (30)	19.9	25.2 (56,000)
Seal ducts in unheated areas	175	5 (5)	3.1	35.0 (78,000)
Caulk worst places	200	3 (3)	1.9	66.7 (149,000)
Total or average	1,660	108 (103)	67.1	15.4 (34,000)

[a]Assumes that water and space heating is by gas.
[b]This table is derived from information in Fig. 23 and Table 34.

residential sector: from the figures in Table 34, we can easily calculate that this amounts to $10/GJ/year of saved energy. This assumption is broadly consistent with another study (Johnson and Pierce, 1980) of energy conservation costs in the commercial sector: the Johnson and Pierce results, when analyzed to show the costs of measures aimed at reducing energy use for heating, indicate that about 60% of the heating energy used in the commercial sector could be saved at a cost of $10/GJ/year or less. Based on the assumption of 50% savings at $10/GJ/year in the commercial sector, and on the domestic conservation measures listed in Table 34, the least expensive combination of domestic and commercial conservation measures (to save a total of 3.25 EJ) is given in Table 35.

This is clearly more cost-effective than implementing the entire list in Table 34, and except for the last item on the list, it uses capital more efficiently than the production of substitute natural gas (see Table 22).

Table 35. The least expensive means of saving 3.25 EJ/year of natural gas after fuel switching in the residential and commercial sectors of federal regions I, II, III, and IX

Activity	Sector	Percentage of gas saved in federal regions I, II, III, and IX	Actual saving (EJ year)[a]	Investment ($ GJ year[b])	Cost (billions of $)
Turn pilot light off, launder in cold water, lower hot water temperature, set back thermostat manually at night	Residential	13.7	0.47	0	0
Install automatic night setback on thermostat	Residential	8.7	0.30	2.9	0.87
Insulate water heater	Residential	4.3	0.15	5.7	0.86
Install low-flow shower	Residential	1.9	0.06	6.7	0.40
Take a combination of several actions designed to save 50% of gas used for heating[c]	Commercial	50.0	1.22	10.0	12.20
Insulate ceiling to R-19	Residential	9.9	0.34	16.9	5.75
Seal attic bypasses	Residential	3.7	0.13	18.3	2.38
Insulate walls to R-11[d]	Residential	11.5	0.58	25.2	14.62
Total or average			3.25	11.4	37.08

[a]Total usage in these sectors for space and water heating in federal regions I, II, III, and IX after the switch from oil but before these additional conservation measures is 3.41 EJ year (residential) × 2.44 EJ year (commercial).

[b]See Table 35 for equivalent ($ bble d).

[c]This analysis assumes that the level of investment required to save 50% of the gas used for heating is the same in the commercial sector as in the residential sector.

[d]90% of homes only.

The total investment required in these conservation items is about $40 billion.

There are many caveats associated with this analysis. Some of them arise from an extrapolation—to a wide range of sizes and climates—of the small, northern California home studied by Maulhardt, et al (1979). The extrapolation works under the assumption that costs and savings vary linearly with initial energy use. This is almost certainly not true. Furthermore, it assumes that the relative magnitude and cost of domestic conservation options—e.g., space heating vs. hot water systems—do not vary. This is even more certainly untrue. Nevertheless, these uncertainties do not affect the broad conclusion that a combination of fuel switching and conservation can save oil more effectively than either production or conservation alone.

Another part of the proposal made here is for federal regions other than 1, 2, 3, and 9 to switch from oil heating to electric heat pumps and resistance heaters. Space heating by heat pumps works at about 150% efficiency (compared to oil or gas at 75%*), and water is heated at 100% efficiency by electric resistance (compared to oil or gas at 75%). The increase in electricity use when it is used in place of oil for space and water heating would be 1.46 EJ/year. Once again, this could be offset by conservation measures.**

Table 36 shows the average energy uses identified in Figure 23, but modified to reflect the use of heat pumps and resistive water heaters. Table 37 ranks the conservation opportunities identified and priced by Maulhardt, et al (1979) in order of capital investment per unit saving. We can make a valuable comparison between the conservation measures and the option of increasing electrical supply by observing the relative capital costs. The final column of Table 37 shows the investment cost per unit of power station capacity saved, assuming the use of a power plant running at a 60% load factor: this is a figure that could be used by a utility in deciding whether to invest in a new plant [at approximately $800/kW(e) for a coal-fired plant] or in building conservation.

Note that because of the large savings available at no (monetary) cost by using cold water for laundering, by lowering domestic hot water temperatures, and by night setback, the average cost of the first half of the savings is admirably low. The next question is what would be the capital costs involved in reducing electricity use in federal regions 4, 5,

---

*As previously noted, there is growing evidence that the seasonal efficiency obtained in practice in present day systems is much lower, in the range of 35-50% (Burwell, 1980 and Hise, 1975).

**Data for evaluating this are again taken from Figure 23.

Table 36. Residential use of electricity,
assuming electric space and water heating

	Annual usage per household (kWh)	Percentage of total household usage
Space heating	16,700"	51
Water heating	7,300	22
Appliances	3,800	12
Space cooling	3,600	11
Lighting	1,200	4
Total	32,600	100

"No pilot light is needed for a heat pump, so the figure here is slightly lower than the one used by Maulhardt et al. (1979).

6, 7, 8, and 10 sufficiently so as to offset the increase caused by switching from oil to electricity. Present electricity use in the domestic and commercial sector in these regions is approximately 3 EJ [1.7 EJ (houses) + 1.3 EJ (commercial buildings (Roberson, 1979). After the switch from oil it would rise to 4.46 EJ (see Table 29). If 33% of this were conserved, the total electricity use would not change despite the fuel switching.

To calculate the cost of saving 33% (1.46 EJ/year) of the electricity used, we once again assume that savings of this order would cost the same in the commercial as in the domestic sector. Table 37 shows that actions down to, and including, sealing the attic bypasses would save 33% of the energy use in an individual household. The cost would be $500, and the amount of electricity saved would be 10,600 kWh/year. The cost per unit of saving is therefore 500 per 10,600 $/kWh, or 4.7¢/kWh. At this rate, the cost of saving 1.46 EJ/year would be only $15 billion.

The calculations above relate to a specific proposal: how to conserve gas and electricity sufficiently to substitute them for fuel oil in the domestic and commercial sectors without an overall increase in gas and electricity usage. The general conclusion is that this is not only feasible, but desirable. The numerical conclusion is that the investment in conservation would need to be approximately $50 billion. This is less than the investment required to supply additional electricity and to make synthetic gas, and it is much less than would be required to set up syn-

Table 37. Electricity conservation opportunities in order of capital investment effectiveness[a]

Action[b]	Annual savings per household (kWh)	Savings as % of total usage	Cost per household ($)	Investment cost of savings ¢ MJ year[c] (¢ kWh year)	$ kW(e)[d]
Launder in cold water, lower hot water temperature, set back thermostat manually at night	3,500	10.7	0	0 (0)	0
Install automatic night setback on thermostat[e]	1,800	5.5	40	0.61 (2.2)	120
Insulate water heater	1,400	4.3	40	0.81 (2.9)	150
Install low-flow shower	600	1.8	20	0.92 (3.3)	180
Buy an energy-efficient refrigerator	400	1.2	20[f]	1.39 (5.0)	260
Insulate ceiling to R-19	2,100	6.4	270	3.58 (12.9)	680
Seal attic bypasses	800	2.5	110	3.83 (13.8)	720
Insulate walls to R-11	5,500[g]	16.9	805	4.06 (14.6)	770
Install fluorescent lights in kitchen	300	0.9	50	4.64 (16.7)	880
Seal ducts in unheated areas	700	2.1	175	6.9 (25.0)	1,310
Improve energy-efficiency rating of air conditioning to 10[h]	1,500	4.6	440	8.14 (29.3)	1,540
Caulk worst places	400	1.2	200	13.9 (50.0)	2,630
Total or average	19,000	58.1	2,170	3.17 (11.4)	600

[a]From Fig. 22.
[b]Excludes switching to gas for cooking and drying.
[c]This is the capital cost per unit of energy saved annually. The approximate payback period of a conservation option can easily be inferred by comparing the listed cost with the local price of electricity (e.g., if local electricity is 5¢ kWh and the investment is 10¢/kWh/year, the payback period is two years).
[d]Cost per kW(e) of electrical capacity saved, assuming a 60% load factor.
[e]The savings made by using night setback with heat pumps are determined by the heat pump balance point and the minimum outside temperature.
[f]Cost in excess of ordinary refrigerator's price.
[g]Includes cooling savings shown in Fig. 22.
[h]This might give rise to some double counting, because cooling load has already been decreased.

thetic oil production facilities to make the 6.1 EJ/year (2.7 million bbl/d) of actual oil that would be saved by the fuel switch. The $50 billion does not include the cost of replacing the oil furnaces with gas or electric heating systems, and that would add approximately $20 billion to the cost of the total proposal. The cost per unit of oil saved is therefore only $70 billion/6.1 EJ/year, or $4,200/GJ/d ($26,000/bbl/d).

There is no net increase in the amount of gas or electricity used in any of the federal regions.

The effects of the measures described above can be displayed in terms of hypothetical conservation investment curves derived from Tables 34 and 37 (Figs. 24, 25, 26). These show the savings in gas or electricity versus the required investment.

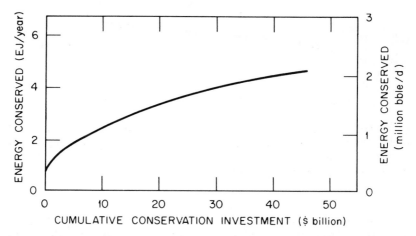

Fig. 24. The cumulative investment in buildings required for achieving various levels of natural gas conservation nationwide appear here with the most cost-effective measures taken first.

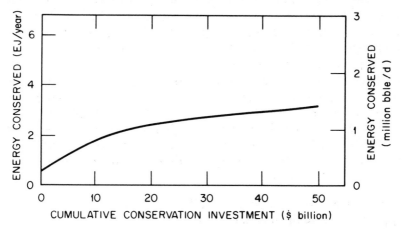

Fig. 25. This is a curve of natural gas saving in federal regions 1, 2, 3, and 9 versus the cumulative investment in conservation measures (the most cost-effective steps being taken first), assuming that gas is substituted for oil in residential and commercial buildings;

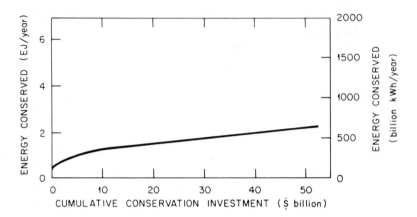

fig. 26. This is a curve of electrical energy saved in federal regions 4, 5, 6, 7, 8, and 10 versus the cumulative investment in conservation measures (the most cost-effective steps being taken first), assuming electricity is substituted for oil in residential and commercial buildings.

When viewing the question from a homeowner's perspective, the list of options that are cost-effective broadens. The conservation option leveled (life-cycle) costs are given in Table 37. Everything but caulking can be implemented for less than 4¢/kWh. In comparison, the leveled cost of electricity is about 11¢/kWh [assuming an average 1980 residential price of 5.5¢/kWh, from DOE/EIA-0035 (80/11), and a leveling factor of 2.03 from Appendix C. Thus, all of the options listed in Table 38 represent a good buy from the homeowner's perspective.

Although conservation requires individual action and investment by a large fraction of the U.S. population, it is, undoubtedly, achievable. It is reasonable, therefore, to suppose that an effective program can be established to save gas and electricity in sufficient quantities to equal that consumed by replacing oil-burning in the residential and commercial sectors. An accelerated program might accomplish one-third of the goal by 1985, with the remainder completed by 1990.

Comparative Assessment of Technical Approaches to Reducing Oil Imports

We have outlined a number of effective approaches to reducing the need for the U.S. to import oil. While many of these appear attractive, it is important to choose the best combination of approaches in order to

Table 38. Analysis of conservation costs for homeowners

Action	Annual savings (kWh)	Initial cost ($)	Annual cost ($ year)	Annualized investment cost of annual saving[a] (c kWh)
Launder in cold water, lower hot water temperature, set back thermostat manually at night	3500	0	0	0
Install automatic night setback on thermostat	1800	40	4.24[b]	0.2
Insulate water heater	1400	40	4.24[b]	0.3
Install low-flow shower	600	20	2.12[b]	0.4
Buy an energy-efficient refrigerator	400	20[c]	2.62[d]	0.7
Insulate ceiling to R-19	2100	270	28.62[b]	1.4
Seal attic bypasses	800	110	11.66[b]	1.5
Insulate walls to R-11	5500	805	85.33[b]	1.6
Seal ducts in unheated areas	700	175	18.55[b]	2.7
Install fluorescent lights in kitchen	300	50	10.3[e]	3.4
Improve energy-efficiency rating of air conditioning to 10	1500	440	57.64[d]	3.8
Caulk worst places	400	200	41.2[e]	10.3

[a] If the cost in this column is less than the levelized cost of electricity (11.2c kWh), the option is favorable to the homeowner.

[b] Annualized using capital recovery factor of 10.6%; corresponds to 30-year life and 10% interest rate.

[c] Cost in excess of ordinary refrigerator's price.

[d] Annualized using capital recovery factor of 13.1%; corresponds to 15-year life and 10% interest rate. Replacement cost not included.

[e] Annualized using capital recovery factor of 20.6%; corresponds to 5-year life and 10% interest rate. Replacement costs not included.

provide the best strategy. Therefore we must develop a common basis of comparison in order to make choices. Although there are innumerable factors involved in such a comparison, the most significant include the rate at which oil can be saved (by conservation/efficiency actions), the rate at which domestic supplies of petroleum or petroleum-like products can be produced, the price per unit of energy saved or produced in relation to the leveled price of $9/GJ ($55/bbl) of imported oil, and the factors that might limit savings or production. Table 39 lists the conservation actions along with comparative judgements. Once again, the *ultimate* potential production or savings are indicated and should not be construed as the suggested rate of action.

It is interesting to compare costs for some of the energy options. To provide a common basis for comparison, we calculated the costs per unit of the energy they directly replaced (Table 40). The table also gives the ratios of their leveled cost in relation to imported oil. From this comparison it is apparent that coal and nuclear generating stations are cost-effective replacements for those burning oil, and producing gasoline from coal or shale is also less expensive than foreign oil. Solar water heating, at today's collector prices, is not cost effective even compared to oil-fired water heating, and neither is the construction of coal-fired power plants solely to provide peak load service to heat pump home heating. However, a summer-peaking utility with coal and nuclear capacity lying idle during the winter months can power home heat pump systems at a cost (including the heat pump) competitive with oil-burning furnaces.

Non-Technological Approaches to Solving the Oil Import Problem

This section will briefly discuss the ways that the national energy problem might be solved by focusing public policy on economic or institutional systems rather than on specific technology options. First, we will outline several general approaches that, while helping with such specific problems as national vulnerability, are broader in scope than any single problem. Then we will identify a number of non-technological approaches to reducing national vulnerability through increased domestic liquid fuel supply, fuel switching, energy conservation, emergency planning, and international policy.

General Approaches

There are several policies concerning energy that are not technological in orientation and that are aimed at energy decision making in

Table 39. Technical approaches to reducing oil imports[a]

Oil-saving or production technique	Possible production levels[b] [EJ year (10⁶ bble d)]						Assumed limiting factors
	1985		1990		2000		
	Less costly	About as costly	Less costly	About as costly	Less costly	About as costly	
Conventional oil production	18.7 (8.5)		15 (6.6)		10–15 (4.7–6.6)		Limited domestic reserves
Enhanced oil recovery		1.1–2.9 (0.5–1.3)		1.1–6.2 (0.5–2.8)		1.1–18 (0.5–8.2)	Limited domestic reserves
Heavy oil		0.44 (0.2)		0.9–1.1 (0.4–0.5)		2.2 (1.0)	Logistics of establishing the industry and limitations of reserves
Oil from shale		0.18–0.29 (0.08–0.13)		0.9 (0.4)		2.2–11 (1–5)	Logistics of establishing the industry and local air quality standards
Oil from coal		0.24 (0.11)		2.4 (1.1)		16.5 (7.5)	Logistics of establishing the industry
Direct coal combustion substituted for gas burning	0.21 (0.09)		0.32 (0.14)[c]		0.53 (0.24)		**Logistics of boiler conversion and local air quality standards**
Direct coal combustion substituted for oil burning	0.21 (0.09)		0.32 (0.14)[c]		0.53 (0.24)[d]		**Logistics of boiler conversion and local air quality standards**

Table 39. (continued)

Intermediate-Btu gas from coal	2.0 (0.9)[e]		6.0 (2.7)[f]	6.0 (2.7)[f]	Logistics of establishing regional plants
Power wheeling	4.2 (1.9)				Accelerated construction of coal and nuclear units under way and strengthened interties
New coal and nuclear units replacing oil in utility sector	1.7 (0.78)		4.4 (2.0)	7.5 (3.4)[g]	Logistics of unit conversion and construction of new capacity and their financing
Natural gas replacing oil in space and water heating	0.71 (0.32)[h]		1.4 (0.63)[i]	2.8 (1.3)[j]	Logistics of system replacement
Electricity (non oil-fired or non gas-fired) replacing oil in space and water heating	0.63 (0.28)[h]		1.3 (0.56)[i]	2.5 (1.1)[j]	Logistics of system replacement
Substitute natural gas replacing oil in space and water heating		0.63 (0.28)[h]	1.3 (0.56)[i]	2.5 (1.1)[j]	Logistics of system replacement
Oil conservation in transportation (savings over 1978)	3.8 (1.7)		5.6 (2.5)	7.2 (3.2)	Penetration rate of new vehicles
Conservation of gas for use as an oil substitute in residential and commercial sectors	0.94 (0.42)[k]		2.82 (1.26)[l]	2.82 (1.26)[l]	Action by a large fraction of the U.S. population

Table 39. (continued)

Oil-saving or production technique	Possible production levels [EJ/year (10^6 bbl/d)]						Assumed limiting factors
	1985		1990		2000		
	Less costly[b]	About as costly[b]	Less costly[b]	About as costly[b]	Less costly[b]	About as costly[b]	
Conservation of electricity for use as an oil substitute in residential and commercial sectors	0.43	(0.19)[k]	1.29	(0.58)[l]	1.29	(0.58)[l]	Action by a large fraction of the U.S. population

[a]Figures in this table were obtained directly from appropriate discussions in the chapter. Assumes 1978 demand.

[b]Cost judgements determined by comparison with \$9/GJ (\$55/bbl) levelized price of imported oil.(For industrial financing. see the standards in Appendix C).

[c]Assumes atmospheric fluidized bed combustion technology is available.

[d]Assumes advanced fluidized bed combustors are available.

[e]Assumes 33% of maximum substitution.

[f]Assumes 100% of maximum substitution.

[g]Assumes all oil and gas electrical generation has been replaced by coal or nuclear.

[h]Assumes 25% of maximum substitution (by heat pump for electricity).

[i]Assumes 50% of maximum substitution (by heat pump for electricity).

[j]Assumes 100% of maximum substitution (by heat pump for electricity).

[k]Assumes 33% of maximum needed conservation effort.

[l]Assumes 100% of maximum needed conservation effort.

the most general sense. Because they are not problem specific, they may help solve other policy problems at the same time (e.g., market imperfections) or improve our ability to solve future problems as well as current ones. Their generality, however, may limit their efficiency in solving specific problems. These approaches can be characterized as changes in the rules of the game and changes in the players in the game.

Changes in the Rules of the Game. Of the possible means we have to influence how we make decisions and view the attractiveness of various alternatives, two general approaches seem particularly powerful: changes in pricing policy and changes in regulations.

Changes in pricing policy: A number of recent studies suggest that the most promising approach to solving our energy problems is through appropriate pricing policies (Landsberg, et al, 1979; *Low Energy Futures for the United States*, 1980; Kalt and Stillman, 1980; Webb, 1978). Essentially, they argue that if we simply decontrol the prices of all energy resources, products, and services, letting the interaction of suppliers and consumers in the marketplace determine the prices, the price of energy will rise to reflect its true value or its market price. At this price, when consumers make energy related decisions, their preferences will reflect the actual value to them of the goods and services required from the future energy supply. The consequences will include economically efficient substitution of capital and labor for more expensive energy and more incentives for developing alternative sources of energy.

The contribution of such a pricing policy to solving our energy problems is difficult to determine precisely. Generally, the response of energy demand to a price increase is relatively small in the short-term but much larger in the longer-term, as people and firms replace their capital stock with more efficient items and adjust their preferences to the new market conditions.

In addition, higher energy prices would accelerate the introduction of new supply options that are economically competitive with real market prices of current options but not with average or controlled prices. The greatest beneficiaries would probably be synthetic fuels, and perhaps other renewable/inexhaustible energy alternatives.

Another pricing policy option is to require the federal government to be evenhanded toward competing resource and technology options. People have argued that, because the federal government supported research and development in nuclear energy and provided depletion allowances for oil and gas production, these options are priced relatively low in comparison with newer technologies such as solar energy and conservation. Recent enactment of tax credits, however, now provide a

Table 40. Comparative costs of selected technical means of displacing oil[a] (i.e., cost per unit of displaced oil)

	Capital investment in 1980 $[b] [$ GJ d ($ bble d)]		Levelized cost (capital + operation and maintenance)[c]	
	For oil displacement capacity	For oil displaced	$ GJ ($ bble)	Fraction of imported oil cost[d]
Utility fuel substitution				
Nuclear power plant (LWR) replacing oil-fired power plant[e]	3.870 (23.700)	5.530 (33.800)	3.29 (20)	0.26
Coal-fired power plant replacing oil-fired power plant[e]	3.100 (19.000)	4.430 (27.100)	4.93 (30)	0.39
Hydrocarbon production[f]				
Oil from shale	Not applicable	2.160–6.100 (13.200–37.400)	3.29–5.48 (20–34)	0.33–0.56
Intermediate-Btu gas from coal[g]	2.500 (15.400)	2.780 (17.000)	4.37 (27)	0.44
Gasoline from coal[h]	7.170 (43.800)	7.970 (48.700)	6.45 (39)	0.64
Substitute natural gas from coal[g]	6.100 (37.300)	6.780 (41.400)	6.51 (40)	0.66

Table 40. (continued) [a]

	Capital investment in 1980 $ [$ GJ d ($ bble d)]		Levelized cost (capital + operation and maintenance) [c]	
	For oil displacement capacity	For oil displaced	$ GJ ($ bble)	Fraction of imported oil cost [d]
Buildings				
Nuclear power plant supplying power to heat pump that replaces an oil furnace [i,j]	17,800 (109,000)	Variable	10.62 (65)	0.83
Coal-fired power plant to supply power to heat pump that replaces an oil furnace [i,j]	14,500 (89,000)	Variable	15.87 (97)	1.24
Solar water heater [k]	19,000 (116,000)	38,000 (233,000)	20.5 (125)	1.6
Solar water heater target costs [k]	8,970 (54,500)	17,900 (110,000)	9.63 (59)	0.76
Heat pump operated in winter by a summer-peaking utility (50% nuclear and 50% coal-fired) to replace oil furnace [l]	6,210 (38,000)	Variable	8.97 (55)	0.71

Table 40. (continued) [a]

	Capital investment in 1980 $ [$ GJ d ($ bble d)]		Levelized cost (capital + operation and maintenance) [c]	
	For oil displacement capacity	For oil displaced	$ GJ ($ bble)	Fraction of imported oil cost [d]
Industrial fuel substitution				
Coal-fired boiler[m] replacing an oil-fired boiler	2,030–3,140 (12,400–19,200)	2,540–3,930 (15,500–24,000)	6.11–7.20 (37–44)	0.61–0.72
Electricity (50% coal and 50% nuclear) replacing oil-fired boiler[o]	10,500 (64,000)[n]	7,320 (44,800)	12.35 (75)	0.97

Table 40. (continued)[a]

Capital investment in 1980 $[b] [$/GJ of ($/bbl of)]		Levelized cost (capital + operation and maintenance)[c]	
For oil displacement capacity	For oil displaced	$/GJ ($/bbl)	Fraction of imported oil cost[d]

[a]Numbers in this table were obtained directly from appropriate discussions in this chapter.

[b]Oil displacement capacity investment is based on the assumption that each system is 100% efficient and operates at 100% capacity. The investment for oil displaced assumes reasonable efficiencies and capacity factors.

[c]Real resource financing (Appendix C).

[d]Assumes 1980 price of $4.90/GJ ($30/bbl), 20-year levelized price of $10/GJ ($61/bbl), and 30-year levelized price of $13/GJ ($78/bbl). Twenty-year value used for industry; thirty-year value used for buildings and utilities. See Appendix C.

[e]Oil-burning power plant assumed to have 33% thermal efficiency. Nuclear or coal-fired plant has 30-year life and a 60% capacity factor.

[f]20-year plant lifetimes are assumed.

[g]Onstream factor of 90%.

[h]Plant efficiency of 60% and a 90% onstream factor. For the cost comparison it was assumed that gasoline from natural oil is produced at 100% efficiency.

[i]Assumed heat pump capital cost of $3500 and 1%/year O&M cost for Boston single-family home (Kelly et al. 1978).

[j]Power plant built solely to meet heat pump demand.

[k]Data for current cost from Solar King Corporation with further assumptions and projected costs from Kelly et al. (1978). Assumed 50% capacity factor and 30-year life. Oil furnaces assumed to have 70% efficiency.

[l]Assumed only power plant fuel cost plus heat pump capital and O&M costs.

[m]20-year life, 80% capacity factor.

[n]Bus-bar power.

[o]Assumed 70% efficiency for oil-fired boiler and 100% efficiency for electric boiler (zero capital cost) plus previous assumptions for electricity generation.

subsidy for solar and conservation technologies to compensate for any previous bias or neglect.

Changes in regulations: Other than price, the main determinant of the rules of the game is our body of statutes and regulations. One current concern is to simplify these rules by eliminating overlaps, inconsistencies, and redundancies without changing the basic policies that the rules reflect. This is difficult to do because specific groups benefit from some of the existing procedures, but many agree that simplification is a good idea. For example, the Northwest Alaska Pipeline Co. blames the delays caused by the National Gas Policy Act of 1978 and the lack of timely governmental decisions, for a $5 to $6 billion cost increase in their proposed pipeline ("AGA Hears Effect of Delays on Cost of North Slope System," 1980).

Suggestions for changes in regulations have been directed mainly at two areas: environmental regulations (e.g., the Clean Air Act is presently being re-examined to see if it is unnecessarily stringent) and the relationship between the public and private sectors (e.g., changes in antitrust or patent laws to encourage a more cooperative, less competitive approach to solving problems—the Japanese model). One recent innovation in the first area is EPA's so-called "bubble concept," which increases flexibility in fuel switching by allowing plant managers to increase emissions in certain areas if they reduce them elsewhere. The concept should make conversion to coal easier in such industries as steel, aluminum, and copper (Betts, 1979).

Changes in the Players in the Game. The energy decision making process can also be altered by changing the parties involved or the roles they now play in the process.

Adding players: Few people are suggesting that any of the present parties involved in our pluralistic system of policy making can or should be eliminated. However, a number of proposals have been made to create new institutions to fill gaps in the system. Focusing largely on nonprofit public sector organizations, these proposals are aimed at developing energy resources and providing credible energy resource information (e.g., a public oil exploration and production company); at developing energy sources (e.g., an AEC-like organization for solar energy); or at removing decision-making bottlenecks (e.g., the Energy Security Corporation). Others have suggested there is a need for new institutions that would provide for local and regional resource use (e.g., rural electric cooperatives and municipal utilities). There is growing evidence that energy decision making on a local level can be more resolute than decision making on a broader, more diverse scale. A reinforcement of current trends toward local planning and action could speed up the use of available conservation and domestic supply options (Wilbanks, 1980).

Some Specific Approaches Related to the Oil Issue

Again, the specific concern is one of reducing the national vulnerability that results from our dependence on oil imports. The following paragraphs outline some approaches to meeting this particular need.

Reducing Vulnerability by Reducing Imports. One possible approach to reducing our vulnerability is to put legal restraints on imports. For example, a quota could be set that limits imports of crude oil and/or refined products. Another legal restraint is an import tariff (or tax or fee), which adds to the world market price and makes imported oil more expensive, thus reducing the demand for it.

The idea of a tariff on oil imports has been suggested in several papers (Cox and Wright, 1978; Tyner and Wright, 1978), which reason that regardless of the source, oil prices should include the expected cost of a disruption of normal supplies. An import tariff imposed on oil could reflect such costs. One problem with a tariff, however, is that by spurring increased domestic energy production it may deplete domestic resources too fast. In other words, "the tariff [alone] would buy too much current independence, at the expense of future independence, by reducing imports too much in the current period." A tax on domestic oil production can offset such effects.

Import tariffs designed to reduce our vulnerability have also been suggested by Nordhaus (1974) and by Tolley and Wilman (1977). They argue that a tariff forces domestic suppliers and demanders of oil to operate on short-term supply and demand curves that correspond to higher oil prices. Thus, although the tariff decreases our oil surplus during normal periods, it also reduces the expected surplus losses of periodic import disruptions. An optimal tariff would maximize the expected net surplus gains. The tariff results in lower oil imports, but that is not its main objective.

Tariffs that reduce our vulnerability to imported oil must not be confused with protectionist tariffs or quotas, such as the pre-1973 quota on oil imports. That tariff was designed to protect domestic oil producers from very cheap oil imports, mostly from the Middle East. In effect, that quota subsidized oil consumption for Western Europe and elsewhere, either lowering their consumer prices (including consumption by industry competing with our exports) or increasing the excise tax receipts of foreign governments (Mead, 1979; Bohi and Russell, 1978).

The tariffs proposed now are designed to reduce our vulnerability to sudden world price changes or supply disruptions. These tariffs or quotas would, if they work as intended, reduce the domestic costs of a severe price increase or disruption in supply. The pre-1973 quota was not designed to provide such benefits because our vulnerability was not as severe at that time. Although the benefits of the pre-1973 quota were less than its costs, we cannot conclude that the same is true for tariffs that deal with our vulnerability to foreign oil.

   Reducing Vulnerability by Increasing Domestic Production. There are four types of policy options for boosting domestic liquid fuel production that are not technology-oriented: government activity as a developer, government incentives for private developers, actions to ensure a market for liquid fuels from new sources, and institutional initiatives to remove bottlenecks for developers and consumers.

   Government activity as a developer: Government can increase domestic liquid fuel production by doing the job itself, in whole or in part. For example, it can take actions to develop energy resources on federal lands and the Outer Continental Shelf (OCS) (e.g., providing leasing policies that require lease-holders to develop the resources on a specified schedule). To get new technologies started, government can build demonstration plants and pioneer commercial plants, and then lease them to operators. Or it can pay part of the cost of such facilities. It can also make use of quasi-governmental entities such as the Tennessee Valley Authority (TVA) to undertake development efforts that are in the public interest.

   Government incentives for private developers: Government can encourage private developers to increase domestic production either by making it more attractive economically or by shifting all or part of the risk to the public sector. Economic incentives include tax credits for investments in synfuel production (NEP-II proposed a 50¢/GJ or $3/bbl tax credit for shale oil production) and treatment of investment in synfuels as an annual operating expense—as petroleum exploration and development are treated—rather than as capital investment (Cochran, 1980). An example of a risk sharing initiative is a loan guarantee program: If the new facility turns out to be a loser, the government guarantees that the construction loan will be repaid anyway—a powerful incentive to conventional lenders; or if the facility has a capital cost overrun, the government pays part of the excess costs, which also reduces the risk to a lender.

   Actions to ensure a market for liquid fuels from new resources: If developers are sure that the liquid fuels from new sources can be sold at a fair price, they will be encouraged to make them available. Policy choices include government purchases of unconventional liquid fuels, such as synfuels or ethanol, regardless of price (the state of Illinois has announced that 10,000 state vehicles shifted to gasohol in 1980). Another option is the Synthetic Liquid Utilization Plan, considered in formulating NEP-II, which would have mandated synfuel purchases by refineries and other market entry points by a specified date. For instance, a refinery might have to assure that 10% of its feedstock is synthetic crude oil by 1995 or pay a heavy penalty, or a gas pipeline company might be required to include a certain amount of gas from coal in its supply streams.

Institutional initiatives to remove bottlenecks for developers and consumers: Finally, government can take action to remove impediments to domestic energy development, (e.g., capital supply shortages [the Synthetic Fuels Corporation]). Incentives are an especially promising method to reduce conflicts over the siting of new facilities and to provide insurance against the uncertainty in future environmental regulations.

Reducing Vulnerability by Encouraging Fuel Switching. Aside from an arbitrary requirement by law or regulation, fuel switching can be encouraged by making it more economical or by emphasizing the risk of oil supply cut-offs. In addition, institutional changes may be able to remove the impediments to switching. Essentially, there are four policy approaches to consider.

Legal requirement: In principle, fuel switching can be brought about by mandating it. For example, the Power Plant and Industrial Fuel Use Act of 1978 requires that most base-load electric power generators shift from oil and gas fuels to alternatives by 1990. Except in circumstances where compliance would cause unacceptable consequences, a failure to comply would mean severe penalties. Requirements for industry to switch from oil, at least in some cases, are also incorporated in the law. This approach sounds straightforward, but implementation is complicated by litigation, requests for exemptions, and questions of definition (e.g., does the requirement apply to all sectors and to all sizes of facilities?).

Economic incentives: In many cases, switching from oil to another fuel already makes good economic sense, but it can be made even more attractive. For example, the DOE Office for Conservation and Solar Energy has discussed the possibility of a tax (perhaps 30¢/GJ or $2/bbl) on oil consumed by industry, with the revenue returned to industry in the form of grants or loans for fuel switching (e.g., grants for engineering design work or loans for boiler conversions which are forgiven if the investment doesn't pay for itself in three years). Other economic incentives include investment tax credits for conversion costs, accelerated depreciation of new equipment, and economic incentives for the early retirement of outdated capital stock.

Risk aversion: An effective way to encourage fuel switching, especially by industry, is to remind consumers that they are taking risks if they do not switch. For instance, an emergency allocation formula that gives a current oil consumer a low priority—if well publicized—encourages switching.* In fact, an awareness of the energy crisis may affect even high priority users. Recent ORNL research indicates that residential energy users in New England, after the 1973 oil embargo, switched to energy forms other than oil in greater numbers than price alone could account for. The most plausible explanation is risk aversion (Tepel, 1980).

Institutional factors: There are a number of institutional barriers to fuel substitution. For example, as vestiges of natural gas shortages in the mid-1970's, some geographical areas have restrictions on natural gas hookups, even though natural gas may now be a desirable substitute for oil in many cases. Also, coal distribution systems are in disrepair, to say the least, in many parts of the U.S. Another significant obstacle seems to be the parochialism of those involved in electric utility decision making. Because a public service commission may view expansion of a utility's generating capacity only in terms of pressure for an unpopular rate increase to pay for the new plant, it is difficult to convince these regulating agencies that the additional capacity is, in fact, necessary. It is likewise hard to convince public service commissions that shutting down an oil-fired plant and buying electricity from another utility is a good interim arrangement. Some new thinking about policy is needed. Possible solutions might be: allocation of part of the oil tax revenue (windfall profits tax, oil import tariff, etc.) for payments to electric utilities based on the amount of electricity exported; regulatory protection of importers against unfairly high costs for electrical imports and pass-through systems; regulatory protection of importers in the event of electric power shortages; and federal government representation at state public service commission hearings to provide additional information and perspectives (for instance, about national needs when the "certificate of convenience and necessity" for a new power plant is being considered).

These policy approaches for encouraging fuel switching are inseparable from the technical approaches required. They are not alternatives to technical approaches; they are mechanisms for getting the job done.

---

*However, if all current oil consumers are given low priority, then no one gets oil unless they are new customers. If the allocation formula were developed to give certain classes of existing customers low priority, and not allow any new customers, it would encourage existing customers to switch and would prevent new ones from being added as old ones switch to other fuels.

Reducing Vulnerability by Encouraging Conservation. Energy conservation can contribute to reducing our vulnerability to imported oil by reducing oil demand directly, by reducing demand for other energy forms that can be substituted for oil (such as gas and electricity), or by increasing the acceptance of substitutes. The major opportunity for oil conservation is in the transportation sector, as explained earlier in this chapter. This discussion will be limited to a very brief treatment of non-technological approaches to transportation energy conservation and to a summary of other types of conservation policies.

Transportation energy conservation: Oil can be saved by mandating higher fuel efficiency standards for vehicles, ridesharing, and accelerated market penetration of new technologies through demonstrations and information dissemination.

Significant accomplishments have already been made in conserving energy used for transportation. In 1974, the automobiles sold by General Motors averaged EPA ratings of 5.1 km/L (12 mpg). Through a combination of higher gasoline prices and fuel efficiency standards, General Motors expects their 1985 average to be an EPA rating of 13 km/L (31 mpg). This represents the largest peacetime revolution in transportation in U.S. history (Irwin, 1980). The 1985 estimate, of course, is well beyond the federal government requirement, reflecting price-responsive shifts in consumer demand.

Major policy alternatives to promote further conservation include pricing, efficiency standards, government assistance to industry, and government incentives for retiring inefficient vehicles. A number of observers have proposed gasoline taxes ranging from 1.3 to 13¢/L (5 to 50¢/gal). These revenues might be returned to consumers through the income tax or social security systems so that the overall cost of living does not rise. This would certainly encourage increased efficiency (see the earlier discussion of pricing policies), but it would be politically unpopular while inflated living expenses are a more sharply focused issue than energy.

It is clear now that the 1985 EPA fuel efficiency standard of 11.7 km/L (27.5 mpg) will be met easily, and further standards are being discussed, such as 17 km/L (40 mpg) or higher by 2000. According to the Mellon study (Shackson and Leach, 1980), domestic cars will probably average about 20 km/L (47 mpg) by 2000 even if no standards are applied. A recent ORNL study suggests that a 23 km/L (55 mpg) fleet average is attainable by 2010 (Samuels, 1980). Although the corporate average fuel economy (CAFE) standards have been helpful in signaling a national commitment, the time for them has probably passed; the marketplace can now take over.

A more urgent need may be for government assistance to industry. Just as in, for example, the synfuels industry, automobile makers are exposed to the risks of possible future changes in government policy. Specifically, the federal government should stabilize its regulations on auto emissions and safety standards so that industry does not have to deal with moving targets in this area

Energy efficiency could also be improved by accelerating the retirement of less efficient vehicles. Mechanisms to accomplish this include tax credits or subsidized low-interest loans for buying efficient vehicles, taxes or increased licensing fees on inefficient vehicles, direct government purchases of inefficient vehicles, and price subsidies for efficient ones

Energy conservation in other sectors: There are too many non-technological policies in conservation to describe each in detail, but they fall generally into five different approaches: minimum performance standards (e.g., building or appliance efficiency standards); taxes and other pricing policies (e.g., decontrolling prices); financial incentives for investment in more energy-efficient facilities or equipment (e.g., tax credits, accelerated depreciation, guaranteed loans for capital expenditures); information programs (e.g., free energy audits); and efforts to remove institutional barriers to conservation (e.g., rate structure changes). At current energy prices, a relatively small—say 20%—additional front-end investment in conservation will repay itself quickly, in many cases, through lower operating costs. Actually, the main challenge is to communicate such conservation facts to the public so that they can make appropriate energy decisions. For example, programs that monitor energy use and feed cost data back to the consumer may reduce building energy consumption by 10 to 30% (McClelland and Cook, 1980; Winett and Neale, 1979).

Reducing Vulnerability Through Emergency Planning. Finally, we are less vulnerable if we are better prepared to absorb the effects of an interruption in supply. Besides actions to eliminate the cause of the shortfall, there are three principal preparation strategies: strategic petroleum storage, development of emergency fuel-switching capabilities, and contingency planning.

Strategic petroleum storage: If, for example, we were to have a stockpile of 8.6 EJ (1.4 billion bbl), we could replace 17 EJ/year (7 million bbl/d) of oil imports for half a year. In addition there would be two months of supplies "on the high seas" after a supply cutoff at the source. One approach attaining the stockpile is through the salt-dome storage program that is underway in the public sector. Another alternative is a decentralized approach, where incentives are provided to industry to increase its oil storage capacity at points of production and use.

Contingency planning for emergencies: We are more vulnerable—economically and socially—to a supply interruption if we are less prepared to deal with it. Careful planning that includes participation by a wide range of interests can significantly increase our resilience by increasing our understanding of what actions are necessary and why.

Besides identifying actions that can reduce the likelihood or severity of an emergency (such as petroleum storage, transportation conservation, or fuel switching), contingency planning includes schemes for emergency fuel allocation and policies for emergency conservation. A number of short-term measures have been analyzed (Boercker, et al, 1980), but there is little agreement as to which actions make the most sense. Energy savings from familiar transportation conservation measures—odd-even day restrictions of gasoline purchases, minimum or maximum purchase restrictions, Sunday closings of service stations, or price increases through surcharges—are likely to save less than 20% in the aggregate (Harrington, et al, 1980). Energy savings from such policies as a 40-hour-a-week limit on business hours occur at the expense of a significant increase in unemployment.

Without prior agreement on a strategy, energy savings depend upon happenstance rationing (closed gasoline stations, power blackouts) or upon decisions made on an ad hoc basis, which often overlook relationships within the system. For example, if diesel fuel allocation formulas favor truck freight transportation over other uses for fuel, crops may not get harvested or coal barges may not operate.

Reducing Vulnerability Through International Policy. In a variety of ways, the U.S. can lessen the impact of a cutoff of imported oil by increasing the effectiveness of its international relationships. Alternatives include action in policy areas other than energy, in international cooperation on energy policy, and in technology transfer policies.

Non-energy policies: The strategies for dealing with something as pressing as a significant interruption of imported oil during the early 1980's lie outside the purview of energy policy. The principal concerns here are U.S. relations with oil exporting countries, U.S. relations with developing countries, and our defense expenditures.

The U.S. government should seek to maintain good relations with oil exporting countries, to support governments in those countries (although this can backfire as in Iran), and to continue to diversify imports among a large number of countries. It is especially desirable to reduce the proportion of U.S. imports coming from the Middle East (see "International cooperation" below).

Our energy economy is vulnerable to disruptions that result from international instability, even if it is not directly related to events in the Middle East. Instability can cause friendly nations to become hostile or can interfere with ocean transportation. Aside from the Middle East, the biggest danger in the 1980's and 1990's probably lies in the possibility that some developing countries will encounter major catastrophes, such as economic collapse or large-scale starvation. Actions to help avert such catastrophes, besides being desirable on humanitarian grounds, could be part of a self-interest strategy to protect our energy domain.

Defense expenditures that increase our capabilities will contribute to international stability and will give us the option of military intervention in extreme situations.

International cooperation: A number of important policy choices have to do with bilateral or multilateral agreements between the U.S. and other countries. These include agreements among oil importers, cooperation in the Western hemisphere, and cooperation with developing countries.

Coordinated by the International Energy Agency, there are already agreements among most of the industrialized countries to help each other in the event of a shortfall of imports for one country and to cooperate in limiting or reducing imports. Beyond this, some people believe that oil importers could change the nature of the international oil market by acting as a unified consumer cartel in negotiations with the exporter cartel.

In addition to providing capital supply assistance and technology transfer to developing countries, the U.S. and other industrialized countries could reduce their competition with these countries for scarce world oil supplies; this would contribute powerfully to the resolution of the world energy problems described in Chapter II.

OPTIONS ADDRESSING THE LONG-TERM ISSUES

Summary Statement of the Issue

While resolving the immediate import problem, the U.S. must also face the energy issues that will concern the nation well into the next century. The predominant issues are the need for adequate energy supplies at the lowest economic and environmental cost, and the need to avoid a severe disruption of supply. disruption adversely affecting the population. The needs of other nations must also be taken into account because the fortunes of the rest of the world will influence the fortunes of this country. Thus global concerns are expected to become increasingly important in evaluating domestic energy policy as the population and desire for a better life grow in the developing countries.

We expect and hope that world energy demands will grow rapidly in the coming decades, as needed economic growth takes place in the developing countries. As illustrated in the previous chapter, we may see a total primary energy demand in the world of 1500 EJ* in 2030 compared with the 1975 level of 250 EJ: a six-fold increase. This level of consumption by 2030 would require the cumulative use of only 25% of the globe's conventional fossil and uranium fuel resources (3% if breeder reactors are widely used). Conventional oil, however, will be in short supply before the end of the century. Conventional sources of natural gas may be sufficient to meet demand until 2010 or 2020, at which time production limits will have been reached.

The response of the developed countries to the pending shortfalls in oil and gas will necessarily be the development of non-traditional resources, but these technologies are capital intensive and not enticing to the developing nations. It would therefore be prudent for the developed world to act early to remove itself as much as possible from the international oil and gas market and become, if possible, a supplier of energy resources. Such a policy will not fall upon all developed nations with equal grace or ease, but it is most important nonetheless.

In light of the above, the important energy issue for the U.S. becomes the societal cost associated with a rapid transition from conventional petroleum and natural gas resources to a much greater use of long-term domestic energy sources. Additionally, it must be recognized that some of the major alternative energy sources presently available face serious potential constraints due to possible environmental impacts, risks to safety, and high economic costs. Prudence dictates assembling a number of options, in case some promising technology or system fails to meet its potential.

Long-Term Energy Source Options

The mid-and long-term future (1990–2050) described in the previous chapter is still observed with considerable uncertainty. It is certain,

---

*This estimate exceeds the reference scenario estimated by the International Institute for Applied Systems Analysis (IIASA), primarily because of differing assumptions on GNP growth rates (Haefele, et al. 1981).

however, that the U.S. and the rest of the world will need significant quantities of liquid and gaseous fuels and electricity. It is appropriate then to take stock of the various energy-producing technologies that could provide for these needs. In this section we explore these technologies, estimate the potential contribution they might make, and look at the difficulties and constraints that each might encounter. As in the discussion of the technical options for solving the oil import problem, our aim here is not to outline a comprehensive strategy, but to delineate the reasonable maximum contributions of each energy source.

Oil

The world runs basically on petroleum, yet the outlook for a continued supply at low-cost is very doubtful. So we will first investigate the capability of the U.S. to produce oil from domestic resources. These resources are considered either conventional or unconventional. Conventional sources of oil are those that provide low-cost petroleum using widely accepted recovery techniques. Unconventional sources are typically not in major use, usually because of their higher cost and uncertain availability and technology. We will examine the ability of these sources to produce oil beyond the short term, as the nation enters the twenty-first century.

Outlook for Conventional Resources. As noted in the discussion of the oil import problem, the likely future for conventional sources of oil is one of declining production. The year 2000 may see domestic production of only 10 to 15 EJ/year (4.7 to 6.8 million bbl/d), if no major oil field discoveries are made.

Outlook for Unconventional Resources. Unconventional sources of oil are those recovered with enhanced oil recovery (EOR) techniques, from heavy crudes, from tar sands, and from oil shales. We have discussed EOR at some length in this chapter in relation to the oil import problem. Approximately 1400 EJ (230 billion bbl) of oil is unrecoverable by conventional techniques, and is a target for EOR. It is estimated that 130 to 700 EJ (20 to 110 billion bbl) of this is amenable to EOR techniques (Robel, 1978; Pasini, 1980). This is a modest though not insubstantial quantity, the equivalent of 3 to 17 years of oil consumption at the 1978 U.S. level. The technology, however, is costly, and its future depends upon the price of oil and the availability of capital. Opportunities for technical improvements that will dramatically change this situation are limited and unlikely to occur. Greater knowledge of opportunities (sites and appropriate techniques) would best enhance the potential of EOR. Projections for the long-term production of oil via EOR range from about 1.1 EJ/year (0.50 million bbl/d) (Pasini, 1980) to 18 EJ/year (8.2 million bbl/d) (Robel, et al, 1978) in the year 2000. The relatively small resource base and high costs for EOR are likely to keep recovery through the next century close to the lower figure.

The heavy crudes, also discussed earlier, are an even more limited resource in this country, equaling about 450 EJ (74 billion bbl). They face recovery difficulties similar to those associated with the EOR of light oil. Olszewski (1980) projects a recovery rate of 1.1 EJ/year (0.50 million bbl/d), and Pasini (1980) estimates 0.9 EJ/year (0.4 million bbl/d) for the period beyond 2000.

Tar sands are a minor U.S. oil resource which equal about 180 EJ (30 billion bbl) (Pasini, 1980). They face constraints similar to those facing EOR. A further difficulty is the uncertain economics of the small-scale mining and production facilities necessary to take advantage of such a geographically distributed resource. Pasini (1980) estimates that production might reach 1.1 EJ/year (0.50 million bbl/d) by 2010.

In contrast with the other unconventional oil resources, oil from shale is a phenomenally large resource. The western deposits contain in excess of 12,000 EJ (2 trillion bbl), of which approximately 3700 EJ (600 billion bbl) are high-grade shales (Pasini, 1980). Shale formations in the east contain 18,000 EJ (2.9 trillion bbl), although it is not clear how much is recoverable (Olszewski, 1980). Such an immense resource base clearly deserves considerable attention as a long-term energy source, one that is for all practical purposes inexhaustible.

The development of shale oil can be extended for several centuries without concern for depletion. Pasini (1980) and Olszewski (1980) foresee 2.2 EJ/year (1.0 million bbl/d) of shale oil production by 2000, and Pasini (1980) expects this to double by 2010. Lewis (1979) believes that the production of 2.2 to 4.4 EJ/year (1 to 2 million bbl/d) in 1995 and 11 EJ/year (5 million bbl/d) in 2000 is possible.

The establishment of a mining industry greater than the world has previously known will raise environmental concerns, perhaps severe enough to constrain production. *In situ* recovery of shale oil, if feasible, might relieve these concerns. The other limitation is the cost of recovering and producing oil from the shale, which is still uncertain.

It is possible that the sources of oil described above, when combined with conventional resources, will allow domestic production to remain at the present level for some time. And domestic production could rise of substantial oil shale development takes place.

Natural Gas

As demonstrated earlier in this chapter, natural gas is an extremely valuable fuel, particularly when used as a direct and immediate substitute for oil. Although the short-term availability of adequate gas supplies is good, the longer term outlook is considerably more uncertain.

Outlook for Conventional Resources. The total recoverable conventional natural gas resource is estimated to be between 788 and 1107 EJ, which is a 38- to 55-year supply at 1978 consumption levels (Olszewski, 1980). This is a considerably brighter picture than that for conventional oil, but recent trends are somewhat disappointing. From 1947 to 1954 the yearly additions to reserves were in the range of 10 to 20 EJ/year, and from 1955 to 1967 they averaged about 20 EJ/year. Except for Alaskan gas in 1970, however, reserve additions since 1967 have averaged only about 11 EJ/year. The reserve to production ratio fell from a value of 20 in 1960 to 11 in 1976. A ratio of 11 is the lowest level considered acceptable for normal production (Olszewski, 1980).

Olszewski (1980) has examined two possible cases for future natural gas production. In the optimistic case, reserve additions continue at 10.7 EJ/year until 2000. Production drops from the present 20.9 EJ/year to 16.2 EJ/year in 1985, to 14.0 EJ/year in 1990, and to 11.8 EJ/year in 2000. In the second and more pessimistic case, a direct extrapolation of the historical trend of decreasing reserve additions indicates that production will fall to 12.9 EJ/year in 1990 and to 7.5 EJ/year in 2000. If the potential supplies in the Prudhoe Bay field of Alaska are tapped, an additional 1 EJ/year might be available. The clear message is that conventional domestic sources of natural gas are not reliable long-term supplies.

Outlook For Unconventional Resources. There is reason for considerably more optimism concerning the longer-term availability of natural gas from unconventional sources. However, these will be more expensive to recover than the conventional resource. Unconventional sources of natural gas include western tight sands; Devonian shale deposits; Appalachian coal beds; geo-pressured aquifers; and the deep formations, below 5000 m. The first four sources are estimated to contain recoverable natural gas quantities equivalent to 118 to 236 EJ, assuming a price of $3.50/GJ can be obtained (Samuels, 1979). The deep formations probably contain an additional 650 EJ of gas obtainable at that price (Sanuels, 1979). Samuels (1979) estimates that as much as 10 to 15 EJ/year of gas from unconventional sources could be produced by the year 2000.

Coal

In the previous discussion about solving the oil import problem, we outlined a number of uses for the nation's coal resources, as well as the environmental and health problems of recovering coal. Coal resources are even larger than the oil shales, and can be recovered economically. It is possible to view this resource as a mainstay of a long-term energy future for the U.S., and perhaps for the rest of the world.

Supply Outlook. Considering the resource base (43,300 EJ or 1.8 trillion tons) and the fact that the 1978 level of coal consumption was 14.6 EJ (625 million tons), the reserves could support a very large expansion in production. Most of the lignite and all of the sub-bituminous coal is found west of the Mississippi. Eastern coals are more valuable for heating than western coals, but 80% of the eastern coal requires underground mining compared with only 60% in the west. Furthermore, western coal is primarily low-sulfur, while eastern is predominantly high in sulfur (Olszewski, 1980).

An aggressive coal mining program to expand production by 7.5% per year has been evaluated by Kuhlman (Greenstreet, et al, 1980). In recent years the growth rate has been a little over 4% per under-utilized industry. At a growth rate of 7.5% per year, coal production would reach 71.3 EJ/year (3 billion tons/year) by the year 2000. Such rapid expansion would have to contend with the lead times (5 to 12 years) for opening new underground mines. Surface mining constraints are related to equipment size, since greater capacities require larger excavation equipment. The greatest potential lies in the western states. They have been depleted the least and significant portions of their deposits are strippable.

Most coal used in the U.S. is shipped via rail, with the rest transported by truck and water, in that order. Although the nation's rail system is having problems, Greenstreet, et al (1980) project that transportation inadequacies will not limit coal use if the growth rate is 7.5%/year through 2000.

Combustion. There has been considerable discussion in this chapter about the direct combustion of coal. Many of the conclusions are directly related to the longer term. A general quantitative relationship is easily established between the magnitude of coal combustion and its environmental impact. Craig and Salk (1979) believe that coal use will be constrained—by air quality standards—at some level less than five times the current rate of burning (i.e., at less than 70 EJ/year or 3 billion tons/year). Even with the best current control technology operating on new units, total emissions from burning coal could continue to increase if the emissions from old units are not reduced. The retrofit or retirement of older coal-fired systems, however, could lead to an actual decrease in pollutants.

Conversion. The long-term prospects for converting coal to liquid and gaseous fuels are similar to those for coal combustion: The resource base is extensive and conversion technologies exist; and significant improvements are likely to develop. As described earlier, a coal conversion industry could be established to provide as much as 18 EJ/year (8 million bbl/d) of liquids by the year 2000. Cochran (1980) has estimated that liquid and gases produced from coal could total approximately 50 EJ/year (23 million bble/d) by 2050, if one considers only the technical constraints of plant construction.

Nuclear Energy

Nuclear fission is likely to be used primarily to produce electricity through the mid-term. The contribution fission makes will be determined by political considerations in the short-term, and by technical realities in the long-term.

Nuclear fusion seems to lie outside the present debate over fission. Fusion is being developed at a good pace. Its greatest unknowns lie in the realm of technical and economic feasibility. If used at all, it too is likely to contribute principally to electricity generation, although other uses are possible.

Uranium Supply Outlook. Nuclear fission is now used commercially in thermal reactors, of which the light water reactor (LWR) is the most common type in the United States. These reactors require uranium slightly enriched in the isotope ^{235}U. Although the recycling of both the unused ^{235}U and the plutonium produced as the reactor is operated has the potential to extend the uranium resource by about 50%, thermal reactors do require a continuing supply of uranium.

The magnitude of the conventional uranium resource is under considerable dispute. The National Uranium Resource Evaluation puts proven reserves of uranium [at a cost of up to $156/kg U ($60/lb U_3O_8)] at 3.4 billion kg (4.4 million short tons U_3O_8) (*Nuclear Fuel, 1979*). This would support roughly 800 GW(e) of LWR's, without fuel recycle, over their 30-year lifetime.

Beyond these resources, there are lower grade ores that yield uranium at greater cost. Unconventional sources of significant quantities of uranium include: Chattanooga shale, coal and lignite, phosphate rock, Conway granite, and seawater (listed in the order of increasing cost of uranium recovery). In some cases it will be economical to recover the uranium from unconventional resources along with the recovery of other materials (e.g., simultaneous recovery of oil and uranium from Chattanooga shale or of phosphate and uranium from phosphate rock) (Vath, 1980).

A major difference between fission and fossil fuel electrical generation is that the cost of nuclear fuel is a minor portion of the total electricity cost. Uranium as the hexafluoride (unenriched) comprises only one-half the cost of the LWR fuel cycle, which itself is only one-quarter of the bus-bar cost. This is in contrast to a coal-fired station, where fuel costs represent about one-half the cost of the electricity, and to natural gas- and oil-fired stations where fuel costs are even higher (Reichle, 1979). Nuclear electric power costs are therefore not highly sensitive to the price of uranium and can withstand substantially higher fuel prices without substantially increasing electrical rates.

Fission Reactors. As has been demonstrated both in the U.S. and abroad, thermal fission reactors can produce competitively priced electricity. The U.S. has the capacity to construct an average of perhaps 30 GW(e) of nuclear units per year. Substantial amounts of uranium are likely to be available well through the mid-term, albeit at somewhat higher prices. Thus thermal reactors are potential major contributors to electricity production into the next century.

The breeder reactor system, while in limbo in the U.S., is being vigorously pursued overseas and has a substantial technological base. The breeder will have to compete with the lower-grade and unconventional sources of uranium. Its commercial introduction will therefore be timed to coincide with the rising price of that uranium. Eventually the breeder's efficient consumption of plutonium produced both in breeder systems and in thermal reactors can, in a fully developed industry, make it unnecessary to depend on uranium resources.

Acceptance of breeder reactors in the United States will depend on economics, on the safety of the reactors, and on the real and perceived security issues of a plutonium-based fuel cycle.

The greatest constraint to the expanded use of fission appears to be regulatory uncertainty. This climate of uncertainty stems from the lack of genuine support at the federal and state levels of government, coupled with the sensitivity of the regulatory apparatus to actions by groups opposed to fission reactors. It is compounded by uncertainties in electrical demand, which has grown at rates lower than predicted. These factors combine to produce the present stagnation in fission development.

Although repeated public opinion polls [by Louis Harris and Associates (Spiewak and Cope, 1980), Roger Seasonwein Associated, Inc. (1979/80), and *National Geographic* (1981)] indicate that the majority of Americans believe in an expanded role for fission, the further development of the industry is thwarted for the moment. Utilities and financial institutions looking at investment in nuclear power do not know what the final requirements for plant construction will be and thus cannot gauge the final cost. They are not even sure whether the plants will be allowed to be completed (Spiewak and Cope, 1980).

In essence, fission faces many of the same political and social difficulties as do other major technologies (such as coal combustion), but its choice as the target of a number of groups has given it more visibility. Thus, the means for achieving agreement on how to proceed with nuclear energy will be little different in concept from the techniques required by other technologies. The discussion of these will be left to those sections involving domestic decision making.

Radwaste Issues. Radioactive wastes have been generated in the United States since the inception of the nuclear weapons programs during World War II. For many years defense wastes were the major source of radwaste, and they continue to be produced at a significant rate. Although we confine our discussion here to the disposal of commercially generated waste, defense wastes pose similar problems, and solutions to one are likely to be applicable to the other.

Radioactive waste from a nuclear power facility is classified as either high level waste (HLW) or low level waste (LLW). The only commercially generated material which falls into the HLW category is the waste separated from spent fuel by reprocessing. Concern about the disposal of high level waste is a significant obstacle to further construction of fission reactors. This is the only part of the nuclear fuel cycle that has not been demonstrated on any significant scale in the U.S.

The magnitude of the technical problem is not great, due to the small volume of HLW material that will be generated. A major power reactor will produce approximately 0.03 m^3 (8 gal)/year of pure waste (fission products), although more typically the waste is diluted in the spent fuel. There appears to be general agreement within the international technical community that HLW can be safely disposed of in geological formations (i.e., buried in carefully chosen sites deep underground), assuming reasonable measures are taken. This would require only the use of already existing technology or simple extensions of existing technology. The added cost of disposal would be a factor of about ten below present day electricity costs. The environmental impact in either the short- or long-term (many generations) from the geological disposal of HLW has been estimated as negligible. (Report to the President by the Interagency Review Group on Nuclear Waste Management, 1979; Roy, et al, 1978; Special Workshop on Radwaste, 1979, DOE/EIS-0046 D).

The production of LLW is not confined to the power industry. Large quantities are produced by medical establishments, research institutions, and other industrial activities. By definition, LLW is only slightly contaminated with radioactive substances, which are often short-lived. Disposal is generally accomplished by shallow land burial, which for the most part has proven successful. Over the last few years the states of Washington and South Carolina have balked at becoming the only disposal sites in the nation. Other states are being encouraged to handle their own LLW disposal or to enter into compacts to provide regional facilities.

Perhaps the greatest difficulty in radioactive waste management is finding states and communities willing to host disposal facilities. The federal agencies considering this problem believe that social consensus can be obtained by bringing state and local officials, and members of the public, closer into the decision-making process (Report to the President by the Interagency Review Group on Nuclear Waste Management, 1979). The implication is that public participation guarantees acceptance. This approach, however, ignores the possibility of reaching an impasse in the development of the technology and the siting of a facility. It is possible to foresee a situation in which only a small minority could block an effort unless certain safeguards are included in the decision-making apparatus. Public participation in reaching a consensus on disposal technology and facility siting will probably not work on its own. Without explicit incentives for states and communities to accept waste terminals, there is no reason for them to expedite their establishment. Clearly, institutional and social mechanisms are necessary to guarantee the timely completion of safe disposal facilities. There will be further discussion of these generic issues in the sections of this chapter dealing with decision making.

Fusion Reactors. Nuclear fusion reactors are only a possibility for the long term. Their technical feasibility is yet to be demonstrated, but the possibility of producing essentially unlimited, low-cost power from fusion exists. This has led the U.S. and other nations to invest in extensive research and development. Assuming that the numerous and formidable technical problems can be overcome, commercial units that generate electricity at a competitive cost might appear by the year 2025. Magnetic confinement will probably be the early choice for a commercial system, although inertial confinement may supplement or even replace magnetic confinement should unforeseen constraints or breakthroughs occur (Wertheim, 1980).

While fusion power systems would have the advantage of an essentially limitless fuel supply (provided the fusion system does not require lithium for breeding), the envisioned commercial systems are not without their difficulties. These include sufficient containment of large amounts of tritium and the need to dispose of large reactor components activated by the neutron flux in the reactor. While the magnitude of the waste problem will not equal that of fission, it will probably face similar social problems. Furthermore, magnetic confinement currently requires the use of superconducting magnets cooled with liquid helium.* There is considerable debate as to the size of the helium resource that will be available in the future, and as to whether or not sufficient efforts are being made to hold or recover helium from its major source (natural gas) before it is lost to the atmosphere.

Solar Energy

Solar energy encompasses a wide range of energy sources and technologies. Most of the significant sources of energy on earth are or were derived from the sun's rays (nuclear energy and geothermal energy are obvious exceptions). For purposes of this study, however, solar technologies are those that either use direct solar radiation, such as space heating and photovoltaics, or are the indirect result of solar radiation, such as hydroelectricity, wind power, and fuels from biomass. It is obvious that most forms of solar energy will be available through the long term. Although not quantitatively demonstrated, it is generally perceived that some of these technologies have lower environmental and social impacts than many of their competitors. Solar energy is inherently intermittent, especially in the direct forms. This provides a unique set of problems. Solar energy will need to be supplemented by more conventional forms of energy in any given application (or vice versa), and therefore the relationship between the systems will be of considerable importance.

Direct. Passive solar space heating is a function of building design, and its use, to a significant extent, is practical at today's energy prices. It is likely to be used extensively in new residential and commercial construction. Thus the long-term outlook is quite favorable. A simple calculation that assumes new housing is appropriately oriented and built with somewhat less glazing than the present stock, indicates a passive solar contribution of 1 to 1.5 EJ in 2010.

---

*It is possible that adequate superconducting materials not requiring liquid helium may be developed in the future.

Active solar space and water heating systems, which gather the sun's heat by warming a circulating fluid, are presently too costly to replace most fuels economically. Most of the cost of energy from these systems is in the capital expenditure required for the collection and storage hardware. Should projected cost decreases be achieved (about one-half the present cost), such systems may become competitive (Kelly, et al, 1978). Recent history, unfortunately, has not indicated any drop in commercially available collector prices, which have been increasing with inflation (Zehr et al. 1981). It may be reasonable to assume, however, that perhaps 10% of all water heating in 2010 will be solar, yielding 1.3 to 1.5 EJ/year.

The difficulty of integrating active solar space heating systems with their back-up or supplemental heating sources can be great. In industrial or commercial applications the use of back-up energy sources that require extensive distribution systems (electricity and natural gas) may cause the solar system to become non-competitive. The ultimate solution to such difficulties would lie in solar systems which do not require back-up, but these have been avoided because of the prohibitive capital cost (even at the lower prices projected for the future) of the necessary extra collector area and storage capacity.

The technical viability of solar thermal electric power has been demonstrated on a small scale (Kreith, 1979), but economic viability rests on the development of cost-effective heliostats. Achieving the cost goal of $70 to $100/m² would require the development of new concepts and designs that reduce weight and simplify construction and installation. Estimates do exist, however, that indicate these cost goals might be reached using standard mass production techniques (Solar Energy Research Institute, 1979). Due to the inherent intermittency of the availability of such systems and the costs of storing large amounts of energy, it is most likely that they will be used as fossil fuel savers rather than firm power sources. Simmons, et al (1979) noted that should cost goals be reached, about 0.21 EJ or 15 GW(e) of capacity would be available in 2000 and 0.57 EJ or 40 GW(e) of capacity in 2010.

The technical viability of direct conversion of solar radiation to electricity (photovoltaics) has been demonstrated for many years, but the technology remains far from large-scale commercial realization. Given the information available to date, it is not certain that commercial viability will ever be achieved. Breakthroughs are needed to bring the cost of the cells down by at least a factor of ten, to extend their lifetimes to 10 or 15 years, and to provide a means of inexpensively storing large amounts of electrical energy (which would also provide an advantage for other forms of electricity generation, thus making photovoltaics relatively less attractive). It is our view that it would not be prudent to plan for the availability of competitive photovoltaic systems. Rather, we should strive for such a goal. If major improvements in photovoltaics occur, the projections of Simmons, et al (1979) of a year 2000 capacity of 33.5 GW(e) peak, generating 0.18 EJ/year, and a year 2010 capacity of 41 GW(e) peak, generating 0.22 EJ/year, could be realized.

Base load photovoltaic power could be provided by an orbiting central power station beaming energy via microwaves to a terrestrial receiver. The main advantage would be the availability of continuous sunlight with no losses because of the earth's atmosphere. Caputo (1977) estimates that such systems would have a capital cost of $7900/kW(e) ($75,000/GJ/d) (converted to 1980 dollars), which is six and one-half times greater than the capital cost for a light water reactor. This does not include the projected investment of $85 billion (converted to 1980 dollars) in research and development required to establish the technology. A more recent cost estimate (U.S. Department of Energy, 1980) indicates that the capital costs could be as low as $3000/kW(e) ($28,000/GJ/d) but are more likely to be closer to $15,000/KW(e) ($140,000/GJ/d).

Indirect. Hydroelectricity is a widely used form of indirect solar energy. The long-term outlook for continued use of hydro power is excellent, although its prospects for expansion may be modest. There are already 60 GW(e) of existing capacity in the U.S. with an estimated potential for another 120 GW(e). The constraints of available water resources and the difficulty of siting new dams are likely to lower the achievable capacity considerably. For 1990, this capacity is estimated to be only 82 GW(e) yielding 1.1 EJ/year. In recent years, much of the hydroelectric resource in the U.S. has been reserved for intermediate- and peak-load requirements, and so the energy by generated hydro has been considerably less than capacity. This is a prudent use of hydroelectric power for directly or indirectly displacing petroleum and natural gas. By the year 2010, about 1.8 EJ may be generated by hydropower, not because of greatly increased capacity, but because of shifts in the proportion devoted to base load (Davis, et al, 1979).

A major area of interest for using indirect solar energy is in harnessing the power of the winds. Estimates indicate that the cost of electricity generated from wind may approach that of some conventional systems (Yeoman, 1978). The wind's intermittent quality, however, suggests that it will be of little value for base-load electrical generation (Coste and Lotker, 1977). It may find use in intermediate- and peak-load applications where it can become a fossil fuel saver, especially if coupled with an economical storage system. Lane (1977) noted that hydroelectric pumped storage and compressed air storage are the least costly approaches. He estimated that by the year 2000, 46 to 80 GW(e) of capacity may exist, yielding 0.34 to 0.44 EJ/year, with further development possible, depending on the availability of suitable wind sites. Once again, these solar electric applications need to be viewed as saving fossil fuels that would ordinarily be used to meet nonbase-load demand, and not as reducing needed base-load capacity.

Ocean thermal energy conversion (OTEC) uses the temperature difference between the solar-heated surface waters of the ocean and the colder waters found at greater depths. Such systems would either produce electricity for direct distribution or would be used to produce other fuels or energy-intensive products (ammonia, aluminum, and so on). Since OTEC systems can operate continuously, they are one of the few solar options which offer the possibility of meeting base-load electrical requirements. Estimates for capital costs vary widely, but most of them yield power costs well in excess of those projected for base-load nuclear and coal-fired plants. Furthermore, OTEC systems have little or no operating experience and are still in the experimental stage (Schurr, et al, 1979). Finally, OTEC powerplants would necessarily be located in waters in the most southern regions of the U.S. (Hawaii and Puerto Rico), further limiting their usefulness (Francis, et al, 1980).

Biofuels encompass a wide range of indirect solar energy sources derived from vegetable and other organic matter. The energy equivalent of the present commercially unused biomass has been estimated to be between 10 and 32 EJ/year (Johns, et al, 1980; Lee, 1980). The primary conversion methods that are commercially available are fermentation, thermal conversion, and physical extraction. The fermentation methods produce ethanol from glucose or sucrose (or, eventually, cellulose), and methane from manure or sewage sludge. Thermal conversion methods are combustion, gasification, liquefaction, and pyrolysis which can produce solid, liquid, and gaseous fuels. Physical extraction involves pressing and filtering the oil from vegetable matter such as sunflower seeds or peanuts.

Biomass fuels in the U.S. are primarily used for burning wood and wood-derived wastes in the forest products industry and in the residential sector. A recent estimate places this energy consumption at 2 EJ/year (Norwood, 1980). Fuel ethanol, anaerobic methane, and the combustion of food processing and municipal wastes also make small contributions of energy. Between now and the year 2000, there may be opportunities to increase the quantity of energy derived from biomass.

However, there are barriers to the growth of biomass fuel use. There will be direct competition between the use of resources to produce food or fiber as opposed to the production of fuels. Biomass feedstocks are highly dispersed, and their harvest and transportation to end points for use are costly. There is no commercial infrastructure in place for these activities. Further, the environmental effects of large-scale biomass use are unclear. For example, we do not yet understand what the effects of removing leaves and small branches for biofuel use during lumbering will be on soil fertility.

The direct combustion of biomass usually has a greater end-use efficiency than its conversion to liquid or gaseous fuels. Where biomass combustion can replace oil or gas fuel use directly, there would be a more efficient use of resources. These applications would frequently be in competition with the direct combustion of coal, however, which is a more economical fuel in most regions of the U.S.

Ethanol from grain, a liquid fuel option, is currently receiving much attention. If 10% of the automotive needs in the U.S. were satisfied with ethanol from grain, 40% of the U.S. grain harvest would be required as feedstock (Segal, 1980). If only farmland that is currently idle were used to produce grain for ethanol, only 2% of the U.S. automotive fuel needs would be met. It has also been estimated that meeting more than 3 to 5% (0.6 to 1 EJ/year) of the 1978 demand for transportation fuel would adversely affect U.S. food supplies (Lee, 1980). As world and U.S. food demands grow, the potential for affecting food supplies will, of course, occur at values lower than these. Furthermore, cost estimates for such fuels, including credit for byproduct materials usable as livestock feed, indicate that they will, at best, approximate the present price of unleaded gasoline, $5.52–7.86/GJ (Lee, 1980), but probably will be substantially higher.

Methanol from woody biomass and waste materials could supply a maximum of 15 to 20% (3-4 EJ/year) of the 1978 level of transportation fuel demand by the year 2000 with little immediate impact on U.S. food supplies and environmental quality. The extensions of present technology to these future production levels, however, indicate product costs of $14 to $16/GJ ($0.95 to $1.09/gal).

Refined (filtered) vegetable oils typically have about 90% of the fuel value of no. 2 fuel oil, or 36 MJ/L. The direct use of soybean, sunflower, and peanut oils as fuels in diesel engines has been successfully attempted at a fuel cost of approximately $0.42/L ($1.60/gal) or $11.70/GJ. The credit for the seed cake left after pressing, however, equals $0.165/kg ($150/ton) and amounts to $0.20/L ($0.78/gal) (Mullins, 1980). This yields a fuel price of $0.22/L ($0.82/gal) or $6.10/GJ. Assuming it replaced all diesel fuel use on farms it would be produced at 0.46 EJ/year in 2010.

The outlook for the production of gaseous fuels from biomass may be somewhat brighter than that for liquids, although it is also well known that methane can be reformed to methanol and, in sequence, to gasoline. The use of aquatic biomass (e.g., water hyacinths) is expected to be cost-effective because of the low feedstock costs. However, culture techniques are not yet perfected enough to assure a reliable source of feedstock. Therefore development of this option will be slow. With advanced gasification techniques, it is estmated that up to 8.9 EJ/year may be available by 2010 to 2020 (Lee, 1980). However, it is likely that actual production will be much lower and consist primarily of anaerobic digestion of manure and sewage sludge, possibly using 40 to 50% of this substrate by the year 2000 to obtain 0.16 to 0.19 EJ/year (Lee, 1980).

The production of liquid and gaseous fuels from biomass must compete in national markets against synthetic fuels from coal and oil shale. Coal-based synfuel plants are generally expected to be close to the mine and large, and their products will be cheaper than biomass-derived fuels.

As a result, expansion of biomass fuel use would have to be based on a number of dispersed applications. These would involve a variety of feedstocks and technologies. Expansion of wood combustion in the forest products industry, and possibly in other industries and in residences, is the most obvious. Expanded combustion of municipal solid wastes to generate steam appears feasible and desirable.

Other promising applications would have to be based on technological improvements. The agricultural sector could substantially increase its use of biomass fuels. Space heating and crop drying could use agricultural residues or gas derived from anaerobic digestion of manure and compost.

In discussing the use of biomass, we must recognize the unique situation with regard to waste materials. These require investment for disposal, and thus they may be available at zero delivered cost. Municipal solid waste is produced in the U.S. at a rate of 1.2 EJ/year, of which about 0.6 EJ/year is judged to be available, and sanitary waste is produced at the equivalent of 0.4 EJ/year (Lee, 1980); it is likely that much of this potential will be in use before the year 2000.

Other Resources

Geothermal. Geothermal energy is the heat generated in the earth and available near the surface of the earth's crust. This includes hydrothermal sources, geopressured zones, hot dry rock, and magma. Although the extent of the resource is highly uncertain, a conservative estimate places it at a recoverable 3600 EJ (Loftness, 1978). The vapor-dominated (>150°C) hydrothermal resources are the smallest portion of the resource base, representing only 4 EJ, but they are the only ones currently developed to any significant scale in the U.S. The magma resources (340 EJ) are thought to be renewable by natural resupply from the earth's core and represent a potentially large, renewable source of energy (Loftness, 1978).

There are two major uses for geothermal resources: electricity production and direct heat applications. On a worldwide basis, direct thermal applications for residential, commercial, and industrial uses are more significant than electric power production. Global geothermal electrical power output in 1975 was about 1.1 GW(e), while use in direct applications amounted to the equivalent of 5.5 GW(e) (Schmitt, et al, 1976). In some countries development of low-temperature (40–150°C) geothermal energy has been extensive. In Reykjavik, Iceland, for example, approximately 95% of the 85,000 inhabitants live in geothermally heated houses (Schmitt, et al, 1976; Lund, 1976).

In the U.S., emphasis has been placed on power production using vapor-dominated, hydrothermal convection (>150°C) resources. By 1983 about 1.5 GW(e) of capacity should be on line, all in the Geysers field in California (MacLachlan, 1979). Estimates for the year 2000 indicate that anywhere from 4.4 to 75 GW(e) of capacity could be on line (Loftness, 1978).

The current non-electric usage in the U.S. is about 15 MW (Schmitt, 1976) at four locations (Lund, 1976). The two major applications are for space heating in Boise, Idaho and Klamath Falls, Oregon. In addition, recent research efforts have been exploring the use of low-temperature (50 to 150°C) geothermal heat for industrial applications (*Chemical Engineering*, 1976). Increased use of this resource base of 350 EJ (Loftness, 1978) for direct non-electric uses could make a significant contribution to long-term U.S. energy supplies.

Tidal. Power from the tides can be obtained by building dams and sluice gates across suitable ocean bays and estuaries. The movement of waters in and out of the enclosures can be channelled through hydraulic turbines, and power can be stored by impounding the waters until required. An estimate of the peak capacity in the U.S. is 120 GW(e), although only a few sites are considered favorable. Various cost assumptions indicate that power will be generated at a somewhat higher price than from more conventional base-load generating systems (Schurr, et al, 1979). The tidal power concepts may face similar opposition as that faced by proposed hydroelectric dams because they inhibit the access of marine life and people to the enclosed areas.

Comparative Assessment of Technical Options

Although a wide range of energy options is available for meeting the long-term requirements of the U.S., some would clearly be better choices than others. Table 41 lists the options along with estimates of their magnitude, possible longer-term production levels, and likely constraints or uncertainties.

Conventional oil resources are obviously not a long-term energy option because of the small resource base. With the exception of oil shale, unconventional resources are not much more attractive. Oil shale is a vast resource whose long-term use will be limited only by the ability to establish a shale oil industry within environmental constraints yet to be established. Cost uncertainties may be a hindrance, but should be resolved within the short term.

Both conventional and unconventional sources of natural gas are limited resources which, while greater in magnitude than all the oil resources except shale oil, still are not attractive in the long-term.

Coal, like shale oil, is an enormous U.S. energy resource. Whereas the opportunities for the direct combustion of coal are presently considerable, coal will likely be able to be converted economically to provide liquid and gaseous fuels as well. Its use over the next 70 years will be constrained only by environmental restrictions, which presently allow for considerable expansion of coal use, and by the ultimate cost of the coal conversion products.

Nuclear energy in the form of thermal reactors is a considerable resource which could be magnified enormously by the use of fast breeder reactor systems. Uncertainty in nuclear regulation and uncertain costs for breeder reactor systems, which still require further development, plague the industry.

Like the breeder reactor, nuclear energy in the form of fusion represents an essentially infinite energy source (assuming limited lithium or helium resources do not impose a constraint), if its technical and economic feasibility were established. The extensive R&D program required for fusion makes it unlikely to contribute in a major way before 2025.

Solar energy is a very large resource with equally large unknowns. The key to significant solar energy use in the long term rests on reducing the capital cost per unit of energy delivered. Furthermore, its introduction as an often intermittent source of energy into a society that operates continuously, will likely provide further cost disadvantages. A number of specific applications for solar energy, however, are cost effective and may see expanded use in the future (e.g., passive space heating).

Table 41. Long-term U.S. technical options[a]

Technical option	Magnitude of usable resource[b]	Possible production level	Major constraints or uncertainties
Oil			
Conventional resources	624 1,080 EJ (102 170 × 10⁹ bbl)	10 15 EJ year (4.7 6.8 × 10⁶ bbl d) in 2000	Dependent on level of reserve additions
Unconventional resources			
Enhanced oil recovery	700 EJ (115 × 10⁹ bbl)	1.1 18 EJ year (0.5 8.2 × 10⁶ bbl d) in 2000	Dependent on world oil price for these higher-cost extraction techniques
Heavy crudes	135 EJ (22 × 10⁹ bbl)	0.1 1.1 EJ year (0.4 0.5 × 10⁶ bbl d) after 2000	Limited resource base
Tar sands	180 EJ (30 × 10⁹ bbl)	1.1 EJ year (0.5 × 10⁶ bbl d)	Limited and geographically dispersed resource base
Shale oil	12,000 EJ(2.0 × 10¹² bbl) western, 18,000 EJ (2.9 × 10¹² bbl) eastern	2.2 EJ year (1 × 10⁶ bbl d) in 2000, doubling by 2010	Environmental constraints on mining and uncertain cost of production
Natural gas			
Conventional resources	964 EJ	7.5 12.8 EJ year in 2000	Modest resource base
Unconventional resources (including deep formations)	769 886 EJ	10 15 EJ year in 2000	Cost of recovery somewhat greater than current gas prices
Coal			
Direct combustion	42,800 EJ (1,800 × 10⁹ tons)	70 EJ year (3 × 10⁹ tons year) ultimate	Environmental and health impacts of mining and transportation; Environmental impacts of emissions using current technology
Conversion		18 EJ year (8 × 10⁶ bbl d) of liquids by 2000	Potential environmental impacts

Table 41. (continued)

Technical option	Magnitude of usable resource[b]	Possible production level	Major constraints or uncertainties
Nuclear Energy			
Thermal reactors (no recycle)	1,630 EJ (4.4×10^6 tons) of U_3O_x	Minimum 730 units at 1000 MW(e). Construction capacity = 30 GW(e)/year	Uranium resource. Lead time of 10–14 years per unit. Uncertainty about regulation
Breeder reactors	200,000 EJ	Not resource limited	Unavailable until 2000 because of necessary research and development. Cost may prove prohibitive until later in the twenty-first century
Fusion	Essentially inexhaustible[d]	Unavailable until after 2025	Technical and economic feasibility unproven
Solar energy			
Direct			
Passive	e	1–1.5 EJ in 2010	Introduced with new housing stock
Active	e	1.3–1.5 in 2010	Hot water heating. Other uses require major collector cost reduction. Cannot function economically with natural gas or electricity back-up
Thermal electric	e	0.21 EJ [15 GW(e)] in 2000 and 0.57 EJ [40 GW(e)] in 2010	Requires significant heliostat cost reductions (assumes DOE cost goals met). Will likely provide only intermediate-and peak-load power economically (fossil fuel saving)
Photovoltaics	e	0.22 EJ [41 GW(e)] in 2010	Economic feasibility not established (assumes DOE cost goals met)
Indirect			
Hydroelectricity	180 GW(e) capacity	1.1 EJ/year in 1990, saturating at 1.8 EJ/year in 2010	Availability of adequate sites. Likely restricted to meeting intermediate- and peak-load electricity demand

Table 41. (continued)

Technical option	Magnitude of usable resource[b]	Possible production level	Major constraints or uncertainties
Wind	e	0.34–0.44 EJ [46 80 GW(e)] in 2000	Availability of suitable sites. Probably economic only for intermediate- and peak-load power (fossil fuel saving).
Ocean thermal energy conversion	e	Unknown	Likely to be competitive with coal and nuclear base-load capacity only in a few restricted regions (Hawaii and Puerto Rico) if at all
Biomass	10 32 EJ year		
Direct combustion		3.8 EJ in 2010	Production waste products
Methanol		3 4 EJ in 2000	Wood biomass and waste
Vegetable oil		0.46 EJ in 2010	Applicable primarily for on-farm use
Gas		0.16 0.19 EJ in 2000	Manure and sewage source
Other resources			
Geothermal	3600 EJ	4 75 GW(e) of electrical production in 2000	Resource could have significant (large impact if direct uses expand from current level of 15 MW(e)
Tidal	120 GW(e) peak capacity	Unknown	Higher cost than conventional base-load requirements but may be economical for electrical peak- and intermediate-load requirements

[a]Figures in this table are obtained directly from the appropriate discussions in this chapter.
[b]Based on resource and reserve information developed in Chapter 2 and in previous portion of Chapter 3.
[c]The higher production level includes Alaskan gas.
[d]Assuming fusion does not require lithium.
[e]Not applicable.

Tidal resources in the U.S. are limited and therefore are not likely to play a significant role on a national scale. Geothermal resources applied to space heating have not seen much development, but have the potential for a significant future role.

RELATIONSHIPS OF SELECTED TECHNICAL OPTIONS TO NATIONAL ENERGY ISSUES

In the following section we shall summarize many of the important technical options in relation to the national energy issues they address. This is necessary because it is often easy to lose sight of the objective of an activity when one is caught up in examining its characteristics.

As described in previous sections, the most urgent and immediate U.S. energy problem is national vulnerability due to oil imports, and the solution is a reduction in these imports. Any examination of an energy option must consider its direct or indirect impact on this issue. The longer-term challenge of providing energy at the lowest cost to society is another issue by which options must be compared. Other considerations are the potential magnitude of an energy source's contribution and the time frame of its availability. Table 42 addresses these issues in relation to their time scale.

INCREASING THE EFFECTIVENESS OF ENERGY DECISIONS

The Issue

A fundamental problem is that we are having trouble making and sustaining major energy technology and policy decisions (Chapter II). Consensus has been elusive, accommodation difficult, and the perspectives of those making decisions about energy tend to be short-sighted. This results in a lack of resolution and in a lack of action, and this in turn, affects our ability to solve any and all of our problems.

If we could increase the effectiveness of our structures for making major energy decisions, we would improve our capability to solve short-, mid-, and long-range energy problems. This section will briefly describe the policy alternatives for rendering our decision making more effective. In general, we characterize the alternatives as being focused on either technology or social action (technological or social fixes), and distinguish them as being either best suited for business-as-usual decision-making structures or emergency decision-making structures. In many cases, the options are attractive because (a) actions that help us to solve

Table 42. Effects of selected technical options.

Energy technology option	Short term (1980–1990)	Mid term (1990–2010)	Long term (2010–2050)
Unconventional sources of oil			
Enhanced oil recovery			
Heavy crudes	Increases domestic gas production		Declining production
Tar sands			
Shale oil			
Unconventional sources of natural gas	Increases domestic gas production		Declining production
Coal technologies			
Advanced combustion			
Flue gas desulfurization	Clean combustion of coal		
Fluidized bed combustion	Allows coal to replace oil and gas in industry		
Magnetohydrodynamics	Not available	Efficient electricity generation from coal	
Liquefaction			
Indirect	Replaces oil in all applications		
Direct			
Pyrolysis	Replaces oil and natural gas in all applications		
Gasification			
Substitute natural gas	Replaces natural gas in all applications and replaces oil in nontransportation applications		
Intermediate-Btu gas	Replaces oil and natural gas in industrial applications		
Low-Btu gas	Replaces oil and natural gas in limited (large-scale) industrial applications		
Nuclear technologies			
Light-water reactor	Provides base-load electricity		
Breeder reactor	Not available	Provides base-load electricity and produces plutonium	
High-temperature gas reactor	Technology available	Provides base-load electricity	Provides base-load electricity and process heat
Fusion	Not available		Provides base-load electricity

Table 42. Effects of selected technical options. (continued)

Energy technology option	Short term (1980–1990)	Mid term (1990–2010)	Long term (2010–2050)
Solar technologies			
Direct			
Passive space heating	Partially replaces fossil fuel (an energy-saving effect)		
Active space and/or water heating			
Thermal electricity	Provides peak- or intermediate-load electricity (a fossil fuel-saving effect)		
Photovoltaics	Not available		
Indirect			
Hydroelectricity	Provides peak- or intermediate-load electricity (a fossil fuel saving effect		
Wind electricity			
Ocean thermal energy conversion	Not available	Provides base-load electricity or production of energy-intensive products (confined to the southern United States)	
Biofuels	Replaces oil or gas, provides for waste disposal		Possible declining production because of replacement by food production
Geothermal	Provides direct heat or base-load electricity		
Tidal	Not available	Provides peak- or intermediate-load electricity	

our short-term decision-making problems are likely also to help us solve problems in the more distant future; (b) their possible benefits per federal budget dollar may be very large; and (c) they may be able to make a difference in how quickly a major new technology can be demonstrated and made commercial.

Alternative Approaches for Improving Decision-Making Processes

Domestic energy decision making can be improved in a variety of ways. Although all of the alternatives concern both technology and society, they can be divided between those that focus action on the technologies and those that do not.

Technology Fixes

There are two types of technology-fix approaches: technology choices and technology improvements.

Technology choices. Obviously, consensus is easier to reach the less disagreement a proposed technology provokes. One way to reduce impediments to decision making is to choose combinations of technology, resource, site, and institution that are easier to agree upon, even if engineering cost estimates indicate that they are slightly more expensive. The reasoning here may appear to be circular, but the point is in fact a powerful one: If decisiveness has social value, then achieving our long-range goal of minimizing total social cost for energy may mean paying a price for the hardware above the minimum.

Technology improvements. A classic approach to accommodation is through R&D to mitigate undesirable characteristics of a technology. Environmental control technologies are an example. Another kind of technology improvement is through R&D to enlarge the range of choices, e.g., R&D of new resources and technologies or R&D to increase the scale of an existing technology. Both of these R&D approaches can enlarge the range of acceptable choices, which makes the "technology choice" alternative more feasible. But part of the R&D challenge is to orient the process toward acceptability (a social judgment) rather than risk reduction (a scientific judgment); this requires better information about human attitudes than is generally available.

Social Fixes

There are four general non-technical approaches to making more effective decisions: information, incentives, legitimacy, and institutional changes.

Information. A central reason for irresolution is uncertainty about the characteristics of technology and its impacts, energy demand, and institutional roles and responsibilities. Some of these uncertainties are irreducible, but in other cases accommodation might be facilitated by offering credible information (Kash, et al, 1976). When disagreements are based on poor or incomplete sets of facts, reliable and full information can reduce the disagreements. And even when a conflict is not based on questions of fact, but on differences in the values and priorities of participants in decision making, an agreement on the facts can help to focus the accommodation process on the essential issues. Table 43 lists some policy options that have been suggested as ways to create consensus through better information. The major drawback of an information approach is that is usually takes a considerable amount of time to have an effect. And, of course, better information in some cases may sharpen disagreements rather than reduce them.

Incentives. A promising way to get broad agreement about particular decisions is to offer compensation to individuals or groups for accepting real or perceived adverse impacts, risks, or other costs. These costs can also be offset by subsidies or other incentives (O'Hare, 1977) In its simplest form, compensation works through normal economic markets to bring about accommodation. A developer, for instance, pays more for a parcel of land if he also gets permission to use it for an energy facility site, or the owner of an energy resource is paid higher royalties so that he will agree to the development of his resource. But things are seldom this simple. Besides the fact that many of the markets are highly regulated (and thus limited in their potential for a market solution), there are often disagreements about who gets the compensation and what form it will take. Projections of benefits are uncertain, and they are often not very credible to the concerned parties. As a result, bottlenecks often result when parties who will bear most of the costs of an energy decision believe that they will get a much smaller share of the benefits, while parties who want the benefits try to avoid bearing the costs. Debates over the siting of energy facilities are a common example of this.

Structures of incentive can redistribute costs and benefits more equitably, and they have often been successful in getting widespread agreement on major decisions. Table 44 indicates some of the possible approaches. The most common problem in an incentive approach is getting a commitment of fiscal resources from either the government or the energy developer, and there are nearly always powerful interests that would prefer to see the funds used in other ways.

Legitimacy. A very different approach to making decisions is to give a body a special right to decide. Familiar examples include the use of ar-

Table 43. Examples of information alternatives

Alternative	Methods for implementation
Generate reliable and credible information	Conduct technology assessments during technology development
	Demonstrate new energy technologies at commercial scale before widespread utilization
	Support costs of supplying the public with information involved in decision making
Establish a national energy data center	Standardize data bases
	Collect baseline data
	Collect information about the effects of energy programs, development projects, etc.
	Require that quality information (i.e., "truth in packaging") be provided for energy facilities
Disclose site early	Establish a national energy siting schedule
	Establish a regional site disclosure mechanism
Ensure local participation in decision making	Develop community statements of goals and objectives
	Use state or local referenda to stimulate interest and to judge preferences
	Create an information network that reaches to local level
Disseminate information about the "rules of the game" (procedures, statutes, etc.)	

bitration to settle labor disputes and the role of the federal court system in deciding constitutional questions. In the former case, the parties agree to let an external person or group make an independent judgment and to accept that judgment. In the latter case, the body with final decision-

Table 44. Examples of incentive options: compensation

Compensation opportunities	Methods for implementation
Direct compensation in exchange for accommodation ("buying in")	Offer monetary reward to first party that will agree to a needed action ("Dutch auction")
	Assure the party of abundant and/or cheap energy
	Offer social improvements in lieu of monetary payments
	Make energy production/efficiency a variable in the revenue-sharing formula
Ensure positive impacts (where impacts are focused)	Guarantee a generous minimum level of compensation (e.g., tax revenues)
	Prepay expected benefit payments
	Make more use of severance taxes
	Ensure that the public sector receives benefits (e.g., royalties from the project, public ownership of adjacent property, and a value-added tax in affected areas)
	Offer a local share in facility/institution ownership and operation
Ensure compensation for negative impacts (where impacts are focused)	Establish an impact compensation fund (as has been done in coastal zone management legislation)
	Provide specific assistance for adversely affected groups or areas
	Have government assume long-range liability
Allow for public participation in allocating compensation	
Compensate parties for accepting higher-cost or higher-risk choices (where costs or risks are diffuse)	Subsidize part of the costs (e.g., tax credits)
	Protect parties against such risks as reliability uncertainties and legislative or regulatory changes (e.g., loan guarantees for large facilities)

making authority is defined by law. A more subtle influence of this type is a threat of decision making by an external authority, encouraging parties to reach their own agreement to avoid having to abide by someone else's judgment.

Legitimacy generally takes the form either of pre-emptive decision-making (I will decide) or regulation that narrows the range of acceptable decisions (you can decide, but only from a limited range of options). Table 45 indicates some of the policy alternatives in this area. The main

Table 45. Examples of legitimacy options

Legitimacy options	Methods for implementation
Preemptive decision making	
Apply current constitutional and statutory powers of the government	Apply federal powers to preserve national security
	Use federal powers of eminent domain to develop resources or locate facilities
	Limit energy imports
Assign new preemptive powers by statute	Allow higher jurisdictions to override lower-level decisions or vice versa
	Permit state-level preemptive decision making in emergency situations
	Pass a federal site acquisition law
Create new bodies with a role in resolving disputes	National, regional, or state-arbitration boards
	A "science court"
	An Energy Mobilization Board
	A state energy board with such powers as power plant site selection
Regulation	
Limit the impacts or costs of energy resources or technologies	Environmental standards or pollution taxes
	Price controls or rationing
	"Self-destruct" mechanism for facilities that are found to have unacceptable impacts
Limit the site of facilities	

drawback to pre-emptive decision making is that it seldom reduces conflicts and tends to be ineffective except in a time of crisis. Regulation,
on the other hand, has the disadvantages of administrative costs, market
distortions (creating costly inefficiencies), and requirements for information that is unavailable.

Institutional changes. Finally, it is sometimes possible to facilitate
a consensus—either by making procedural changes or by changing the
roles and responsibilities of the institutions involved. Procedural re-
forms usually streamline decision-making processes that are cumber-
some or that cause delays by waiting too long to consult all the inter-
ested parties. Other institutional changes are aimed at decision-making
structures that, in the eyes of some, have not kept up with the times,
have become impediments to consensus-building, and fail to do their
jobs properly. Clearly, a change in the system for supplying and using
energy could have a much greater long-term effect than a change in any
specific decision about energy.

Table 46 lists some of the policy options that have been suggested.
Many of these choices run into considerable opposition because their
consequences can be so far reaching. An imperfect but familiar decision-
making structure is often preferred to an alternative that might be
better—but that also might be worse.

An attractive possibility is to increase the role of local energy planning and decision making (Wilbanks, 1980). As the demand for participation has grown in the past twenty years, people who were outside the
traditional decision-making frameworks have realized that their only
legitimate channel for entering the process is through government: by
voting for or against candidates, by getting legislators to take actions
that give people a way to use the courts or formal hearings to get involved, etc. And the government unit or jurisdiction to which most
people have ready access is relatively small: a ward, a city, an election
unit, at most a state. One result has been that the balance of power in
our federal system has shifted, at least to some degree, away from func-
tional subdivisions toward units defined more by scale than by function,
where a person's right to participate (in a sense, his or her share of
ownership) is determined by residence rather than by status. Both this
experience and social science theory suggest that consensus (or accommodation) is easier to reach if the social and geographical size of the
decision-making unit is relatively small.

In fact, many communities and regions are moving ahead more
resolutely than the nation as a whole. For example, in 1975 Davis, California, adopted a building code that promotes energy efficiency and the
use of passive solar energy in new houses. They are also promoting trans-

Table 46. Examples of institutional change options

Institutional change	Methods of implementation
Procedural changes	
Streamline energy facility siting[a]	Establish a one-stop decision-making system
	Separate the site review process from the facility review process
	Standardize energy supply technologies
	Assign responsibility for site selection clearly
Reexamine the National Environmental Policy Act[b]	Simplify the requirements for environmental impact statements in order to focus on issues rather than nonessentials (routine boiler plate)
	Emphasize early identification of alternatives
	Increase attention given to generic, regional, and programmatic assessments relative to single-facility EIS
Establish a statute of limitations on settled issues	
Changes in institutional roles	
Increase the role of local planning and decision making	Increase incentives or requirements for local planning (e.g., advance planning for water resources in the United States and community heating in Sweden)
	Involve the local government or community in planning for impact mitigation
Create new institutions to fill gaps	Establish publicly owned firms to ensure competition (e.g., Outer Continental Shelf development, oil product pricing)
	Establish institutions to provide capital for energy investment (e.g., the Energy Security Corporation)
	Establish institutions to develop ''infant'' energy resources and technologies (e.g., Solar Energy Research Institute, Atomic Energy Commission)
Change the institutional structure of the energy supply system	Change the organization and regulation of the electric supply system (e.g., change the scale at which utilities operate or the way public service commissions are constituted)
	Encourage industries and municipalities to meet part of their own energy needs [e.g., provide incentives for cogeneration (non-oil fueled) or decentralized oil storage]

[a]See also Tables 43 and 45. [b]See also Table 43.

portation energy conservation. In 1976, Seattle decided that it was cheaper to spend money conserving electricity than to spend it on two new power plants; in the first year, electricity demand dropped 7.7% from the previous year. Springfield, Vermont, is trying to set up a municipal utility to develop the hydroelectric energy potential of existing low-head dams on the nearby Black River. San Diego and Santa Clara, California, are encouraging the use of solar energy. Trenton, New Jersey, is looking at large-scale cogeneration. St. Paul, Minnesota, is considering district heating systems. Boise, Idaho, has developed local geothermal resources in connection with a downtown redevelopment project. Dade County, Florida, is putting in the biggest facility in the country to recover energy from wastes. Memphis, Tennessee, is proposing a coal gasification facility. Montgomery County, Maryland, has implemented an extensive energy conservation program.

Recognizing these early experiments as a possible key to solving our nation's energy problems and urging other places to follow the examples of these pioneers is a promising policy alternative.

We should provide more incentives at the federal level for community energy planning; remove legal and regulatory barriers to community action; make information and technical help available; and assist local institution-building where a new organization is needed to get things done. Local political processes can contribute as their leaders (and their would-be leaders) compete to show that their programs are in the best interests of the voters.

Comparative Assessment of Decision-Making Approaches

The possibilities outlined above are so diverse, and so subtly related to each other and to alternatives described in other sections of this chapter, that it is hard to assess the specific contribution of any of them individually. Some of them, for instance, are mutually supportive, while others are mutually exclusive. Many of them might play a significant role in solving our national energy problems if they were combined with other actions.

One very important point is that the options for increasing the effectiveness of domestic energy decisions involve basic philosophical choices:

Strong lead vs. consensus formation. We can base decisions on a clear assignment of powers and responsibilities or on policies and procedures that facilitate a broad consensus among a range of participants.

Avoidance vs. compensation. We can handle the problematic consequences or risks either by avoidance or by a mechanism to compensate the affected parties.

Large vs. small-scale. On various issues, we can give priority to national needs and plans or local needs and plans.

In forming a national energy strategy, we can choose to resolve any of these issues in terms of one end of the energy continuum or another, or we can seek a mix of policies that puts us somewhere in between the poles.

But the most profound differences between the alternatives are their effects under emergencies (Table 47). Some options that are suitable when a crisis is not upon us (e.g., information options) are of little value in an emergency. Others that are effective in an emergency (e.g.,

Table 47. Comparison of decision-making approaches

Situation	Approach	Speed with which the approach works
Normal	Legitimacy: regulation	Reasonably quick
	Incentives	Reasonably quick
	Technology choices	Reasonably quick
	Institutional changes: procedures and local roles	Reasonably quick
	Information	Slow
	Technology research and development	Slow
Emergency[a]	Legitimacy: preemptive decision making	Very quick
	Institutional changes: new institutions and structural changes	Reasonably quick

[a]To work, these approaches require exceptional circumstances.

pre-emptive decision making) are unacceptable under less urgent conditions. Consequently, we might need a strategy to distinguish between normal policies and emergency policies. Normal policies work slowly and are more consensual in nature. Emergency policies work quickly; they substitute a consensus about the emergency for a consensus about the energy decision and they usually have some provision for re-evaluation when the emergency ends. In between lie certain policies for accelerated (as contrasted with ''business as usual'') solutions to problems, emphasizing incentives, choices of technology, and institutional changes.

IV. NATIONAL ENERGY ISSUES—ENERGY SERVICE AND SUPPLY

Earlier sections of this report dealt with energy issues (Chapter II) and individual technologies and actions that might resolve those issues (Chapter III). The purpose of this section is to clarify our position on an overall energy strategy through the use of a detailed quantitative discussion of future energy demand and supply.

There is no attempt here to take on the role of energy seer, nor to rely on detailed models of the economy. Instead, we examine fuel use in each consuming sector, and calculate straightforward estimates of energy demand. We will examine energy supply separately in order to focus on the availability of domestic resources.

It is not our intention to explore how the energy market responds to changing prices, levels of demand, and quantities supplied. In fact, energy prices are implicit in this analysis. The assumption is that energy demand can be characterized in terms of its relationship with the future growth of the economy. Given this level of energy demand, we will examine the potential sources of supply. We assume that the markets are in equilibrium, and that prices are set at the market-clearing level.

Addressing the question of an energy strategy requires some assumptions or statements about the future. In recent years it has become fashionable to employ complex quantitative models of the economy as a means of "predicting" the future. Although we *did* do some analyses using existing quantitative models [LEAP (Peele, 1981) and WEM (Parikh, 1979)], and we *did* carefully examine the results obtained by others [U.S. Department of Energy, 1980b; Gibbons, 1979; Haefele, et al, 1981 , it is our judgment that the value of such efforts lies in gaining insights about interactions, not in predicting the future.

Our approach is simpler and minimizes the investigation of interactions. The advantage is that the reasoning behind each projection can be understood and discussed. Large, computer-based models, on the other hand, require lengthy theoretical and empirical justification for results that are often no more reliable than the approach outlined here.

We thus chose not to attempt to predict the future. Rather, we proceeded to identify a desirable future and to examine what energy strategy could make that desirable future possible.

What is a desirable future? This depends on who formulates the answer, and we recognize that this simple question is at the heart of the energy debate. In our study, a desirable future is one that satisfies the national goals stated in the preface; two of them are worth repeating because of their influence in developing the strategy.

- To maintain a relationship with the rest of the world that improves its well-being, contributes to international stability, and leaves the United States free to follow relatively independent policies.
- To provide for future U.S. energy needs so that economic aspirations can be fulfilled and lifestyles remain a matter of choice.

The Broad Path

In this investigation, as in all energy studies, certain goals and principles from the foundation for the conclusions about an energy strategy. The basic tenets underlying this work are that the United States should *1.* maintain its position as a world political and economic leader, *2.* improve the opportunities for low income countries to acquire energy needed for economic development, and *3.* ensure that its people are able to enjoy increasing levels of prosperity through economic growth.

It will be exceedingly difficult, if not impossible, to achieve these goals if the nation's present political and economic vulnerability to imported oil countries. In broad outline, the energy-related actions that would help overcome this vulnerability include the following:

- Implement an accelerated fuel substitution program
    - Electric utilities
    - Space and water heating
    - Industrial steam raising and process heating
- Encourage improvements in end-use efficiency with emphasis on improvements related to reducing oil imports
    - Transportation
    - Space and water heating
    - Industry
- Accelerate production of domestic energy resources on improvements related to reducing oil imports
    - Coal and nuclear power plant construction, with emphasis on nuclear

— Oil and gas exploration, enhanced oil recovery, and development of unconventional gas
— Movement toward a major synfuels and oil shale industry

The above outline *does not* represent a shopping list from which the nation can pick and choose. The *entire* program must be undertaken if we are to accomplish our goals. In developing the strategy we assumed that only commercial or near-commercial technologies would be implemented. This conservative approach yields a strategy that is known to be achievable. We fully expect that during our planning horizon R&D breakthroughs and the major development of other technologies will occur to improve the energy situation greatly (on either the demand or supply side). However, it would be imprudent to develop a strategy that *requires* R&D breakthroughs since the consequences of not achieving the necessary development could be disastrous. Our strategy posits a conservative but steady rate at which U.S. dependence on foreign oil can be reduced. New technologies could help us meet our energy goals much sooner and at considerably reduced costs.

DEMAND FOR ENERGY

In this study, end-use rather than primary energy constitutes the measure of energy needed to accomplish the goals of society. End-use energy is the energy delivered to the ultimate consumer. Primary energy, or the raw energy required to provide end-use energy, is considered later in the chapter in the analysis of energy supply.

A Desirable Rate of Economic Growth

One determinant of the demand for energy is the level of economic activity measured by GNP. In keeping with our overall approach, we did not attempt to *predict* economic growth—we *chose* a desirable rate for per capita GNP, and obtained total GNP by factoring in population.

The judgment of what constitutes a desirable growth rate in per capita GNP was made by looking at history. As shown in Fig. 27, the constant-dollar per capita GNP has grown at an average rate of nearly 2% per year over the past 70 years. The growth trend is remarkably consistent considering that the period examined included four wars, a major world economic depression, and numerous recessions.

The future will include an evolving set of economic conditions. Real energy prices will probably continue to increase. This contrasts

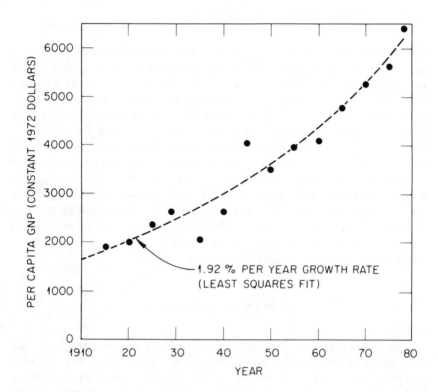

Fig. 27. The historical trend in per capita GNP shows that it has grown at near-ly 2% per year for the past 70 years. Data for the years 1915 through 1975 were derived from information given in *Statistical Abstract of the United States: 1976*, U.S. Department of Commerce, Bureau of the Census, (97th edition), 1976; source for 1979 data was *Information Please Almanac Atlas and Year-book: 1980* (34th edition) Simon and Schuster, New York (1979).

Note: Currently, economic data are typically discounted for inflation using 1972 dollars as the fixed standard. This report adheres to that procedure when discussing data pertaining to the overall economy.

sharply with our history of declining energy costs, which prevailed until the early 1970's. High inflation rates and erratic credit markets, both of which contribute to the dampening of private investment, may con-tinue for at least a decade. Changes in tax policy, environmental regula-tion, and defense spending will all have an impact on the future level of GNP. However, it is widely believed that in the long run the economy will be able to adjust to all of these factors and that the historical trend of economic growth will be sustained well into the future. Thus, we selected a 2% growth rate in real per capita GNP as a reasonable goal. Table 48 illustrates a summary of the population and GNP data used in this study.

Table 48. Population and GNP assumptions

Year	Population[a] ($\times 10^6$)	GNP (1972 dollars)	
		Per capita[b]	Total ($\times 10^9$)
1977	216.8	6,167	1,337
1985	233.0	7,226	1,684
1990	244.0	7,978	1,947
1995	253.0	8,808	2,228
2000	260.0	9,725	2,528
2005	268.0	10,737	2,877
2010	275.0	11,854	3,260
2015	283.0	13,088	3,704
2020	290.0	14,450	4,191
2030	300.0	17,615	5,284
2040	308.0	21,473	6,614
2050	316.0	26,175	8,271

[a]Bureau of the Census Series II figures (replacement-level fertility rate and 400,000 immigrants per year) (U.S. Department of Commerce 1977).

[b]Based on 2% per year growth rate in real per capita GNP.

We recognize that neither GNP nor any other economic indicator can properly measure the so-called quality of life. In addition, we are well aware that much of the debate about energy policy is really a debate about growth. The issue is complex. Concerns about environmental damage and resource depletion, on the one hand, are matched by apprehensions about social rigidity, loss of mobility, and greater difficulty in achieving social equity within our own society. From the beginning, our nation has been viewed, at home and abroad, as a land of opportunity. It still is, and an essential element of this, we believe, is economic growth. While we are unable to justify in detail a particular rate or pattern of growth, the prevailing judgment in our group is that

continuation of the historical growth of average per capita GNP, as
noted above, is a sound basis for planning.

Defining The Demand Band

Overall

The range of end-use energy demand developed for this study is
shown in Fig. 28. This level of end-use demand is sufficient to allow
economic growth, expanded use of personal transportation, and a dispersed pattern of living similar to that which prevails now. For any given
year, all points within the demand band provide the same level of
energy service; the range represents uncertainty about economically
achievable end-use efficiency.

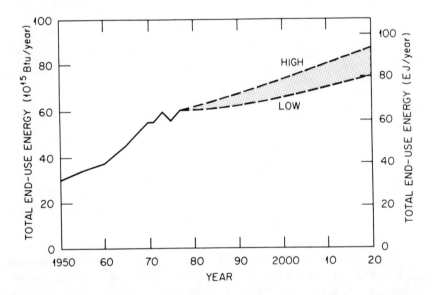

Fig. 28. Total end-use energy demand shows only modest growth because of
strong conservation measures.

The overall demand in Fig. 28 is the sum of three consuming sectors: transportation, buildings, and industrial. The level of energy service and the end-use energy* required to provide the service is described

---

*Electricity end-use demands are reported at 3600 kJ/kWh (3412 Btu/kWh).

for each sector. We shall discuss the extent of conservation implicit in the level of energy demand later.

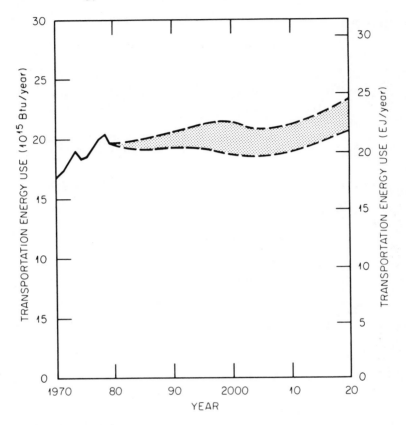

Fig. 29. Transportation end-use energy demand increases only slightly to 2020 because of the increase in efficiency.

Transportation

Transportation energy demand through 2020 is shown in Fig. 29. Distribution of energy use by particular modes of transportation is given in Table 49, and assumptions about the future levels of transportation service are summarized in Table 50.

Generally, end-use energy demand for transportation is projected to increase only slightly over the next 40 years. But the growth in transportation service will be substantial. For example, the number of cars on the road and distance traveled per year will probably increase at the rela-

Table 49. Energy use by mode of transportation
[EJ/year (10^{15} Btu/year)]

	1970		1985		1990		2000		2010		2020	
Low energy use												
Cars	10.580	(10.028)	9.69	(9.18)	9.28	(8.80)	7.84	(7.42)	6.89	(6.52)	7.17	(6.79)
Motorcycles	0.059	(0.056)	0.06	(0.06)	0.06	(0.06)	0.07	(0.07)	0.07	(0.07)	0.08	(0.08)
Buses	0.139	(0.132)	0.15	(0.14)	0.16	(0.15)	0.17	(0.16)	0.18	(0.17)	0.19	(0.18)
Light trucks	1.803	(1.709)	1.73	(1.64)	1.71	(1.61)	1.60	(1.52)	1.54	(1.45)	1.39	(1.32)
Other trucks	3.373	(3.197)	3.54	(3.36)	3.67	(3.48)	4.00	(3.80)	4.45	(4.22)	4.96	(4.70)
Air	1.706	(1.617)	1.91	(1.81)	2.07	(1.96)	2.10	(1.99)	2.35	(2.23)	2.68	(2.54)
Water	1.164	(1.103)	1.43	(1.36)	1.62	(1.54)	2.05	(1.94)	2.56	(2.43)	3.17	(3.00)
Pipeline	0.593	(0.562)	0.59	(0.56)	0.59	(0.56)	0.59	(0.56)	0.59	(0.56)	0.59	(0.56)
Other	1.705	(1.616)	1.13	(1.07)	1.32	(1.12)	1.32	(1.25)	1.42	(1.35)	1.59	(1.51)
Total	21.12	(20.02)	20.23	(19.18)	20.34	(19.28)	19.74	(18.71)	20.05	(19.00)	21.82	(20.68)
High energy use												
Cars	10.580	(10.028)	10.41	(9.87)	10.36	(9.82)	9.73	(9.22)	8.17	(7.73)	8.50	(8.06)
Motorcycles	0.059	(0.056)	0.06	(0.06)	0.06	(0.06)	0.07	(0.07)	0.07	(0.07)	0.08	(0.08)
Buses	0.139	(0.132)	0.15	(0.14)	0.16	(0.15)	0.17	(0.16)	0.18	(0.17)	0.19	(0.18)
Light trucks	1.803	(1.709)	1.83	(1.73)	1.84	(1.74)	1.80	(1.71)	1.71	(1.62)	1.60	(1.52)
Other trucks	3.373	(3.197)	3.64	(3.45)	3.88	(3.68)	4.35	(4.12)	4.93	(4.67)	5.70	(5.40)
Air	1.706	(1.617)	1.91	(1.81)	2.07	(1.96)	2.37	(2.25)	2.74	(2.60)	3.21	(3.04)
Water	1.164	(1.103)	1.43	(1.36)	1.62	(1.54)	2.05	(1.94)	2.56	(2.43)	3.17	(3.00)
Pipeline	0.593	(0.562)	0.59	(0.56)	0.59	(0.56)	0.59	(0.56)	0.59	(0.56)	0.59	(0.56)
Other	1.705	(1.616)	1.13	(1.07)	1.18	(1.12)	1.29	(1.22)	1.42	(1.35)	1.59	(1.51)
Total	21.12	(20.02)	21.15	(20.05)	21.76	(20.63)	22.42	(21.25)	22.37	(21.20)	24.63	(23.35)

Table 50. Basis for future levels of transportation demand[a]

Mode	Basis
Cars	Linear increase in number of cars by 2.8 million per year through 2020. Annual average of 17,700 km (11,000 miles) per car
Motorcycles	Distance traveled per year proportional to population
Buses	Distance traveled per year proportional to population
Light trucks	Distance traveled per year proportional to number of households
Air	Distance traveled per year proportional to GNP
Medium and heavy trucks	t-km (ton-miles) per year proportional to GNP
Water	t-km (ton-miles) per year proportional to GNP
Pipeline	Constant
Rail and other	Proportional to GNP

[a]Levels for 1970 through 1979 are based on actual data. Levels for future years assume increases proportional to growth in the factors indicated.

tively high rates established in the first half of the 1970's. By 2020, the average family household will have two cars and each one-person household, one car, for a total of 220 million cars and a total travel distance of over twice the 1978 value.

Buildings

The energy use through 2020 projected for residential and commercial buildings is shown in Fig. 30 and in Table 51. In general, the buildings sector shows very little growth in energy demand even though the number of units is expected to increase much faster than the population.

We estimated the total number of housing units using the population projections of Table 48 and assuming that the historical decline in occupancy rate (persons per housing unit) continues as shown in Fig. 31 [historical data from U.S. Department of Commerce, (1970)]. We further assumed that changes in the pattern of housing stocks (single-fam-

Table 51. End-use energy demand for residential and commercial buildings

	End-use demand [EJ year (10^{15} Btu year)]			
	1980[a]	1990	2000	2010
Residential	13.2 (12.5)			
Aggressive conservation[b]		10.2 (9.7)	9.8 (9.3)	9.9 (9.4)
Nominal conservation[c]		13.4 (12.7)	14.0 (13.3)	12.7 (12.0)
Commercial[d]	7.1 (6.7)	7.4 (7.0)	8.9 (8.4)	10.8 (10.2)
Total	20.3 (19.2)			
Aggressive conservation		17.6 (16.7)	18.7 (17.7)	20.7 (19.6)
Nominal conservation		20.8 (19.7)	22.9 (21.7)	23.5 (22.2)

[a]Data from U.S. Department of Energy (1980a), Hirst and Jackson (1977), and Corum (1980).
[b]As detailed in this chapter's sections about buildings, aggressive conservation includes standards for new building construction, standards for appliance efficiencies, and retrofits of 42 million pre-1980 single-family and 7 million multiple-family dwellings in the 1980 and 1990 period.
[c]Includes only building thermal integrity standards and retrofit of 22 million residences.
[d]Includes aggressive implementation of improved building construction, optimized lighting levels, better control equipment, and improved appliances.

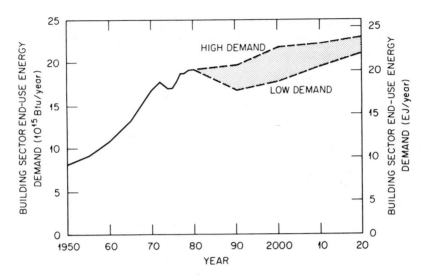

Fig. 30. The building sector end-use energy demand shows only moderate growth because of increases in the energy efficiency of new units and conservation retrofits for existing untis.

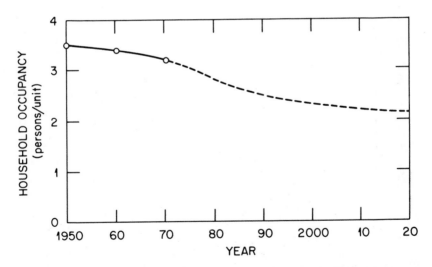

Fig. 31. Household occupancy rates continue their historical decline as the population shifts toward older age groups.

ily vs. multi-family residences), as correlated with the age of the head of the household, will continue the trend established in the 1960 to 1970 period. The projected number and types of housing units are shown in Table 52. [This projection corresponds to the CONAES B projection (Gibbons, 1979)].

Table 52. U.S. housing stock, 1980 to 2010

Type of housing unit	Number of units (× 10⁶)			
	1980	1990	2000	2010
Single family	51.9	61.1	69.4	74.2
Multifamily	24.2	31.7	37.6	43.5
Mobile homes	3.6	5.6	7.4	9.0
Total	79.7	98.4	114.4	126.7
Annual net additions	2.6	2.6	2.7	2.8

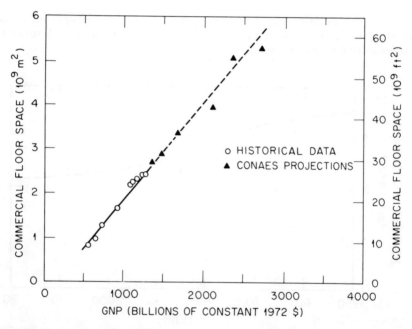

Fig. 32. Commercial floor space has been closely linked to growth in GNP and is generally forecasted in such a fashion. Historical data are from U.S. Department of Commerce, Bureau of the Census, *Historical Statistics of the United States, Colonial Times to 1970,* Part 2, 1970. Projections are from National Academy of Sciences, *Alternative Energy Demand Future to 2010,* Washington, D.C., 1979.

For the commercial buildings subsector, we assumed that total floor space was proportional to GNP. The floor space versus GNP correlation, which was derived from historical data, is shown in Fig. 32 (Hirst and Jackson, 1977; U.S. Department of Commerce, 1970). It should be noted that the correlation is also consistent with the assumptions used in the CONAES demand study (Gibbons, 1979). The resulting commercial buildings floor space is given in Table 53.

Table 53. Commercial building floor space[a]

Year	Floor space 10⁹m²	10⁹ft²
1980	2.9	(31.2)
1990	4.0	(42.6)
2000	5.3	(57.3)
2010	7.2	(77.9)

"Data from Gibbons et al. (1979).

Industry

The end-use demand for energy by the industrial sector is shown in Fig. 33. The projected demand is based on the GNP data of Table 48, the correlation of industrial production with GNP shown in Fig. 34 (derived from U.S. Department of Commerce, 1978), and the very sub-

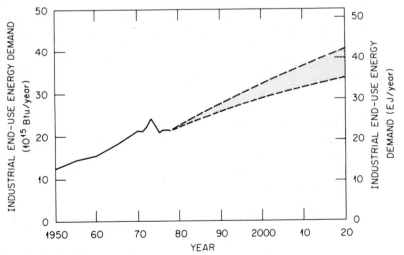

Fig. 33. Even with continued improvements in energy efficiency, industrial energy demand should show substantial growth.

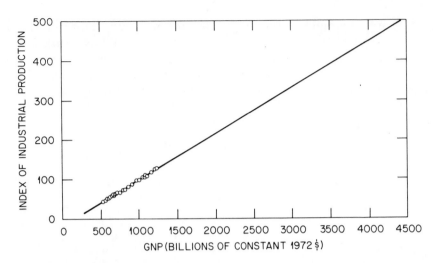

Fig. 34. Historical evidence indicates that industrial production is a strong function of GNP.

stantial energy efficiency improvements described later. Even though industry is expected to become much more energy efficient, substantial growth in energy use is needed because of the growing GNP.

Implicit Level of Conservation

The end-use energy demands discussed above embody considerably more conservation than is being practiced today. Nevertheless, conservation was treated as a means to an end rather than as an end in itself. The conservation measures are both cost-effective and technically achievable. Some general guidelines used in selecting energy efficiency measures are:

- Conservation is to be used as a means of acquiring an energy service at low cost. A reduction in energy service is *not* considered a conservation measure in this study.
- Technical means of reducing energy use are to be based on demonstrated technologies.

This approach is consistent with the use of these estimates as an upper bound on the expected value of future energy demand. If consumers respond to rising energy prices by reducing their thermostat and driving less, one would expect the projected level of energy demand to be lower.

This simplifying assumption is not intended to belittle the potential impact of innovation on energy demand. However, the range of uncertainty expands when one begins to hypothesize conceivable technological improvements. As in the assumption of a non-declining level of energy service, the current-technology assumption contributes to the interpretation of these estimates as upper bounds on the expected value of future demand.

We will discuss the bases for energy efficiency improvements included in the previous demand projections for each of the three consuming sectors.

Transportation

The range of energy intensity for each transportation mode is given in Table 54. Energy intensity is the amount of fuel required for a given amount of service (e.g., gallons per mile for automobiles). We derived these data in part from an ORNL analysis (Samuels 1980) of technically possible improvements in energy efficiency. The bases for the energy intensity values are given below for three of the most important modes of transportation—passenger cars, trucks, and aircraft.

Table 54. Range of energy intensities by mode of transportation

Mode	Relative energy intensity					
	1977	1985	1995	2000	2010	2020
Passenger cars	1	0.75 0.81	0.57 0.65	0.45 0.56	0.34 0.40	0.31 0.37
Motorcycles	1	1	1	1	1	1
Buses	1	1	1	1	1	1
Personal light trucks	1	0.80 0.84	0.64 0.70	0.58 0.65	0.50 0.56	0.43 0.50
Other trucks	1	0.83 0.86	0.68 0.74	0.63 0.68	0.54 0.60	0.47 0.54
Air	1	0.84 0.89	0.71 0.78	0.65–0.74	0.57 0.66	0.50 0.60
Water	1	0.98	0.95	0.93	0.90	0.87
Pipeline	1	1	1	1	1	1
Rail and other	1	1	1	1	1	1

We assumed that by 1995 the entire U.S. fleet of automobiles will satisfy one of two mileage standards established for 1985. (Since the average lifetime for a car is about 10 years, almost all operating cars in 1995 will have been manufactured after 1985.) We considered the corporate average fuel economy (CAFE) standard for 1985 a lower limit on efficiency for the 1995 fleet. The 1985 federal fleet standard, or the fuel economy required of government cars purchased in 1985, was taken to be the upper limit. The resulting fuel economy range for 1995 is given in Table 55. For the years 2000 to 2020, it was assumed that the automobile fleet will be made up of equal numbers of family, personal, and urban vehicles with the characteristics shown in Table 56.

Table 55. Passenger car fleet fuel economy range for 1995

	Fleet fuel economy [km L (mpg)]	
	Low[a]	High[b]
EPA combined driving cycle	11.7 (27.5)	13.4 (31.5)
Estimated actual	9.1 (21.5)	10.4 (24.5)

[a] Based on corporate average fuel economy standard for 1985.
[b] Based on federal fleet standard for 1985 (McNutt et al. 1979).

Table 56. Characteristics and estimated fuel economy of passenger cars—2000 to 2020

Year	Size of cars [kg (lb)]			Efficiency [t-km L[a] (ton-miles gal)]				Fleet[b] estimated actual fuel economy [km L (mpg)]	
				EPA combined driving cycle		Vehicle estimated actual			
	Family	Personal	Urban	Low	High	Low	High	Low	High
2000	1450 (3200)	1135 (2500)	815 (1800)	15.6 (40)	19.5 (50)	12.1 (31)	14.8 (38)	10.6 (24.9)	13.1 (30.8)
2010	1270 (2800)	1000 (2200)	725 (1600)	19.5 (50)	23.4 (60)	14.8 (38)	17.6 (45)	14.8 (34.8)	17.6 (41.3)
2020	1135 (2500)	905 (2000)	680 (1500)	19.5 (50)	23.4 (60)	14.8 (38)	17.6 (45)	16.2 (38.0)	19.2 (45.1)

[a] Metric ton-kilometers per liter.
[b] Fleet assumed to consist of equal numbers of family, personal, and urban cars.

Even though it is assumed that the automobile fleet fuel economy will be very good [16 to 19 km/L (38–45 mpg)] by 2020, neither austerity nor technical breakthroughs are required to achieve this level of efficiency. For example, the 1135-kg (2500-pound) family car assumed for 2020 does not represent a large change from today's technology. Fairly roomy 1135-kg (2500-pound) sedans, including General Motors' X-cars, are being manufactured today. Likewise, the 2020 fuel efficiency of

19.5–23.4 t-km/L* (50–60 ton-miles/gal) seems to be well within reach. Present diesel-powered cars get 19.5 t-km/L (50 ton-miles/gal) and turbocharged diesels get better than 23.4 t-km/L (60 ton-miles/gal).

We categorized trucks into two classifications—light trucks (pickups and vans) and medium/heavy trucks. Light trucks undergo the same kind of changes as automobiles but with less reduction in weight. Medium and heavy trucks undergo improvements in engines, aerodynamics, and frictional losses but with little reduction in weight. We assumed that improvements in efficiency for all classes of trucks would parallel those for automobiles, but light trucks would achieve 60% of automobile improvements and medium and heavy trucks only 50%.

Air transportation efficiency improvements are expected in load factors, engines, and aerodynamics. In this study we assumed that load factors would increase from the present level of 57–58% to 70–75% by 2020. We also assumed that by 2020 fuel efficiency would increase 15–30% through engine improvements and 15% through aerodynamic improvements. The overall improvement in efficiency would be 50–60% by 2020. This should be compared with the 33% improvement in air transportation fuel efficiency that took place between 1971 and 1977 (Shonka, 1979).

Buildings

Consumers have already begun to respond to higher energy costs by purchasing more energy-efficient equipment and through other conservation measures (e.g., installing insulation and storm windows). And it is expected that the energy intensity of providing heating, cooling, and other services within residences will continue to decline. We considered two cases of energy conservation in buildings. The first involved a relatively aggressive conservation policy corresponding to the CONAES B′ case (Gibbons, 1979). This included standards for new building construction as well as retrofits, and standards for new appliance efficiencies (see Tables 57 and 58). The retrofit program is assumed to include, during the 1981 to 1990 period, 42 million single-family and 7 million multi-family pre-1980 dwellings. The second case involved a less aggressive conservation program and included only the building thermal integrity standards and a tax credit program to encourage the retrofit of 22 million single-family homes between 1981 and 1987.

These energy efficiency improvements result in a decreasing energy intensity in the household subsector, as shown in Fig. 35. All energy in-

---

*tonne-kilometers per liter

Table 57. Space heating thermal integrity for new construction and retrofitting in the residential subsector[a]

	1980	1990	2000	2010
New structures				
Single family	1.00	0.65	0.65	0.65
Multifamily	1.00	0.48	0.48	0.48
Mobile home	1.00	0.75	0.68	0.65
Retrofitted structures				
Single family	1.00	0.65		
Multifamily	1.00	0.72		

[a] The thermal integrity of a structure is the delivered heating or cooling energy required to provide space conditioning for a fixed occupant behavior. All values were normalized to 1.0 for 1980.

Table 58. End-use energy intensities of new residential appliances[a]

	1990	2000	2010
Electricity			
Space heating	0.88	0.75	0.66
Water heating	0.85	0.85	0.85
Refrigerators	0.68	0.68	0.68
Freezers	0.77	0.77	0.66
Cooking	0.97	0.93	0.91
Air conditioning	0.75	0.75	0.70
Lighting	1.0	0.90	0.70
Other	0.90	0.90	0.89
Gas			
Space heating	0.81	0.76	0.73
Water heating	0.80	0.79	0.75
Cooking	0.82	0.67	0.62
Other	0.90	0.83	0.80
Oil			
Space heating	0.84	0.78	0.75
Water heating	0.81	0.81	0.79

[a] All energy intensities were normalized to 1.0 for 1980; an intensity of 0.75 indicates a 25% energy savings.

tensities in Fig. 35 have been normalized to 1.0 in 1980; hence an intensity index of 0.75 indicates a 25% saving in energy. In 1980 the energy intensity of the household subsector was estimated to be 166.7 GJ/unit/year (158 million Btu/unit/year).

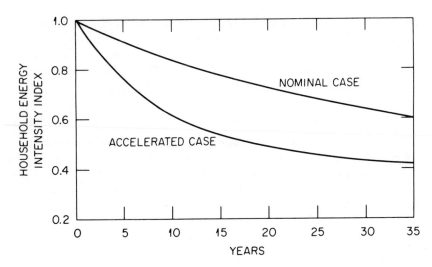

Fig. 35. Continued implementation of conservation options for new and retrofit applications results in household energy intensity showing a steady decline.

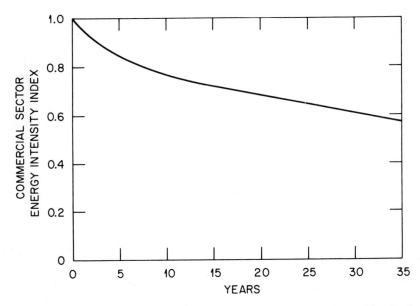

Fig. 36. Conservation efforts also result in declining energy intensities in the commercial subsector.

Energy intensities in the commercial sector also show a decline (Fig. 36). Again, the CONAES B′ case (Gibbons, 1979) was used as the basis for calculating these intensities. Energy conservation efforts in this subsector include improved building construction, optimized lighting levels, better control equipment, and improved appliances. The energy intensity of the commercial subsector in 1980, the base year, was estimated to be 253 MJ/m²/year (223,000 Btu/ft²/year).

Industry

As shown in Fig. 37, industrial end-use energy intensities[*] decreased at an average rate of 1.7% per year from 1950 to 1970. During the mid-70's they declined at an average rate of about 5.5% per year. This increased conservation effort was sparked by the rapid escalation of oil prices and included many housekeeping options.

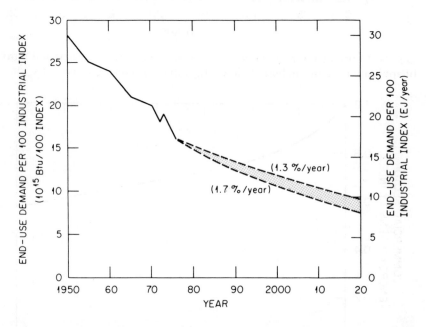

Fig. 37. Higher energy prices are expected to result in the end-use energy demand per unit of output to continue its historic decline in the industrial sector.

---

[*]The numerator of this intensity is the industrial end-use energy demand (historical data from U.S. Department of Energy, 1980a). The denominator is the industrial index of production (Fig. 34) divided by 100. Thus, the intensity used is the end-use demand per 100 units of industrial index of production.

Future industrial energy intensity trends were estimated by examining the factors underlying past trends and determining how important they will be in the future. It is highly unlikely that the recent declines of 5.5% per year can be maintained much longer because many of the conservation actions taken were one-time, housekeeping actions. The decline of industrial energy intensity during the 1050 to 1970 period was primarily due to the following factors:

1. Conversion from coal to oil and gas resulting in higher process efficiencies,
2. The use of larger processing units that made recovery of waste heat economical,
3. New industrial plants situated in southern climates (more than half of the new plants built in the last 30 years),
4. Greater attention to energy consumption by the energy-intensive industries,
5. Technological improvements, and
6. Development and use of new energy-saving devices.

The full potential of factors 1, 2, and 3 has probably been realized, although increasing energy costs could result in factors 4, 5, and 6 contributing significantly to industrial energy conservation in the future. However, these options require capital to buy equipment, and these capital needs compete with the needs for production equipment. There is some evidence that recent industrial trends show much faster growth in the less energy-intensive industries (e.g., computers, electronics), helping to reduce the overall energy intensity of the industrial sector. (Marlay, 1981)

Taking these factors into consideration, we considered two future trends in industrial energy intensity. In the first case, industrial energy intensity was assumed to continue its long-term historic 1.7% per year decline. This case assumes the replacement of existing processes and equipment with those that are more energy efficient and a continuation of the trend toward less energy-intensive industries. The second case assumes that limited capital availability would constrain the introduction of new equipment and processes so that industrial energy intensity would decline at only 1.3% per year. Figure 37 presents the industrial end-use demand intensity associated with these two cases.

A potential increase in the cogeneration of process steam and electricity in industrial applications is not included in these estimates, even though several studies indicate that total energy consumption could be reduced between 3 and 4% through cogeneration (for example, see Resource Planning Associates, 1977). Despite the effort of the National

Energy Act of 1978 to promote the combined production of electricity and steam at industrial sites, cogeneration tends to be a very risky energy-conservation option. Cogeneration reduces energy use while it increases capital requirements, and firms have been hesitant to trade off capital for fuel.

There have been at least four significant deterrents to cogeneration: the fear of regulation as a utility, the inability to sell excess electricity, the high cost of back-up power, and the historically declining price of electricity relative to fuel. If these were removed, the level of cogeneration would probably increase, and the net energy demand in the industrial sector would be lower.

Overall

Total end-use energy per unit of GNP is one index of energy efficiency. Figure 38 shows the historical trend [using data from U.S. Department of Energy (1980a)] in this index, as well as the future values derived from the results for energy demand developed in this study. Also shown in Fig. 38, for comparison purposes, are estimates of the future from other recent energy studies [i.e., the CONAES study (Brooks, et al, 1979); *National Energy Plan II* (U.S. Department of Energy, 1979g); and the ORNL *Rational Energy Use* study (Pine, et al)]. It should be noted that our study embodies a higher level of industrial conservation than almost all other energy demand projections.

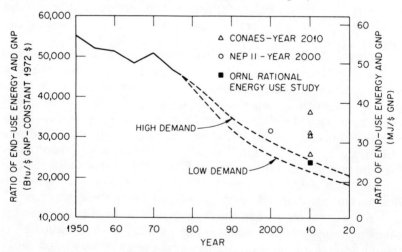

Fig. 38. Our assumptions about achievable improvements in end-use energy efficiency result in a higher level of conservation than do most other studies.

ENERGY SUPPLY ANALYSIS

General Approach

We based the analysis of energy supply on two combinations of end-use demand and domestic production of natural oil and gas. The combinations, low demand-high supply and high demand-low supply, represent limiting cases in the supply analysis. Thus, high supply refers to the higher range estimates of domestic natural gas and oil production. The converse is true for the low supply case. The high and low demand refer to the upper and lower ranges shown on the demand estimate plot in Fig. 38.

Our general approach included examining each consuming sector in detail and determining the end-use demands by function (e.g., domestic space heating). We determined the fuel requirements to meet these demands by starting with the current fuel mixes and following an aggressive fuel switching policy. The objective of this policy was to substitute electricity and gas for oil where possible in the buildings and industrial sectors, and to use coal or nuclear fuels to replace oil and gas in the electric utility sector. We then compared the fuel demands to fuel availability and, where necessary, fuel substitutions were made to bring supply and demand into balance. The allocation of fuel supplies in these projections was generally governed by constraints on fuel availability. As shown in Table 59, the assumed level of domestic production for crude oil and natural gas declines from 1978 levels. Also shown in

Table 59. Natural resource constraint assumptions for supply analysis

	\multicolumn{8}{c}{Projected production [EJ year (10^{15} Btu year)]}							
	\multicolumn{2}{c}{1978}	\multicolumn{2}{c}{1990}	\multicolumn{2}{c}{2000}	\multicolumn{2}{c}{2020}
High-supply case								
Domestic crude oil production[a]	21.8	(20.7)	22.0	(20.9)	21.5	(20.4)	15.8	(15.0)
Natural gas production[b]	20.6	(19.5)	17.0	(16.1)	18.0	(17.1)	14.8	(14.0)
Hydro and geothermal power	1.1	(1.0)	1.3	(1.2)	1.4	(1.3)	1.8	(1.7)
Low-supply case								
Domestic crude oil production[a]	21.8	(20.7)	19.5	(18.5)	15.5	(14.7)	9.5	(9.0)
Natural gas production[b]	20.6	(19.5)	15.5	(14.7)	12.0	(11.4)	6.3	(6.0)
Hydro and geothermal power	1.1	(1.0)	1.3	(1.2)	1.4	(1.3)	1.8	(1.7)

[a]Includes enhanced oil recovery.
[b]Includes unconventional gas sources and Alaskan production.
The 1978 power production was 283×10^{9} kWh (U.S. Department of Energy 1980a) for the electric utility sector. Converting at 3600 kJ kWh (3413 Btu kWh) yields the numbers shown.

Table 59 are the assumed levels of hydroelectric and geothermal power that will be available in 1990, 2000, and 2020.

The primary goal in this study is a reduction in the fraction of oil imported thus we placed a limit on oil imports of 20% of the oil usage in 2000. Although no quantitative limitation was placed on the 1990 level of oil imports, the U.S. must begin to make its intentions clear by then. Thus, a reduction in both the total quantity of oil imported and the fraction of oil demand satisfied by imports was a goal for the 1990 supply picture.

The 20% oil import limitation was the result of a simple analysis of likely oil supply disruptions. The U.S. could absorb a 5 to 10% cut in oil supply without serious economic disruption, as demonstrated by the 1973–1974 oil embargo. At current oil consumption levels, this translates to a shortfall of 2.0 to 4.0 EJ/year (0.9 to 1.8 million bbl/d). imports and represent the least secure U.S. oil supply. Thus, we reasoned that a total Arab-Persian oil cutoff should be allowed to result in only a 5 to 10% oil supply shortfall. To achieve this we need to reduce oil imports until they are only 14 to 28% of total consumption. In our study we used a figure of 20%, near the middle of this range, as a reasonable target.

Because the major uses for natural gas are in industrial production and residential space heating, significant interruptions in gas supply could have even more serious impacts on the U.S. economy than oil supply disruptions. Therefore, to forestall possible problems due to gas imports, we imposed an import limit of 10% of gas usage.

We further assumed that the maximum gas imports available to the U.S. in 1990 would be 2.3 EJ/year (2.2×10^{15} Btu/year). Much of the increase from the present level of 1.4 EJ/year (1.3×10^{15} Btu/year) would come from Mexico, with some from the Middle East via LNG imports.

In addition to the fuel availability constraints presented in Table 59, electric utility expansion between now and 1990 was confined to what is already planned and reported by the electric reliability councils. Under present conditions it would take more than ten years to initiate, plan, license, and construct any new plants. Using data from U.S. Department of Energy (1980a, 1977, 1979a) we calculated the installed capacity and net generation for the base year (1978) and projections for 1990. The results (presented in Table 60) indicate that 3660×10^9 kWh of electrical generation will be available in 1990, and demand for electric power in 1990 was, therefore, constrained to this figure. It was assumed in these calculations that by 1990 oil and gas consumption by utilities will be reduced by 50% through coal retrofits and power wheeling.

Table 60. Summary of 1978 and projected 1990 electric
utility statistics[a]

	Capacity [GW(e)]		Generation (billions of kWh)		Capacity factor (%)	
	1978	1990	1978	1990	1978	1990
Fossil						
Coal	228	470	980	2060	50	50
Oil[b]	145	104	370	180	29	20
Gas[c]	81	46	310	150	43	38
Hydro and geothermal[d]	72	88	280	350	45	45
Nuclear	54	178	280	920	59	59
Total	580	886	2220	3660		

[a]Data from U.S. Department of Energy (1977, 1979a, and 1980a) were used to derive these figures.
[b]Includes internal combustion engines.
[c]Includes gas turbines.
[d]The 1978 capacity factors were 45% for hydro and 49% for geothermal. Because geothermal generation accounted for only 1% of the combined total, the hydro capacity factor was used for this combination.

We assumed that sufficient electrical capacity could be built by the year 2000 to satisfy demand at and beyond that time, and that the new additions would consist of coal and nuclear units. Oil- and gas-fired plants would be used solely for peaking load.

As indicated in Chapter III, vigorous development of hydro and geothermal resources could result in an additional 0.95 EJ/year (0.9 × 10^{15} Btu/year) and at least 3.48 EJ/year (3.3 × 10^{15} Btu/year) of electricity in the years 2000 and 2020, respectively. In addition, other sources of electricity could be on line by 2000. Also, as we indicated in Chapter III, solar thermal, photovoltaics, wind, municipal solid waste and sludge, and biomass sources could, in total, contribute an additional 4.7 to 7.9 EJ/year (4.5 to 7.5 × 10^{15} Btu/year) of electricity by the year 2000. However, the economics of these additional sources of electricity are questionable and therefore they were not included in our supply assumptions.

For synthetic fuel production, we assumed that an aggressive program would be undertaken making available 2.1 EJ/year (1 million bbl/d) of synthetic oil (75% from coal; 25% from shale) and 2.1 EJ/year of synthetic gas being available by 1990. For the year 2000, a

Table 61. Industrial use of energy in 1979[a]

[EJ/year (10^{15} Btu/year)]

End use	Total use	Percentage of total	Source			
			Petroleum	Gas	Coal	Electricity
Feedstock	6.33 (6.0)	25	2.95 (2.8)	0.74 (0.7)	2.64 (2.5)	
Direct heat	5.59 (5.3)	22	1.17 (1.1)	4.00 (3.8)	0.21 (0.2)	0.21 (0.2)
Process steam	2.85 (2.7)	11	1.16 (1.1)	1.27 (1.2)	0.42 (0.4)	
Machine drive	2.11 (2.0)	9	0.95 (0.9)	0.21 (0.2)		0.95 (0.9)
Electricity generation	0.63 (0.6)	2	0.21 (0.2)	0.21 (0.2)	0.21 (0.2)	
Electrolysis	0.42 (0.4)	2				0.42 (0.4)
Other[b]	7.39 (7.0)[b]	29	2.95 (2.8)[b]	2.64 (2.5)	0.32 (0.3)	1.48 (1.4)
Total	25.32 (24.0)	100	9.39 (8.9)	9.07 (8.6)	3.80 (3.6)	3.06 (2.9)

[a]Adjusted fuel-use percentages from Maloney et al. (1978) applied to 1979 industrial fuel use from U.S. Department of Energy (1980g).
[b]Includes asphalt for road surfaces.

total synthetic fuel production capacity (oil and gas combined) of up to 20 EJ/year (9.0 million bble/d) was assumed, with further increases possible.

Sectoral Analysis of Fuel Demand

Industrial Sector

As shown in Table 61 energy demand in the industrial sector can be subdivided into seven major end-use categories, each of which derives its energy from various sources. The demand for each end-use (of purchased fuel only) was estimated using U.S. Department of Energy [1980a,g, and Maloney, et al, 1978].

We estimated the fuel demand using the 1979 fuel-use mix, an aggressive fuel-switching policy, and the end-use energy demands presented in Table 62. In each end-use subdivision we estimated that 25% of the existing (pre-1980) stock would be retired by 1990. Thus, the 1990 stock would include: 75% of pre-1980 stock, replacements for the 25% retired stock, and new stock for expansion. Our assumptions concerning the fuel requirements of new stock and the retrofitting of existing stock were:

1. Direct heat
- New stock fuel profile is 86% gas, 10% coal, and 4% electric.
- 1990 oil use is reduced to 40% of 1979 use through retrofits to gas and retirements.

2. Process Steam
- New stock fuel profile is 80% coal, 15% gas, and 5% oil.
- Oil use level is cut to 40% of 1979 level through retrofits to coal and retirements.

3. Feedstocks
- New capacity fuel profile is 75% gas and 25% oil.
- There is no expansion of steel industry and therefore no increase in the demand for coal used for making coke.
- A proportion of the remaining pre-1980 stock is retrofitted for gas so that oil use is reduced by 25%.

4. Electrical Generation
- New capacity fuel profile is 90% coal and 10% oil.
- Oil and gas use by the remaining pre-1980 stock is reduced by 50% through retrofit to coal.

Table 62. Summary of 1990 industrial end-use fuel demand

[EJ year (10^{15} Btu year)]

	Direct heat	Process steam	Feedstock	Electrical generation	Machine drive	Electrolysis	Other	Total
High-demand case								
Coal	0.42 (0.4)	2.11 (2.0)	2.64 (2.5)	0.63 (0.6)			1.69 (1.6)	7.49 (7.1)
Petroleum	0.53 (0.5)	0.74 (0.7)	2.32 (2.2)	0.11 (0.1)	1.16 (1.1)		1.27 (1.2)	6.12 (5.8)
Gas	5.49 (5.2)	0.63 (0.6)	2.74 (2.6)	0.11 (0.1)	0.31 (0.3)		1.69 (1.6)	10.97 (10.4)
Electricity	0.31 (0.3)				1.16 (1.1)	0.63 (0.6)	2.74 (2.6)	4.85 (4.6)
Total	6.75 (6.4)	3.48 (3.3)	7.70 (7.3)	0.85 (0.8)	2.63 (2.5)	0.63 (0.6)	7.39 (7.0)	29.43 (27.9)
Low-demand case								
Coal	0.42 (0.4)	2.01 (1.9)	2.64 (2.5)	0.63 (0.6)			1.58 (1.5)	7.28 (6.9)
Petroleum	0.53 (0.5)	0.74 (0.7)	2.22 (2.1)	0.11 (0.1)	1.16 (1.1)		1.16 (1.1)	5.91 (5.6)
Gas	5.28 (5.0)	0.63 (0.6)	2.42 (2.3)	0.11 (0.1)	0.21 (.02)		1.58 (1.5)	10.23 (9.7)
Electricity	0.21 (0.2)				1.16 (1.1)	0.53 (0.5)	2.64 (2.5)	4.54 (4.3)
Total	6.44 (6.1)	3.38 (3.2)	7.28 (6.9)	0.85 (0.8)	2.52 (2.4)	0.53 (0.5)	6.96 (6.6)	27.96 (26.5)

Table 63. Industrial purchased energy demand

[EJ/year (10^{15} Btu/year)]

Source	1979[a]	1990 Low-demand case	1990 High-demand case	2000 Low-demand case	2000 High-demand case	2020 Low-demand case	2020 High-demand case
Petroleum	9.4 (8.9)	5.9 (5.6)	6.1 (7.1)	4.3 (4.1)	6.0 (5.7)	5.6 (5.3)	6.6 (6.3)
Gas	9.1 (8.6)	10.2 (9.7)	11.0 (10.4)	13.0 (12.3)	12.1 (11.5)	13.6 (12.9)	16.6 (15.7)
Coal	3.8 (3.6)	7.3 (6.9)	7.5 (7.1)	7.5 (7.1)	9.4 (8.9)	9.7 (9.2)	11.6 (11.0)
Electricity	3.0 (2.9)	4.5 (4.3)	4.8 (4.6)	5.4 (5.1)	5.8 (5.5)	6.8 (6.4)	7.9 (7.5)
Total	25.3 (24.0)	27.9 (26.5)	29.4 (27.9)	30.2 (28.6)	33.3 (31.6)	35.7 (33.8)	42.7 (40.5)

[a] From U.S. Department of Energy (1980g); asphalt for road surfacing is included in the industrial consumption.

5. Machine Drive
- The fuel profile stays about the same because all four industrial subsectors (manufacturing, mining, agriculture and construction) will grow about equally.
6. Other
- Since much of this demand is apparently for steam,* the new stock profile is 25% coal, 20% oil, 25% gas, and 30% electricity.
- The remaining pre-1980 stock oil and gas use is reduced 50% through retrofits to coal and electricity.

The resulting 1990 industrial end uses and their fuel requirements are shown in Table 62. Similar calculations, assuming a continuation of these fuel switching trends, were carried out for the years 2000 and 2020. The results are shown in Table 63, which also summarizes the 1990 figures.

Buildings Sector

We calculated fuel use demands for the buildings sector in the same manner as for the industrial sector. The 1979 fuel use profile [estimated using data in Hirst and Jackson (1977); Blue, et al (1977); and U.S. Department of Energy (1980g)] is given in Table 64. Demand by end-use functions is presented in Table 65. Again the 1979 end-use

Table 64. Summary of 1979 fuel-use profile in buildings sector

End use	Fuel demand [EJ year (10¹⁵ Btu year)]				
	Electricity	Gas	Oil	Coal	Total
Space heating	0.54 (0.51)	5.95 (5.64)	5.75 (5.43)	0.22 (0.21)	12.46 (11.79)
Water heating	0.40 (0.38)	1.02 (0.97)	0.34 (0.32)		1.76 (1.67)
Air conditioning	1.04 (0.99)	0.17 (0.16)			1.21 (1.15)
Lighting	1.06 (1.00)				1.06 (1.00)
Cooking	0.17 (0.16)	0.33 (0.31)			0.50 (0.47)
Refrigeration	0.50 (0.47)				0.50 (0.47)
Food freezing	0.21 (0.20)				0.21 (0.20)
Other	0.49 (0.47)	0.73 (0.69)			1.22 (1.16)
Total	4.41 (4.18)	8.20 (7.77)	6.09 (5.75)	0.22 (0.21)	18.92 (17.91)

*Asphalt for road surfacing is included in the industrial sector tables.

---

* As indicated in Chapter III, much of the "other" category is steam.

Table 65. Summary of buildings sector end-use demands

[EJ year (10^{15} Btu year)]

End use	1990[a]		2000[b]		2020[b]	
	High demand	Low demand	High demand	Low demand	High demand	Low demand
Space heating	11.61 (11.0)	10.96 (10.5)	12.76 (12.1)	10.44 (9.9)	11.50 (10.9)	10.66 (10.1)
Water heating	2.43 (2.3)	1.90 (1.8)	2.64 (2.5)	2.22 (2.1)	2.64 (2.5)	2.43 (2.3)
Air conditioning	2.11 (2.0)	1.37 (1.3)	2.32 (2.2)	1.90 (1.8)	3.17 (3.0)	2.85 (2.7)
Lighting	1.69 (1.6)	1.06 (1.0)	1.90 (1.8)	1.48 (1.4)	2.43 (2.3)	2.22 (2.1)
Cooking	0.63 (0.6)	0.53 (0.5)	0.74 (0.7)	0.63 (0.6)	0.74 (0.7)	0.63 (0.6)
Refrigeration	0.42 (0.4)	0.32 (0.3)	0.42 (0.4)	0.42 (0.4)	0.42 (0.4)	0.42 (0.4)
Food freezing	0.21 (0.2)	0.21 (0.2)	0.21 (0.2)	0.21 (0.2)	0.21 (0.2)	0.21 (0.2)
Other	1.69 (1.6)	1.16 (1.1)	1.90 (1.8)	1.37 (1.3)	2.85 (2.7)	2.74 (2.6)
Total	20.78 (19.7)	17.51 (16.6)	22.89 (21.7)	18.67 (17.7)	23.96 (22.7)	22.16 (21.0)

[a] Using end-use fractions estimated from Blue et al. (1979) and Hirst and Jackson (1977).
[b] Using end-use fractions from Gibbons et al. (1979).

fraction [estimated from U.S. Department of Energy (1980g) and Blue, et al, (1979)] was assumed to apply in 1990.

Between 1980 and 1990 about 12% of the pre-1980 stock of single and multi-family homes will be retired. Also in this period 80% of pre-1980 mobile homes will be replaced. Therefore, in 1990 the housing stock will consist of 71% pre-1980, 13% replacement, and 16% expansion stock.

About 25% of the pre-1980 stock of commercial floor space will be replaced by 1990. Therefore the 1990 stock will include: 55% pre-1980, 18% replacement, and 27% expansion.

The assumptions concerning fuel switching include:

1. Space heat
   • The fuel use profile for new stock is 75% electric, 18% gas, and 7% other (solar and biomass).
   • 50% of the pre-1980 stock that presently uses oil is retrofitted to gas and electricity.
2. Water heating
   • The fuel use profile in 1990 is 40% electric, 45% gas, 5% oil, and 10% other (direct solar and biomass).
3. Cooking
   • The fuel use profile of new stock is 80% electric and 20% gas.
4. Other
   • Fuel use profile in 1990 is 60% electric and 40% gas.

The resulting 1990 fuel use demands for the building sector are given in Table 66, along with the projections, assuming a continuation of fuel switching trends, for the years 2000 and 2020.

Transportation Sector

We assumed that pipeline energy service would remain constant because of the declining use of oil and gas. The remaining demands for oil are calculated on the basis of both the increased use and efficiency of transportation (Table 54). The results, taken from Table 50, are summarized in Table 67.

Electric Utility Sector

Electric utility generation available in 1990 and the electricity demand for 2000 and for 2020 (taken from Tables 63 and 66) are sum-

Table 66. Buildings sector fuel demands

[EJ/year (10^{15} Btu/year)]

Source	1979	1990 Low-demand case	1990 High-demand case	2000 Low-demand case	2000 High-demand case	2020 Low-demand case	2020 High-demand case
Gas	8.2 (7.8)	6.0 (5.7)	6.8 (6.4)	6.3 (6.0)	5.1 (4.8)	4.7 (4.4)	5.2 (4.9)
Oil	6.1 (5.8)	1.7 (1.6)	1.9 (1.8)	0.5 (0.5)	0.6 (0.6)	0	0
Electricity	4.4 (4.2)	9.2 (8.7)	11.3 (10.7)	10.9 (10.3)	16.0 (15.2)	16.1 (15.3)	17.2 (16.3)
Solar and other [a,b]	0.2 (0.2)	0.6 (0.6)	0.8 (0.8)	1.0 (0.9)	1.2 (1.1)	1.4 (1.3)	1.6 (1.5)
Total	18.9 (17.9)	17.5 (16.6)	20.8 (19.7)	18.7 (17.7)	22.9 (21.7)	22.2 (21.0)	24.0 (22.7)

[a] The "solar and other" category for 1979 consists mainly of coal and a negligible amount of solar; for 1990 and beyond, the category consists largely of solar active hot water heating. The role of wood in this sector is being debated. Data from U.S. Department of Energy (1980a) indicate that only 0.01 EJ of wood is used in this sector, primarily by homes that rely solely on wood for heating. An analysis by Norwood (1980) indicates that perhaps 0.5 EJ of wood is purchased for fuel in this sector. Because fireplaces have extremely low efficiencies and because, in fact, net energy losses are not uncommon, it is not clear how much of a net reduction of fuel for the primary heating system is obtained. Thus, the role of wood fuels in the buildings sector was neglected in this analysis.

[b] Space heating demand reductions brought about by passive solar heat gain were accounted for in the demand analysis and are not included here. By 2010, this source should provide about 1.3 EJ/year.

Table 67. Summary of fuel use in the transportation sector
[EJ year (10^{15} Btu year)]

Fuel	1979	1990		2000		2020	
		Low-demand case	High-demand case	Low-demand case	High-demand case	Low-demand case	High-demand case
Petroleum	20.3 (19.2)	19.8 (18.8)	21.2 (20.1)	19.2 (18.2)	22.0 (20.8)	21.3 (20.2)	24.2 (22.9)
Gas	0.5 (0.5)	0.5 (0.5)	0.5 (0.5)	0.5 (0.5)	0.5 (0.5)	0.5 (0.5)	0.5 (0.5)
Total	20.8 (19.7)	20.3 (19.3)	21.7 (20.6)	19.7 (18.7)	22.5 (21.3)	21.8 (20.7)	24.7 (23.4)

marized in Table 68. The various installed capacities, capacity factors, and generation efficiencies are shown in Tables 69 and 70, which also show the declining role of oil- and gas-fired stations as they are phased out of base- and intermediate-load generation and used for peaking only. The corresponding primary fuel usage by the electric utilities is shown in Table 71.

Table 68. Electricity usage and demand

(10^9 kWh)

Fuel	1978 usage[a]	1990 availability	2000 demand		2020 demand	
			Low case	High case	Low case	High case
Coal	980	2060	2350	3500	3400	3800
Oil	370	180	100	100	100	100
Gas	310	150	100	100	100	100
Nuclear	280	920	1650	2000	2300	2400
Other[b]	280	350	400	400	500	500
Total	2220	3660	4600	6100	6400	6900

[a] Data from U.S. Department of Energy (1977, 1979a, and 1980a).
[b] Generation by hydroelectric and geothermal.

Table 69. Electric utility installed capacity by fuel type

[GW(e)]

Fuel	1978[a]	1990	2000		2020	
			Low demand	High demand	Low demand	High demand
Coal	228	470	569	800	769	870
Oil[b]	145	104	125	143	143	209
Gas[c]	81	46	125	143	143	209
Nuclear	54	178	340	385	437	459
Other[d]	72	88	95	95	126	126
Total	580	886	1254	1566	1618	1873

[a] Data from U.S. Department of Energy (1977 and 1979a).
[b] Includes internal combustion engines.
[c] Includes gas turbines.
[d] Hydroelectric, geothermal, etc.

Table 70. Power station capacity factors and generation efficiency by fuel type

	Capacity factor (%)				Efficiency (%)		
	1978[a]	1990	2000	2020	1990	2000	2020
Coal	50	50	50	50	32	32	32
Oil	29	20	8	8	31	25	25
Gas	43	38	8	8	31	25	25
Nuclear	59	59	59	59	32	32	32
Other[b]	45	45	45	45			

[a]Data from U.S. Department of Energy (1977, 1979a, and 1980a).
[b]Generation by hydroelectric and geothermal.

Demand and Supply Consolidation

The next step is to consolidate the projections for domestic supply and demand. For each of the three dates considered (1990, 2000, and 2020), we consider two extreme cases: high demand and low domestic supply availability, and the converse.

Low Demand-High Domestic Supply

In this case 1990 electrical demand totaled 13.7 EJ/year (13.0 × 10^{15} Btu/year) (see Tables 63 and 66). Since the supply projection (Table 68) indicates that only 13.2 EJ/year (12.5 × 10^{15} Btu/year) of electricity will be available in 1990, some adjustment of the actual end-use fuel estimate is necessary. In this case, we simply assumed an additional 0.5 EJ/year of gas heating in buildings and a corresponding reduction in electricity demand. No such adjustment is necessary in 2000 and 2020 because adequate supplies can be made available by then. The corresponding fuel requirements are shown in Table 72.

The primary fuel supply mix to satisfy these demands, within the constraints on both imported and domestic oil and gas availability, is shown in Table 73 (high domestic supply case). These demands include a 92% efficiency for refining crude oil and natural gas for pipelines, an efficiency of 63% for coal liquefaction, and an efficiency of 64% for coal gasification. Table 73 therefore illustrates one of the two extreme cases.

High Demand-Low Domestic Supply

Fuel availability again limited the amount of fuel switching that could take place. In addition to the limitation on availability of electrici-

Table 71. Electric utility primary fuel usage
[EJ year (10^{15} Btu year)]

Fuel	1979[a]	1990	2000		2020	
			Low-demand case	High-demand case	Low-demand case	High-demand case
Coal	11.9 (11.3)	23.2 (22.0)	26.5 (25.1)	39.3 (37.3)	37.9 (35.9)	42.7 (40.5)
Oil	3.8 (3.6)	2.1 (2.0)	1.5 (1.4)	1.5 (1.4)	1.7 (1.6)	2.1 (2.0)
Gas	3.8 (3.6)	1.8 (1.7)	1.5 (1.4)	1.5 (1.4)	1.7 (1.6)	2.1 (2.0)
Nuclear	2.8 (2.7)	10.3 (9.8)	18.6 (17.6)	22.5 (21.3)	25.4 (24.1)	27.0 (25.6)
Total	22.3 (21.2)	37.4 (35.5)	48.1 (45.5)	64.8 (61.4)	66.7 (63.2)	73.9 (70.1)

[a]Data from U.S. Department of Energy (1980g).

Table 72. Fuel type requirements in the low-demand case

[EJ year (10^15 Btu year)]

Sector	Coal	Oil	Gas	Solar	Nuclear	Hydro and geothermal	Electricity[a]
Transportation							
1990		19.8 (18.8)	0.5 (0.5)				
2000		19.2 (18.2)	0.5 (0.5)				
2020		21.3 (20.2)	0.5 (0.5)				
Buildings							
1990		1.7 (1.6)	6.0 (5.7)	0.6 (0.6)			9.2 (8.7)
2000		0.5 (0.5)	6.3 (6.0)	1.0 (0.9)			10.9 (10.3)
2020			4.7 (4.4)	1.4 (1.3)			16.1 (15.3)
Industry							
1990	10.2 (9.7)	7.3 (6.9)	5.9 (5.6)				4.5 (4.3)
2000	7.5 (7.1)	4.3 (4.1)	13.0 (12.3)				5.4 (5.1)
2020	9.7 (9.2)	5.6 (5.3)	13.6 (12.9)				6.8 (6.4)
Electric utility							
1990	23.2 (22.0)	2.1 (2.0)	1.8 (1.7)		10.3 (9.8)	1.3 (1.2)	
2000	26.5 (25.1)	1.5 (1.4)	1.5 (1.4)		18.6 (17.6)	1.4 (1.3)	
2020	37.9 (35.9)	1.7 (1.6)	1.7 (1.6)		25.4 (24.1)	1.8 (1.7)	
Total							
1990	33.4 (31.7)	30.9 (29.3)	14.2 (13.5)	0.6 (0.6)	10.3 (9.8)	1.3 (1.2)	
2000	34.0 (32.2)	25.5 (24.2)	21.3 (20.2)	1.0 (0.9)	18.6 (17.6)	1.4 (1.3)	
2020	47.6 (45.1)	28.6 (27.1)	20.5 (19.4)	1.4 (1.3)	25.4 (24.1)	1.8 (1.7)	

[a]The electricity used in the industrial and buildings sectors is generated with the primary energy shown for the electric utility sector.

Table 73. Primary fuel requirements (low demand–high domestic supply case)
[EJ/year (10^{15} Btu/year)]

Fuel type	1979[a]	1990	2000	2020
Liquid fuel				
Domestic	21.7 (20.5)	22.1 (20.9)	21.5 (20.4)	15.8 (15.0
Imports	17.9 (17.0)	1.6 (7.4)	1.6 (1.5)	0 (0
Oil from shale	0 (0)	0.5 (0.5)	1.1 (1.0)	4.2 (4.0
Oil from coal	0 (0)	2.5 (2.4)	5.1 (4.8)	15.6 (14.8
Total	39.6 (37.5)	32.9 (31.2)	29.3 (27.7)	35.6 (33.8
Gaseous fuel				
Domestic	20.3 (19.3)	17.0 (16.1)	18.1 (17.1)	14.8 (14.0
Imports	1.3 (1.2)	1.6 (1.5)	0.6 (0.6)	0 (0
Gas from coal	0 (0)	3.3 (3.1)	6.6 (6.3)	10.8 (10.2
Total	21.6 (20.5)	21.9 (20.7)	25.3 (24.0)	25.6 (24.3
Direct coal use	15.9 (15.1)	33.4 (31.7)	34.0 (32.2)	47.6 (45.1
Nuclear	2.8 (2.7)	10.3 (9.8)	18.6 (17.6)	25.4 (24.1
Hydro and geothermal[b]	1.1 (1.0)	1.3 (1.2)	1.4 (1.3)	1.8 (1.7
Solar and other[c]	d	0.6 (0.6)	0.9 (0.9)	1.4 (1.3
Total	81.0 (76.8)	100.4 (95.2)	109.4(103.7)	137.4 (130.3

[a]Data from U.S. Department of Energy (1980a); excludes net additions to storage.
[b]Hydroelectric and geothermal are converted at 3412 Btu/kWh.
[c]Only supply-side options are included here. Basically, this solar input is from active solar space and water heating in the buildings sector. Demand reduction options, such as passive solar building design and the use of nonpurchased fuel (e.g., wood and wood waste), in the industrial and buildings sectors were considered in the development of end-use demand levels.
[d]Negligible.

ty, the lack of sufficient gas supplies limits the amount of industrial fuel switching that can be undertaken. The resulting demands for delivered fuel are given in Table 74. The primary fuel supply corresponding to this demand is given in Table 75.

Trends in Primary Energy Demand

As shown in Figs. 39 and 40, the fuel switching policy results in a much different fuel mix from that of 1979. Coal and nuclear fuels, through electricity, assume a much larger role while gas and oil decline.

Other important trends in the supply mix are shown in Table 76. The ratio of primary to end-use demand increases because of a greater dependence on electricity and synthetic fuels.

Table 74. Fuel type requirements in the high-demand case

[EJ year (10^{15} Btu year)]

Sector	Coal	Oil	Gas	Solar	Nuclear	Hydro and geothermal	Electricity[a]
Transportation							
1990		21.2 (20.1)	0.5 (0.5)				
2000		22.0 (20.8)	0.5 (0.5)				
2020		24.2 (22.9)	0.5 (0.5)				
Buildings							
1990		1.9 (1.8)	6.8 (6.4)	0.8 (0.8)			11.3 (10.7)
2000		0.6 (0.6)	5.1 (4.8)	1.2 (1.1)			16.0 (15.2)
2020		0 (0)	5.2 (4.9)	1.6 (1.5)			17.2 (16.3)
Industry							
1990	11.0 (10.4)	7.5 (7.1)	6.1 (5.8)				4.8 (4.6)
2000	9.4 (8.9)	6.0 (5.7)	12.1 (11.5)				5.8 (5.5)
2020	11.6 (11.0)	6.6 (6.3)	16.6 (15.7)				7.9 (7.5)
Electric utility							
1990	23.2 (22.0)	2.1 (2.0)	1.8 (1.7)		10.3 (9.8)	1.3 (1.2)	
2000	39.3 (37.3)	1.5 (1.4)	1.5 (1.4)		22.5 (21.3)	1.4 (1.3)	
2020	42.7 (40.5)	2.1 (2.0)	2.1 (2.0)		27.0 (25.6)	1.8 (1.7)	
Total							
1990	34.2 (32.4)	32.7 (31.0)	15.2 (14.4)	0.8 (0.8)	10.3 (9.8)	1.3 (1.2)	
2000	48.7 (46.2)	30.1 (28.5)	19.2 (18.2)	1.2 (1.1)	22.5 (21.3)	1.4 (1.3)	
2020	54.3 (51.5)	32.9 (31.2)	24.4 (23.1)	1.6 (1.5)	27.0 (25.6)	1.8 (1.7)	

[a] The electricity used in the industrial and buildings sectors is generated with the primary energy shown for the electric utility sector.

Table 75. Primary fuel requirements (high demand–low domestic supply case)

[EJ year (10^{15} Btu year)]

Fuel type	1979[a]	1990	2000	2020
Liquid fuel				
Domestic	21.7 (20.5)	19.9 (18.9)	15.5 (14.7)	9.5 (9.0)
Imports	17.9 (17.0)	16.1 (15.3)	6.6 (6.2)	0 (0)
Oil from shale	0 (0)	0.5 (0.5)	2.6 (2.5)	7.4 (7.0)
Oil from coal	0 (0)	2.5 (2.4)	11.4 (10.8)	26.6 (25.2)
Total	39.6 (37.5)	39.1 (37.1)	36.1 (34.2)	43.5 (41.2)
Gaseous fuel				
Domestic	20.3 (19.3)	15.5 (14.7)	12.1 (11.4)	6.3 (6.0)
Imports	1.3 (1.2)	2.3 (2.2)	2.1 (2.0)	0 (0)
Gas from coal	0 (0)	3.3 (3.1)	9.9 (9.4)	29.0 (27.5)
Total	21.6 (20.5)	21.1 (20.0)	24.1 (22.8)	35.3 (33.5)
Direct coal use	15.9 (15.1)	34.2 (32.4)	48.7 (46.2)	54.3 (51.5)
Nuclear	2.8 (2.7)	10.3 (9.8)	22.5 (21.3)	27.0 (25.6)
Hydro and geothermal[b]	1.1 (1.0)	1.3 (1.2)	1.4 (1.3)	1.8 (1.7)
Solar and others[c]	d	0.8 (0.8)	1.2 (1.1)	1.6 (1.5)
Total	81.0 (76.8)	106.8 (101.3)	134.0 (126.9)	163.5 (155.0)

[a]Data from U.S. Department of Energy (1980a); excludes net additions to storage.
[b]Hydroelectric and geothermal are converted at 3412 Btu kWh.
[c]Only supply-side options are included here. Basically this solar input is from active solar space and water heating in the buildings sector. Demand reduction options, such as passive solar building design and the use of nonpurchased fuel (e.g., wood and wood waste), in the industrial and buildings sectors were considered in the development of end-use demand levels.
[d]Negligible.

End-use energy demand increases slowly, reaching only 79.8 to 91.4 EJ/year (76 to 87 × 10^{15} Btu/year) in 2020, but the increased use of electricity and synthetic fuels results in a much more rapid increase in primary energy use, which could, perhaps, double by 2020. Coal production requirements increase by as much as 9% per year, which is possible, but will require a concerted effort on the part of private industry and government to accomplish.

In the worst case, combining high demand with low domestic supply, oil imports will continue to represent a substantial fraction of U.S. supplies in 1990, with the problem easing quickly thereafter. In the low demand-high supply case, however, oil imports are well below current levels, and almost within acceptable limits even by 1990.

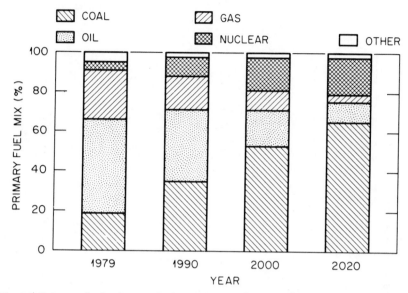

Fig. 39. Primary fuel mix trends through 2020 for the high demand-low supply case indicate a very heavy reliance on domestic coal and nuclear resources will be needed to allow for desirable economic growth and to reduce oil imports to acceptable levels.

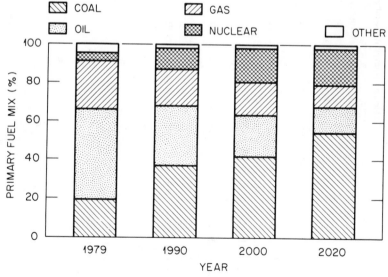

Fig. 40. Primary fuel demand trends through 2020 for the low demand-high supply case show that coal and nuclear sources will become the predominate fuels if oil imports are to be reduced to acceptable levels.

Table 76. Energy demand and supply trends to the year 2020

	Low demand and high supply				High demand and low supply			
	1979	1990	2000	2020	1979	1990	2000	2020
End-use demand. EJ year (10^15 Btu year)	64.0 (60.7)	65.8 (62.4)	68.6 (65.0)	79.8 (75.6)	64.0 (60.7)	72.0 (68.2)	78.7 (74.6)	91.4 (86.6)
Primary demand. EJ year (10^15 Btu year)	81.0 (76.8)	100.4 (95.2)	109.4 (103.7)	137.4 (130.3)	81.0 (76.8)	106.8 (101.3)	134.0 (126.9)	163.5 (155.0)
Synfuel production. EJ year (10^6 bbl d)	0 (0)	4.9 (2.2)	8.5 (3.8)	21.0 (9.4)	0 (0)	4.9 (2.2)	16.1 (7.3)	42.5 (19.3)
Coal mined, 10^9 t year (10^9 tons year)	0.7 (0.8)	1.5 (1.7)	1.7 (1.9)	2.9 (3.2)	0.7 (0.8)	2.2 (2.4)	2.7 (3.0)	4.3 (4.7)
Coal mined for synfuel, %	0	15	26	36	0	15	27	52
Electrical capacity. GW(e)	579	886	1254	1618	579	886	1566	1873
Nuclear capacity. GW(e)	54	178	340	437	54	178	385	459
Oil imported. %	45	24	18	0	45	41	18	0
Gas imported. %	6	7	3	0	6	11	8	0

Trends in Cost of Energy Service

Is it inevitable that the cost of energy service will increase? To get some indication of the answer to that question, we looked at two indices of energy service implied by the supply/demand options considered in this study; the indices are: *1.* the national energy bill as a fraction of GNP and *2.* the fuel component of the cost of driving.

Energy Cost as a Fraction of GNP

Fuel use and prices for 1980 are summarized in Table 77. The fuel prices selected for this analysis include: refiner acquisition costs for oil, natural gas wellhead prices, average retail electricity prices, and mine-mouth coal prices. Preliminary data for 1980 indicate that the GNP (in constant 1972 dollars) is about $1,481 billion (Bernstein, 1981). Thus, energy expenditures represented about 10.8% of the 1980 GNP.

Projected fuel use and prices for 2020 are summarized in Table 78. By 2020 oil and gas prices should be set primarily by the costs to produce them from coal and shale. Therefore the prices shown in Table 78 reflect the cost to manufacture the synthetic fuel (using data from Chapter III and the economic ground rules in the Calculational Standards and Ground Rules) rather than the projected cost of natural oil and gas given in the Ground Rules. As indicated in Table 48, the projected 2020 GNP is $4,191 billion (constant 1972 dollars). Energy expenditures represent between 10.4 and 11.7% of the 2020 GNP.

A useful figure for comparison is the ratio of the 2020 value of energy expenditure as a percent of GNP to that for the base year. For

Table 77. 1980 U.S. energy expenditures

Fuel	Amount used[a] [EJ year (10^{15} Btu year)]	Price[a] [\$ GJ[b] (\$ 10^6 Btu)]	Energy expenditure (10^9 \$ year)
Oil	32.7 (31.0)	2.55 (2.69)	83.4
Gas	17.4 (16.5)	0.74 (0.78)	12.9
Coal	3.6 (3.4)	0.66 (0.70)	2.4
Electricity	7.5 (7.2)[c]	8.06 (8.50)	60.7
Total			159.4

[a]Average prices and total fuel calculated by annualizing data from U.S. Department of Energy (1980g).
[b]1972 dollars.
[c]Converted at 3.6 MJ kWh (3412 Btu kWh).

Table 78. 2020 U.S. energy expenditures

Fuel	Amount used [EJ/year (10^{15} Btu/year)]	Price[a] [$/GJ ($/10^6 Btu)]	Energy expenditure (10^9 $/year)
High-demand case			
Coal	11.7 (11.0)	1.00 (1.06)	11.7
Oil	30.8 (29.2)	4.45 (4.69)	136.9
Gas	22.3 (21.1)	4.79 (5.05)	106.5
Electricity	25.1 (23.8)	9.38 (9.90)	235.6
Total			490.7
Low-demand case			
Coal	9.8 (9.2)	1.00 (1.06)	9.8
Oil	26.9 (25.5)	4.45 (4.69)	119.6
Gas	18.8 (17.8)	4.79 (5.05)	89.9
Electricity	22.9 (21.7)	9.38 (9.90)	214.8
Total			434.1

[a]1972 dollars.

this study the energy cost to GNP index ranges from 0.96 to 1.08. Representative values for other studies are given in Table 79. These data indicate that energy price rises will be kept relatively low if the ONEP strategy is followed. They also indicate that the levels of conservation implicit in the demand band in Fig. 28 are consistent with expected

Table 79. Comparison of energy cost/GNP ratio trends for recent energy studies

Study	Energy cost/GNP index[a]
ONEP[b]	0.96–1.08
CONAES	
A	1.84
B	1.15
B[1]	1.14
C	0.76
REUS[c]	1.06

[a]The base year for ONEP is 1980, and the ending year is 2020. For CONAES (Brooks et al. 1979) and REUS, the base year is 1975 and the ending year is 2010.
[b]This study.
[c]Pine et al. (to be published).

energy price rises, particularly when compared to other studies. These data also indicate that the combination of aggressive energy efficiency improvements and the use of cost-competitive synthetic fuels could result in energy expenditures remaining fairly constant in relation to overall growth in the economy.

Drive More, Pay Less

A relatively common belief is that the age of personal transportation based on the automobile will soon be over. The foundation for this belief is the judgement that fuel prices will increase to the point that people cannot afford to drive. We wondered whether this need be so, and examined the fuel cost per unit driving distance that might be expected using the cost estimates for coal liquefaction given in Chapter III and the automobile fuel consumption figures shown in Table 56.

Gasoline prices to the consumer are summarized in Table 80. The price to the consumer is made up of the producer's price, the producer-to-consumer markup, and taxes. We estimated the producer's price

Table 80. Estimated consumer price for gasoline [a]

Year	Producer's price[b]		Markup[c]		Tax[d]		Consumer price	
	$ L	$ gal	$ L	$ gal	$ L	$ gal	$ L	$ gal
2000	0.29	1.09	0.07	0.27	0.05–0.06	0.18–0.23	0.41–0.42	1.54–1.59
2010	0.29	1.11	0.07	0.28	0.07–0.08	0.26–0.30	0.44–0.45	1.65–1.69
2020	0.30	1.13	0.08	0.29	0.07–0.09	0.28–0.33	0.45–0.46	1.69–1.74

[a]Price expressed in 1980 dollars.
[b]Estimates for Mobil-MTG process.
[c]Assumed 25% markup from producer to consumer.
[d]Road tax on gasoline equivalent to representative 1980 tax per unit of vehicle travel.

using cost data for indirect liquefaction from Chapter III and our Calculational Standards and Ground Rules. The producer-to-consumer markup was assumed to be 25%. We calculated taxes using a typical present day value of 0.45¢/km (0.73¢/mile) a figure based on 83¢/GJ (11¢/gal) tax and 6.4 km/L (15 mpg) average fuel economy.

The fuel component of driving cost is shown in Table 81. What these data suggest is that with continued improvements in automobile efficiency and with the creation of a competitive synthetic fuels industry, the prospects are excellent that by 2010 we could be driving the same distance as today at half the cost of fuel.

Table 81. Fuel cost as a component of driving cost[a]

Year	Fuel economy		Fuel cost		Fuel component of the cost of driving	
	km L	mpg	$ L	$ gal	¢ km	¢ mile
1980[b]	6.4	15	0.33	1.25	5.2	8.3
2000	10.6–13.2	25–31	0.41–0.42	1.43–1.59	3.9–3.2	6.2–5.1
2010	14.9–17.4	35–41	0.44–0.45	1.65–1.69	3.0–2.6	4.7–4.1
2020	16.2–19.1	38–45	0.45–0.46	1.69–1.74	2.8–2.4	4.4–3.9

[a]Price expressed in 1980 dollars.
[b]Representative values actually experienced in 1980.

COMPARISON WITH OTHER STUDIES

Whenever a new energy study appears its conclusions are compared to those of other studies. The ground rules (concerning things such as economic growth, domestic fuel availability, etc.) and purpose of the study (explore U.S. potential energy futures, predict the U.S. energy future, identify the fundamental U.S. energy problem and take steps to solve it, etc.) are seldom included in these comparisons. Since these factors strongly influence the conclusions of any energy study, it is not surprising that there appears to be little agreement among recent assessments as to the necessary U.S. policy.

We performed an analysis to compare our results with those of the CONAES and the *Rational Energy Use* study (REUS) (Pine, et al). The CONAES study was selected because it represents the most thorough analysis of potential U.S. energy futures to date. Its possible future covers a wide spectrum of energy paths ranging from an aggressive conservation path (Scenario I_2) to one that includes substantial synfuel production (Scenario III_3). We also selected the REUS analysis because it is another significant energy study performed at ORNL. The focus of the REUS, however, was substantially different from this study. It sought to determine the maximum possible impact that energy conservation could make by the year 2010 and to examine how oil use could be minimized.

Comparing only the conclusions (see Table 82) reveals several significant differences among the studies. Our results suggest a more ag-

Table 82. Comparison of results from recent energy studies for the year 2010

	This study		REUS[a]		CONAES[b]		
	High demand, low supply	Low demand, high supply	Baseline	I_2	II_2	III_2	III_3
End use, EJ/year (10¹⁵ Btu/year)	83.8 (79.4)	73.4 (69.6)	62.6 (59.3)	54.1 (51.3)	64.1 (60.8)	75.2 (71.3)	103.4 (98.0)
GNP. 1972 dollars × 10⁹	3.260	3.260	2.357	2.357	2.357	2.357	3.317
End-use energy/GNP, kJ/$ (Btu/$)	25.694 (24.355)	22.520 (21.350)	25.540 (25.160)	22.960 (21.765)	27.220 (25.800)	31.915 (30.250)	31.170 (29.545)
Primary energy, EJ/year (10¹⁵ Btu/year)	150.2 (142.4)	125.9 (119.3)	82.6 (78.3)	67.5 (64.0)	87.6 (83.0)	107.8 (102.2)	148.0 (140.3)
Primary energy/GNP. kJ/¢ (Btu/$)	46.080 (43.680)	38.395 (36.395)	35.045 (33.220)	29.720 (28.170)	37.150 (35.215)	45.745 (43.360)	44.625 (42.300)
Primary energy/end-use energy	1.79	1.69	1.32	1.25	1.37	1.43	1.43
Synfuel production.[c] EJ/year (10⁶ bbl/d)	32.1 (13.8)	14.0 (6.0)	0 (0)	0 (0)	8.3 (3.6)	9.6 (4.1)	17.1 (7.4)
Purchased electricity. EJ/year (10¹⁵ Btu/year)	24.3 (23.0)	21.1 (20.0)	9.1 (8.6)	6.0 (5.7)	10.6 (10.0)	12.8 (12.1)	17.0 (16.1)
Purchased electricity/GNP. kJ/$ (Btu/$)	7.445 (7.055)	6.470 (6.135)	3.850 (3.650)	2.555 (2.420)	4.475 (4.240)	5.420 (5.135)	5.120 (4.855)
Solar.[d] EJ/year (10¹⁵ Btu/year)	9.3 (8.8)	9.0 (8.5)	5.3 (5.0)	5.2 (4.9)	3.6 (3.4)	2.6 (2.5)	2.6 (2.5)

[a] Pine et al., to be published.

[b] Roman numerals are the labels given by CONAES to their various scenarios. Brooks et al. (1979).

[c] Includes coal synfuels (gas and oil) and shale.

[d] Includes supply options: active solar space and water heating and hydroelectricity converted at 3.6 MJ kWh (3412 Btu kWh); and demand options: passive solar heating of residences and use of wood and wood waste in the forestry products industry and in residences.

gressive synfuels (REUS and CONAES I$_2$, in fact, indicate that synfuels are not needed) and electrification program. This results in we having a higher primary to end-use energy demand ratio.

There is, however, one indication that suggests similar results are possible. Since our end-use energy demand per dollar of GNP is strikingly close to that calculated in the REUS and CONAES studies, it is reasonable to expect that if all these studies had used the same ground rules the differences in conclusions would be reduced substantially.

To reduce the impact of differing ground rules, we modified the CONAES and REUS results to conform to our ground rules. The CONAES results, which used a 2% per year total GNP growth for all scenarios with a subscript of 2, were modified to include a 2% per capita GNP economic growth and were required to reduce oil imports to zero by 2010. In modifying the CONAES results, the CONAES end-use energy demands per dollar of GNP were multiplied by our 2010 GNP to determine the modified end-use demand. Fuel demands for each sector were then determined using the CONAES sectoral fuel distribution. Oil and gas demands in excess of domestic supply are met via synfuels rather than imports, thus solving the U.S. oil problem.

We modified the REUS results, which also used a 2% per year total GNP growth, to account for differences in the economic growth rate. In addition, our constraints on domestic oil and gas availability were used when determining the supply mix. Synfuels were again used to meet any shortfalls in oil or gas needs.

The results of this analysis, shown in Table 83, indicate that the differences noted in Table 82 (where only the conclusions of the studies were examined) have been reduced substantially. The synfuel and electrification route is now common to all the studies, and the resulting primary to end-use ratio of the modified CONAES and REUS results are within 20% of our results. However, there are still substantial differences in the fuel-supply mix across the modified scenarios. As shown in Table 83, REUS projects the use of approximately half the purchased electricity projected by this study, while CONAES projects between 40 and 80%. This indicates a fundamental disparity in the assumptions of these studies over the future role of innovative energy technologies and the potential for conservation.

This study's assumptions of a constant level of energy service and the application of demonstrated technologies only, form the basis for these differences. The comparison in Table 83 is quite significant because it indicates that the broad energy path espoused here, even with substantial conservation and solar imputs as in REUS and CONAES I$_2$, will require significant synfuel production and increased electricity pro-

Table 83. Comparison of results from recent energy studies for the year 2010, performed using common ground rules

	This study		REUS[a]		CONAES[b]			
	High demand, low supply	Low demand, high supply	High supply	Low supply	I_2	II_2	III_2	III_3
End use, EJ/year (10^{15} Btu/year)	83.8 (79.4)	73.4 (69.6)	86.2 (81.7)	86.2 (81.7)	74.6 (70.7)	87.4 (82.8)	103.7 (98.3)	103.4 (98.0)
GNP, 1972 dollars $\times 10^9$	3.260	3.260	3.260	3.260	3.260	3.260	3.260	3.317
End-use energy/GNP, kJ $ (Btu/$)	25.695 (24.355)	22.524 (21.350)	26.450 (25.070)	26.450(25.070)	22.880 (21.690)	27.125 (25.710)	31.815 (30.155)	31.170 (29.545)
Primary energy, EJ/year (10^{15} Btu/year)	150.2 (142.4)	125.9 (119.3)	121.7 (115.4)	127.7 (121.0)	125.8 (119.2)	129.0 (122.3)	156.9 (148.7)	157.3 (149.1)
Primary energy/GNP, kJ ¢ (Btu/$)	46.082 (43.680)	38.395 (36.395)	37.350 (35.405)	39.145 (37.105)	38.575 (36.564)	39.580 (37.515)	48.125 (45.615)	47.420 (44.950)
Primary energy end-use energy	1.79	1.69	1.41	1.48	1.69	1.46	1.51	1.52
Synfuel production,[c] EJ year (10^6 bbl/d)	32.1 (13.8)	14.0 (6.0)	14.6 (6.2)	30.6 (13.2)	33.7 (14.5)	32.4 (14.0)	34.9 (15.0)	36.8 (15.9)
Purchased electricity, EJ year (10^{15} Btu/year)	24.3 (23.0)	21.1 (20.0)	12.1 (11.5)	12.1 (11.5)	8.2 (7.8)	14.6 (13.8)	17.6 (16.7)	17.0 (16.1)
Purchased electricity/GNP, kJ $ (Btu/$)	7.445 (7.055)	6.470 (6.135)	3.715 (3.520)	3.715 (3.520)	2.520 (2.390)	4.470 (4.235)	5.400 (5.120)	5.120 (4.855)
Solar,[d] EJ year (10^{15} Btu/year)	9.3 (8.8)	9.0 (8.5)	7.4 (7.0)	7.4 (7.0)	7.2 (6.8)	5.0 (4.7)	3.6 (3.4)	2.6 (2.5)

[a] Modified to reflect our gas and oil supply and economic growth rate. Assumptions concerning fuel proportions taken from REUS (Pine et al., to be published).

[b] Modified to reflect our economic growth and to reduce oil imports to zero. Fuel proportions same as in CONAES (Brooks et al. 1979). Roman numerals are the labels given by CONAES to their various scenarios.

[c] Includes coal synfuels (oil and gas) and shale oil.

[d] Includes supply options: active solar space and water heating, hydroelectricity converted at 3.6 MJ kWh (3412 Btu kWh); and demand options: passive solar heating of residences and use of wood and wood waste in the forestry products industry and in residences.

duction if the U.S. is to maintain a healthy economic growth rate and solve the problem of imported oil.

The results of each of these studies are, not surprisingly, sensitive to the assumptions regarding economic growth and domestic oil and gas supply. Adopting similar ground rules results in the three studies (each performed to achieve a different goal) reaching basically the same conclusions regarding the future. As these assumptions change, the future is perceived differently. Therefore, the debate concerning energy policy includes questions about the desirable economic growth rate and the acceptable degree of vulnerability to oil imports, in addition to the means of achieving the desired future.

SOME GENERAL OBSERVATIONS

The foregoing analysis shows that the proposed strategy can reduce oil imports to less than 20% of oil use by the turn of the century, and as we have shown, the prospects are good that the cost for energy service will be no higher, and probably lower, than the price the nation is paying at present.

Although the oil import problem is solvable in a rather straightforward way, this does not imply that the task is trivial. In the next two decades major changes need to be made on both the supply and demand sides of energy. The fuel efficiency of our automobile fleet must approximately double, and the thermal integrity of our homes must be improved by over one-third. Oil and gas use for base- and intermediate-load power generation must be phased out, and this will require that certain utilities be rebuilt essentially from the ground up. Synfuel and oil shale industries will need to be developed with the capability to produce from 4.4 to 17.6 EJ/year (2 to 8 million bble/d) of gas and oil. The electric generating capacity of the country will need to be increased by a factor of 2 to 3, and coal production will need to be increased by up to a factor of 3 even with near-maximum use of nuclear power. These are the kinds of actions needed if oil imports are to be brought under control by the turn of the century.

Beyond the year 2000, both the U.S. and the world will need to supply an increasing fraction of liquid and gaseous fuels from nontraditional sources. The supply of energy will come increasingly from the long-term and the inexhaustible sources. In the context of the long-range global perspective explored in Chapter II, the actions necessary in the short- to mid-term to solve the oil import problem will build a foundation for the future.

The strategy examined in the foregoing analysis is not an exact blueprint for the entire 1980–2020 time frame. Rather, it is an indication of what can be done to solve the oil problem with developed technologies that are cost-competitive today. It is an indication of the actions that must be initiated now to begin solving the energy problem. Technological advances, environmental limitations, voluntary choices of lifestyle, and other factors that cannot be foreseen will occur during this period. These factors could significantly alter the cost-effectiveness of supply and demand options. A few examples include: photovoltaic breakthroughs that allow on-site household electricity generation; acid rain effects that limit direct coal combustion; and environmental control breakthroughs that result in greatly reduced emissions for coal burning, thus solving some environmental concerns. The list of possibilities is almost endless, particularly if vigorous long-range research and development is pursued.

The technology scenarios described in this chapter represent a worst case approach based on current knowledge only. We fully expect that the goals of reduced vulnerability and continued economic growth can be achieved more cheaply, with less environmental impact, and possibly sooner than outlined in this analysis because better technologies and more scientific knowledge will be at hand in the future.

It would be extremely imprudent to delay implementing options that are currently cost-effective because they may not be optimal in the future or because uncertainties exist that may someday constrain them. Because these concerns will always exist, the strategy chosen must be sufficiently flexible to accommodate changing circumstances. The strategy proposed includes all major supply and demand options and can be fine tuned as uncertainties about the future are resolved. Further, there is nothing in the strategy that precludes other options from playing major roles if circumstances change. In summary, future uncertainties should not deter us from beginning to solve today's problems with today's technologies.

V. A BROAD NATIONAL ENERGY STRATEGY

This chapter outlines a broad strategy for shaping the energy future of the United States in a manner consistent with the national goals stated at the beginning of this book. This strategy was developed using the information and perspectives summarized in Chapters II (the problem) and III (the alternatives) and analyzed in depth in Chapter IV. The proposed strategy is distinctive in several respects.

- It is focused on the urgent need to reduce oil imports.
- It avoids doctrinaire, single-path solutions and recognizes, instead, the need for diversity and flexibility in order to respond to unexpected events and to new information.
- It emphasizes what we should do *now* to solve problems for which there are available solutions, without precluding better solutions when they become available (as they most certainly will).

STRATEGY GOALS

Among the many recent energy studies, some have reached substantially different conclusions from this study. As detailed in Chapter IV, these differences in results are generally traceable to differences in underlying values and goals. Thus, in this investigation, as in most other energy studies, certain specific goals and principles form the foundation for the conclusions about an appropriate energy strategy. The primary goals of the strategy outlined here are:

- To reduce oil imports to 20% of total U.S. oil use by 2000, and eventually eliminate them.
- To ensure that the U.S. energy system can continue to support a per capita GNP annual growth rate of 2%.
- To make possible the retention of existing lifestyles, including continued use of personal transportation and dispersed patterns of living.

- To achieve the preceding goals while maintaining overall environmental quality.

REDUCING NATIONAL VULNERABILITY

Our efforts to reduce imports should be directed through efforts in all areas a variety of channels. These inlcude: *1.* improvements in energy efficiency; *2.* fuel substitution; *3.* energy production from domestic resources, such as new electric power plants that use domestic resources other than oil and gas; *4.* enhanced oil recovery, unconventional gas and oil production, and increases in domestic oil and gas exploration; and *5.* development of a major synfuels industry by the year 2000. Even with these efforts we will remain vulnerable for several years, and it is imperative that we also prepare for emergencies through contingency planning and petroleum storage.

The United States will be able to respond to unexpected challenges by improving its technology base and strengthening decision-making capabilities. Any unpleasant surprises such as resource depletion, technology failure, or international unrest, will be handled better if a strong R&D establishment is in place to create new technology options and if government and industry are able to act quickly and decisively.

This has been a broad outline of the path we must follow to reduce oil imports. A more detailed review of some essential elements of the strategy now follows.

Fuel Substitution

Fuel substitution—the use of abundant domestic energy resources in place of oil—represents one of the best near-term approaches to reducing oil imports. The best opportunities for fuel substitution lie in the electric utility, industrial, and residential and commercial sectors. Within these sectors, there are four types of consuming devices which are prime candidates for oil substitutes. These devices, which together consume about 14.3 EJ/year (6.4 million bbl/d) of oil, are shown below along with a listing of possible oil substitutes.

Use	Possible Oil Substitutes
Space and Hot Water Heaters	Natural Gas Substitute Natural Gas (SNG) Electricity

Electric Utility Boilers	Coal Nuclear
Industrial Process Heaters	Natural Gas Intermediate-Btu Gas (Coal) Coal Electricity (Nuclear and Coal)
Industrial Boilers	Coal Natural Gas SNG Intermediate-Btu Gas (Coal)

A vital consideration in a near-term substitution strategy is the fact that natural gas and oil are highly interchangeable in the above end uses. This has two implications:

- Secondary substitution can be an effective way to displace oil. For example, coal can be substituted for gas in the utility sector and the displaced gas can, in turn, be substituted for oil in industrial process heaters or in buildings; we would, in effect, be substituting coal for oil.
- Conservation of natural gas and other oil substitute fuels can also be an effective way to reduce oil imports. For example, we can reduce the amount of gas consumed for heating buildings and use the conserved gas in areas now using oil for heating.

The actions required by the federal government to accelerate fuel substitutions in the near term include new legislative, deregulatory, and financial-assistance initiatives leading toward:

- A major shift away from oil and gas to coal and nuclear electricity generation.
- Conversion of medium-to-large industrial steam generation and some process heating from oil and gas to coal.
- Conservation of substitute fuels with a limited resource base, especially natural gas used in buildings.
- The use of natural gas, released as a consequence of the preceding steps, to displace oil used in buildings, industrial process heaters, and small industrial boilers.

The electric utility industry will need to be a key target in a fuel substitution program.

Total gas and oil used for boiler fuel amount to about 6.6 EJ/year (3 million bble/d), divided almost equally between the two fuels. As noted above, the gas displaced could be used to displace oil presently used in space and water heaters, industrial process heaters, and small industrial boilers. The potential for reduction in oil imports in the utility industry is 6.6 EJ/year (3 million bbl/d), or about 40% of our imports. The technical steps* required to implement fuel substitution in utilities follow,

- Immediately
    - Operate existing coal and nuclear plants at a capacity more nearly corresponding to their availability.
    - Use existing interties, to the fullest extent possible, to move excess power from coal/nuclear utilities to oil/gas utilities.
    - Use the gas released by these measures to displace oil used in industrial process heaters and boilers that have dual-fuel capability.
- Next Five Years
    - Convert existing oil- or gas-fired boilers that were originally designed to burn coal back to coal use (with scrubbers). Convert boilers not designed to burn coal to intermediate-Btu gas produced from coal.
    - Give high priority to completing the nuclear and coal plants currently under construction.
    - Strengthen interties to allow a greater transfer of power to oil- and gas-fueled utilities.
    - Expand natural gas transmission, storage, and distribution systems in order to provide gas service to residential and commercial markets now using oil.
- Next 10 to 15 Years
    - Start and complete construction of new coal and nuclear plants *within the service areas* of utilities now using oil and gas.
    - New capacity should be sufficient [about 150,000 MW(e)] to replace all unconverted oil and gas plants that are not required for peaking operations, and to accommodate any growth.

---

*Policy implications of these steps are discussed in a separate section of this chapter.

The industrial sector uses about 7.57 EJ/year (3.4 million bbl/d) of oil* and 9.0 EJ/year (4.1 million bble/d) of natural gas. Although there are opportunities in the long term for fuel substitutions in almost all industrial end uses, steam raising has the best potential for oil-import reductions within the next five years. The most important substitute boiler fuel is coal. Although some industrial boilers currently burning oil and gas could be converted to coal or coal/oil mixtures, new coal-fired boilers will have to be constructed to bring about a significant reduction in oil use. As with fuel substitutions for utilities, the natural gas replaced by coal in larger boilers can be used to displace oil in small industrial boilers, buildings, and some types of process heaters.

Oil use for space and hot water heating in the residential/commercial sector averages 6.1 EJ/year (2.7 million bbl/d). The major substitutes for this oil are natural gas and electricity (with heat pumps). Both can make a contribution within the next several years, but natural gas is the most important near-term oil substitute. The natural gas would become available by substituting for it in utilities and industry and by conserving it in buildings.

The reduction in imports that could be achieved by 1985 through fuel substitutions is 4.0 EJ/year (1.8 million bbl/d), or approximately one-fourth of our imports (Table 84). The reduction could reach 8.9

Table 84. Preliminary estimate of the potential for reducing oil imports through fuel substitutions in the next five years

	Natural gas available from fuel substitutions and conservation (10^6 bble d)	Potential 1985 import reduction [EJ year (10^6 bbl d)]		
		Oil displaced through use of released natural gas	Oil displaced through direct substitution	Total displaced
Electric utilities[a]	0.9 (0.4)	0 (0)	1.3 (0.6)	1.3 (0.6)
Industry[b]	0.4 (0.2)	1.1 (0.5)	0.4 (0.2)	1.5 (0.7)
Residential commercial[c]	0.9 (0.4)	1.1 (0.5)	0 (0)	1.1 (0.5)
Total	2.2 (1.0)	2.2 (1.0)	1.7 (0.8)	4.0 (1.8)

[a] Oil and gas displaced through interutility transfers.
[b] Oil and gas displaced through use of coal for industrial steam raising.
[c] Gas displaced through conservation (assumed 10% reduction in gas by current residential and commercial gas customers).

---

* Excluding asphalt for road surfacing.

EJ/year (4 million bbl/d) by 1990. The 4.9 EJ/year (2.2 million bbl/d) that comes after would come primarily from the industrial and utility sectors. Additional industrial boiler conversions and some uses of coal-derived fuels for process heating would yield about half of the reduction beyond 1985 (i.e., ∿2.5 EJ/year or 1.1 million bbl/d); full exploitation of interutility transfers plus completion of new nuclear and coal power plants within the service areas of oil- and gas-fueled utilities could yield another 2.4 EJ/year (1.1 million bbl/d).

Efficiency Improvements

As shown earlier in the analysis of energy demand, conservation is an essential element of the strategy. The largest and most direct energy efficiency improvements will come in the transportation sector. As noted earlier the conservation of fuels that can substitute for oil can also be important, but only if coupled with a fuel substitution program.

Conservation can lower the cost of energy service and reduce environmental impacts of production and consumption. But unfocused conservation, that not directed toward a strategic issue, can be and will continue to be, a negative factor in the quest to reduce oil imports. For example, cogeneration based on oil and gas, although energy efficient, results in the substitution of these premium fuels for coal and uranium—a move contrary to the desired national policy. Emphasis on conserving oil in applications where it is no longer an appropriate fuel diverts attention away from the real issue, which is the need to replace the oil with a domestic energy resource. Conservation of electricity with the sole purpose of postponing construction of new coal and nuclear capacity, which, in turn, can displace oil or gas, is in most cases a negative action. Thus, the nation's conservation initiatives need to become more focused.

Although improved efficiency will likely find its own market (if energy is priced at its true market value), we propose several governmental actions as part of the overall strategy. These actions are focused on the sector where fuel substitution is most difficult: the transportation sector.

- Financial aid to accelerate the introduction of more efficient highway vehicles
  - Providing incentives for buyers of energy efficient vehicles would expedite the replacement of inefficient vehicles.
- Cooperation between government and the transportation industry
  - Industry needs stability in emission regulations and in other public policies affecting automobile design.

—Support should continue for the development of promising engine and transmission concepts.
—Cooperation is also needed to develop more reliable and credible efficiency ratings for vehicles.

Production of Oil and Oil Substitutes

Even with aggressive fuel switching and purposeful conservation, it will be necessary to develop a major synthetic fuels industry before the year 2000. Oil from shale as well as oil and gas from coal will be required.

It appears that any serious near- to mid-term effort to solve our oil problem through coal liquefaction will use indirect liquefaction technologies because:

• Indirect liquefaction has been demonstrated as effective and possible.
• The natural products from indirect processes tend to fit the market needs better than the products from direct processes.
• There appear to be fewer adverse health effects than with direct processes.

The production of intermediate-Btu gas from coal as a substitute for oil and natural gas in industry and in utilities can be just as effective as coal liquefaction in reducing oil imports, and somewhat less expensive. The supply analysis presented in Chapter IV indicated that by the end of the century approximately half of the synfuels production should be intermediate-Btu gas.

The analysis in Chapter IV also indicated that we could need a synfuels production capability of 17.6 EJ/year (8 million bble/d) by the year 2000 in order to cut oil imports to 20% or less. On the other hand, the need may be considerably less—less than 4.4 EJ/year (2 million bble/d)—but it is unlikely that the need will be zero. There is a good chance that it will be substantial, and any excess liquid fuels can be exported to help meet world energy needs. Without deciding how much capacity we will need in the year 2000, we believe that there should be immediate action to establish a synfuels industry. This would put us in a position where we would be better informed about characteristics, costs, and consequences as further decisions are made about the eventual size of the industry.

As guidelines, we propose several specific emphases or targets (see Chapter III for supporting information and analysis):

- Use demonstrated technology
  - Build pioneer plants using demonstrated technology: indirect coal liquefaction and surface oil shale retorting. Aim for a product mix biased toward light- to medium-weight hydrocarbons.
  - Give intermediate Btu gas a priority equal to that for synthetic liquids, because it is a stepping-stone for indirect liquefaction, and it can displace oil and gas used by utilities and industry.
- Getting a start
  - Make a commitment by the end of 1982 to start construction on at least six synfuels plants with a capacity of 0.11 to 0.13 EJ/year (50,000 to 60,000 bble/d).
  - Use tax credits, loan guarantees, and assured government buys to encourage private industry to construct and operate these facilities.
  - Initiate plans for government owned facilities to be built and operated if private industry does not respond to incentives for synfuels development.

Emergency Preparedness

Even with our best efforts, the United States will remain vulnerable to oil cutoffs, and threats of oil cutoffs, for many years. We should prepare for such eventualities through planning and through petroleum storage. We should get ourselves in a position to handle—without serious economic, environmental, or social impacts—a 6.7 EJ reduction in oil imports for a one-year period (3 million bbl/d). This is about half of our total current imports, and it represents approximately the level of our dependence on Middle Eastern oil.

Policy Implications

The energy problems of the 1970s brought forth many legislative and regulatory initiatives. Further initiatives will be needed to solve the import problem in a timely manner. To suggest specifics is beyond the scope of this study. Nevertheless, it is useful to examine briefly what has been done and to make a few observations about future directions.

What Has Been Done.

Recent federal policy and legislation have addressed many aspects of energy. These initiatives span a wide range, from price decontrol to policies that promote conservation and energy production.

Price controls on oil and gas have been blamed for the inefficient use of these premium fuels while at the same time discouraging their production. A phaseout of price controls has begun, with oil decontrol occurring in early 1981 and partial decontrol of natural gas expected by 1985.

The most visible federal legislation has been in the field of conservation and solar energy. Some of these programs are directed toward providing the consumer with reliable information on which to base conservation investments (Residential Conservation Service); some are aimed at giving additional incentives for conservation (Residential and Business Tax Credits for Conservation and Solar); some mandate that manufactured items will meet minimum efficiency standards (automobile CAFE standards); and some provide financial assistance (Solar Energy and Energy Conservation Bank).

Several programs address the production of energy. For example, the use of coal as a substitute for oil and gas is encouraged by the Power Plant and Industrial Fuel Use Act. The most significant initiative on the production side was the formation of the Synthetic Fuels Corporation to accelerate the development of a major synthetic fuels industry.

Support for research, development, and technology demonstration has been the most constant element of the federal government's energy programs. The R&D programs cover a broad range of subjects but emphasize long-term technologies.

The "energy crisis" has not suffered from a lack of federal attention. Regulations dealing with the whole spectrum of real and perceived issues have proliferated. Existing legislation directly addresses the oil import issue and is moving the country in the desired direction. The most significant steps thus far are oil price decontrol and the formation of the Synthetic Fuels Corporation.

Future Emphasis

There is much concern and discussion about the future role of government in solving energy problems. Preliminary data for 1980 (US Department of Energy, 1980g) indicate that net imports of oil declined almost 20% compared to 1979. Some see this as an indication that prices and an unregulated market alone will solve the energy problem quickly. Much of this decline, however, is due to sagging industrial output and to consumers foregoing desired services, particularly in the area of personal transportation, because of rising prices and declining real purchasing power. Although it is doubtful that a major fraction of this decline will persist if vigorous economic activity resumes, higher energy prices have resulted in some efficiency gains (particularly for automobiles) and have begun the movement toward optimizing capital stock to reflect current and expected energy prices.

Given sufficient time, all of the steps outlined in this report probably will be undertaken because of forces in the market. Utilities, for instance, realize that gas and oil are no longer economically viable fuels for steam-electric plants; consumers are buying more fuel efficient automobiles; and a number of other steps have been undertaken to adjust to higher fuel costs. However, as indicated in Chapter II, these massive shifts in fuel choices and capital stocks have historically taken 40 or more years to complete. The United States cannot wait 40 or 50 years. The problem of our vulnerability to imported oil is urgent, with both national and global ramifications, and needs to be solved as quickly as possible. Government initiatives to hasten the solution are warranted.

The government needs to focus its attention on strategic issues—those things that affect the health of the nation as a whole. A shotgun approach treating all conceivable energy-related societal ills—real or imagined—is neither necessary nor desirable. Rather, the 1980s require a few bold federal actions directed primarily toward reducing oil imports. Nine important directions for federal attention follow.

1. Government interference in energy pricing, including natural gas pricing, should be eliminated.
2. The licensing process for nuclear power plants should be completely overhauled. The present process is too costly in time and money, and the excessive delays add little, if anything, to safety. Many suggestions have been proposed to streamline the process, but what has been lacking is an apparent resolve by the federal government to do anything about the problem.
3. Steps should be taken to improve the financial health of the electric utility industry. The regulation of electric utilities needs to be altered to promote the capital formation necessary to replace oil- and gas-fired plants and for expansion. But even if rate reform is accomplished, it is likely to be inadequate for utilities that are largely dependent on oil and gas. The strategy to get oil imports under control by the turn of the century requires that the generating capacity of certain utilities be almost completely rebuilt. This seems unlikely without federal assistance, including loans or loan guarantees. This assistance need not, and should not, be a "give away" program. It is already economically feasible to replace gas- and oil-fired base-

load plants with nuclear or coal plants. The financial feasibility is what is in question.

4. The Synthetic Fuels Corporation needs the full support of the federal government, with the goal of fostering a competitive synthetic fuels industry as quickly as possible, but certainly before the end of this century. Again, the problem is not one of economic feasibility; technologies to produce cost-competitive synthetic liquids and gases are available. The problem is that we do not have a synthetic fuels industry, and a laissez-faire approach is not a solution to this problem because major industries normally require several decades to become established—a time lag the nation cannot afford.

5. The rate at which existing automobiles are replaced with more efficient vehicles needs to be accelerated, and the U.S. automobile industry's capability to provide the vehicles should be strengthened. The replacement of inefficient vehicles might be stimulated by providing financial incentives to purchasers of U.S.-produced automobiles that meet or exceed a specified fuel economy standard. This would also stimulate the sagging automobile industry while encouraging the development and production of fuel-efficient automobiles. The stabilization of emission standards and other regulations affecting automobile design would allow the industry to focus on fuel efficiency.

6. A coordinated federal policy on energy and the environment should be developed. What is needed is not a retreat from our commitment to environmental quality, but a recognition that we currently have energy rules requiring industries to switch from, say, oil to coal and environmental rules prohibiting it.

7. Supply incentives to support energy decisions and activities that are socially desirable in general but involve costs, impacts, or risks to some localities or people. For example, if we need certain new energy facilities, such as radioactive waste repositories or synfuels plants, financial incentives should be offered so that, with full public participation and full knowledge of possible consequences and risks, at least some localities will welcome the facilities.

8. Existing institutions for making decisions should be used fully. Given appropriate pricing policies, incentives, and public information, we should rely heavily on decisions by firms and individuals in economic markets and on the planning and decision-making processes of regional and local units of government. The

genius of the American system is decentralized decision making. We should encourage full use of it.

9. Government should provide R&D related to energy issues and technologies that will be important in the next twenty years. On this time scale, R&D cannot play a central role in reducing oil imports, but it can play an important supporting role.* In general, R&D related to the oil issue can 1. improve the technology base and help remove bottlenecks in the implementation of existing technologies; 2. bring into commercial reality a limited number of new technologies; and 3. reduce impediments to action through better information on environmental, health, and policy matters. An outline of national R&D areas is given in Appendix A.

MEETING LONGER-TERM ENERGY NEEDS

The actions necessary in the short- to mid-term to solve the oil import problem will build a firm foundation for the future. Some points to consider are:

- New energy technologies (especially synfuels and energy efficient machines) will put the United States in an excellent position as a future *exporter* of energy, energy products, and energy technologies; and the world market will be large.
- Continued electrification with increased emphasis on nuclear power will put us in a better position to reduce fossil fuel use if CO_2 or other environmental considerations require it.

Although the actions proposed to reduce oil imports are consistent with a desirable long-term future, they are not sufficient by themselves to assure such a future. Even if the oil import problem is solved by the end of the century, we will continue to move away from our dependence on natural liquid and gaseous fuels. These fuels will be replaced by synthetic liquids and gases or by other means. It is likely that primary energy demand will increase much faster than end-use demand. Thus, the "low energy future," or a future calling for a constant energy demand level, may be possible for end-use energy, but it seems unlikely for primary energy, particularly if the economic growth goal is achieved and the oil problem is solved. The same conclusion—that primary energy inputs will increase much faster than end-use energy—applies to the rest of the world as well.

---

*In the long term, however, R&D will play an essential role.

Even though both the United States and the world have sufficient energy resources to supply increasingly large demands for the entire period considered in this study (to 2050), there is some concern that the exploitation of these resources, particular the fossil resources, may lead to serious environmental consequences. Possible climatic changes due to increases in atmospheric CO_2, and the effects of acid rain are examples of potential large-area impacts. Local impacts on land, water, and air from mining and processing large quantities of coal and oil shale are also of concern. But in considering these *potential* environmental risks of producing and using energy, one must also examine the certain human risks of not doing so. In a growing world, much of which is already underfed and poorly housed, the humanitarian answer will most surely be both the efficient use and the increased production of energy.

In view of this dilemma, what do we do *now*? First, we cannot and need not decide immediately on the amount and kind of energy supply and end-use technologies that are to be implemented in the distant future. And lacking scientific information on potential large-scale environmental effects, we have no basis yet for making decisions about the limits of our energy resources—nor do we need to make such decisions at the present time. What is needed now, and can be done now, is a vigorous long-range program of scientific research and technological development that will give us sound options and will allow us to make rational choices in the future. Areas for long-term R&D emphasis are given in Appendix A. The suggested areas for long-term emphasis relate to:

- Health and environmental effects of energy use and production.
- More efficient and cost-effective means of providing energy service.
- Better supply-side technologies.
- Supporting programs of applied and basic scientific research.

IN RETROSPECT

Based on our study of energy problems and alternatives, we are optimistic about the nation's energy future. We can reduce oil imports to an acceptable level within twenty years using presently available technologies.

Furthermore, we can make a smooth transition toward a long-term energy future in which the United States contributes technologies and resources to help meet world energy demand. And we can be resolute in a way that is consistent with our national objectives of participation and equity in public policy.

For these reasons, we do not believe that either the availability or the cost of energy need seriously constrain our rate of economic growth or our choice of lifestyles. Our energy system can support whatever choices the members of our society want to make for themselves.

REFERENCES

"American Council for an Energy-Efficiency Economy. October 1979. *ACEEE: Principles and Proposals*, Washington, D.C.

Barnes, R. W. July 1976. *The Potential Market for Process Heat From Nuclear Reactors*, ORNL/TM-5516 Oak Ridge National Laboratory, Oak Ridge, Tenn.

Bernstein, L.M. February 1981. U.S. Department of Commerce, Bureau of Economic Analysis Personal communication.

Betts, M. 1979. "Lower Energy Costs Seen in EPA Tradeoff: Industry Eyes Bubble Concept." *Energy User News* 4:1,5

Bezdek, R. H. and Cone, B. W. 1980. "Federal Incentives for Energy Development," *Energy* pp. 389-405.

Blue, J. L., et al. 1979. *Buildings Energy Use Data Book, Edition 2*, ORNL-5552. Oak Ridge National Laboratory, Oak Ridge, Tenn.

Boecker, F., et al. January 1980 *Emergency Petroleum Conservation: A Review and Analysis of Selected Measures*. ORNL/TM-7059. Oak Ridge National Laboratory, Oak Ridge, Tenn.

Bohi, D. R. and Russel, M. *Limiting Oil Imports* 1978. Resources for the Future, Washington, D.C.

British Petroleum Co. 1978. *BP Statistical Review of the World Oil Industry*. London.

Bronowski, J. 1974. *The Ascent of Man*. Little, Brown and Co., Boston.

Brooks, H. et al. 1979. *Energy in Transition 1985-2010*, W. H. Freeman and Company, San Francisco.

Burwell, C. C. "Electric Home Heating—Is It A Loser?" *Institute for Energy Analysis Newsletter*, Vol. 3, No. 3, pp. 1, 3.

Business Week. July 30, 1979. "The Oil Crisis Is Real This Time," pp. 44-60.

Caputo, R. 1977. *An Initial Comparative Assessment of Orbital and Terrestrial Power Systems.* JPL 900-780. Jet Propulsion Laboratory, California Institute of Technology.

Carpenter, J. A., Jr. January 1980. "Unconventional Mix of U.S. Energy Carriers," Overview Paper. Oak Ridge National Laboratory, Oak Ridge, Tenn.

Cochran, H. D. January 1980. "Liquid and Gaseous Fuels from Coal," ONEP Overview Paper Number 12.

Cone, B. W. and Bezdek, R. H. 1978. *Incentives Report Overview,* CONF-7805161 Pacific Northwest Laboratory, Richland, Wash.

Corum, K. April 1980. Oak Ridge National Laboratory. Personal communication to M. Olszewski.

Coste, W. H. and Lotker, M. 1977. *Power Engineering.* pp. 48-51.

Cox, J. C. and Wright, A. W. 1978. "The Effects of Crude Oil Price Controls, Entitlements and Taxes on Refined Product Prices and Energy Independence." *Land Economics,* Vol. 54, No. 1, pp. 1-15.

Crabbe, D. and McBride, R. 1979. *The World Energy Book,* MIT Press, Cambridge, Mass.

Craig, R. B. and Salk, M. S. October 1979. "Environmental and Health Implications of Present Energy Systems in the Future." Overview Paper. Oak Ridge National Laboratory, Oak Ridge, Tenn. Addendum (December 1979).

Craig, R. B. and Salk, M. S. February 1980. Addendum to Walsh (1980).

Davis, W. K., et al. 1979. *U. S. Energy Supply Prospects to 2010.* National Research Council.

Delene, J. G. Oak Ridge National Laboratory. Personal communication.

Edison Electric Institute. December 17, 1980. *Recommendations for Restoration of Financial Health to the U.S. Electric Power Industry.* Report of an informal task force to the Reagan Energy Transition Team. Also known as Cory Report.

Electrical World. 1979. "Loss of Another Year's Growth Shaves Construction Program." Vol. 192, No. 6 p. 80.

Energy and Environmental Analysis, Inc. July 1981. *Regional and Seasonal Trends in Fuel Economy and Travel*.

Fox, E. C. 1980. Oak Ridge National Laboratory. Personal communication.

Fox, E. C. and Graves, R. L. January 1980. "The Outlook for Coal Combustion," Overview Paper. Oak Ridge National Laboratory, Oak Ridge, Tenn.

Francis, E. J., et al. June 1980. "Comparison of Cost Estimates, Sharing Potentials, Subsidies and Uses for OTEC Facilities and Plantships." Presented at the 7th Ocean Energy Conference, Washington D.C.

Gibbons, J. H., et al. 1979. *Alternative Energy Demand Futures to 2010*, National Academy of Sciences.

Graves, R. L., Fox, E. C. and Cleveland, J. C. June 1980. "An Engineering Economic Comparison of Electric and Internal Combustion Vehicles." Oak Ridge National Laboratory, Oak Ridge, Tenn.

Greenstreet, W. L., et al. February 1980. "The Coal Fuel Cycle." Overview Paper. Oak Ridge National Laboratory, Oak Ridge, Tenn.

Haefele, W. et al. 1981. *Energy in a Finite World — A Global Systems Analysis*. Energy Systems Program Group, International Institute for Applied Systems Analysis. Ballinger Publishing Co., Cambridge, Mass.

Harrington, I., et al. July 1980. *Contingency Planning for a Gasoline Shortage: A Technical Handbook*, Massachusetts Institute of Technology, Center for Transportation Studies.

Hirst, E. February 1978. *Energy and Economic Benefits of Residential Energy Conservation RD&D*, ORNL/CON-22, Oak Ridge National Laboratory, Oak Ridge, Tenn.

Hirst, E. 1979. "Effects of the National Energy Act on Energy Use and Economics in Residential and Commercial Buildings." *Energy Systems and Policy*, Vol. 3, No. 2, pp. 171-190.

Hirst, E. and Jackson, J. 1977. "Historical Patterns of Residential and Commercial Energy Use," *Energy*, Vol. 2, pp. 131-140.

Hirst, E. and O'Neal, D. 1979. "Contributions of Improved Technologies to Reduced Residential *Energy Growth.*" *Energy and Buildings*, Vol. 2 pp. 217-224.

Hise, E. C. and Holman, A. S. 1975. *Heat Balance and Efficiency Measurements of Central, Forced Air, Residential Gas Furnaces.* ORNL/NSF-EP-88 Oak Ridge National Laboratory, Oak Ridge, Tenn.

Hogan, W. W. October 1979. Interview with S. C. Parikh and T. J. Wilbanks. Cambridge, Mass.

Hutchins, P. F., Jr. and Hirst, E. November 1978. *Engineering-Economic Analysis of Single-Family Dwelling Thermal Performance,* ORNL/CON-35. Oak Ridge National Laboratory, Oak Ridge, Tenn.

Hudson, C. R. February 1980. Personal communication.

Iammartino, N.R. 1976. "Will the U.S. Geothermal Resources Win a Role in Process Plants?" *Chem. Eng.* Vol. 83, No. 24, pp. 79-81.

Information Please Almanac Atlas & Yearbook: 1980. 1979. (34th edition), Simon and Schuster, New York.

Irwin, R. W. August 11, 1980. "A Look at Cars Coming Over Next Five Years," *Automotive News* p. 1, 42.

Johns, L. S., et al. 1980. *Energy from Biological Processes,* Office of Technology Assessment.

Johnson, W. S. and Pierce, F. E. April 1980. *Energy and Cost Analysis of Commercial Building Shell Characteristics and Operating Schedules,* ORNL/CONS-39 Oak Ridge National Laboratories, Oak Ridge, Tenn.

Kalt, J. P. and Stillman, R. S. February 1980. *The Role of Government Incentives in Energy Production* Discussion Paper KSG #80-D. Energy and Environment Policy Center, Harvard University.

Kaserman, D. L. and Tepel, R. C. *The Impact of the Automatic Adjustment Clause on Fuel Purchase and Utilization Practices in the U.S. Electric Utility Industry,* ORNL/TM-7595 (to be published).

Kash, D. E., et al. 1976. *Our Energy Future.* University of Oklahoma Press, Norman, Okla.

Kasten, P. March 1981. Personal Communication. Oak Ridge National Laboratory. Oak Ridge, Tenn.

Kelly, H., et al. 1978. *Application of Solar Technology to Today's Energy Needs*. Office of Technology Assessment.

Keyfitz, N., *Population Projections of the World and Its Regions 1975-2050*, IIASA WP-77-7. Pergamon Press, New York.

Klepper, O. H., et al. August 1979. "Solvent Refined Coal Market Penetration Study," Draft, Oak Ridge National Laboratory. Oak Ridge, Tenn.

Kreith, F. "A Technical and Economic Assessment of Three Solar Conversion Technologies," SERI/TP-34-262 Presented at U.N. Economic Commission for Europe Seminar on Cooperative Technical Forecasting, Tenerife (2–7 July 1979).

Landsberg, H. H. 1979. *Energy: The Next Twenty Years*. Ballinger Publishing Co., Cambridge, Mass.

Lane, J. A. 1977. *Wind Energy*, ORNL/CF-77/92. Oak Ridge National Laboratory, Oak Ridge, Tenn.

Lee, D. D. May 1980. "The Outlook for Biofuels," Overview Paper. Oak Ridge National Laboratory, Oak Ridge, Tenn.

Lemon, R. September 1, 1980. *Energy Topics*. A Periodic Supplement to *IGT Highlights*.

Lewis, A. E. August 1979 *Oil from Shale: The Potential, the Problems, and a Plan for Development*, ICRL-83236. Lawrence Livermore Laboratory, Livermore, Calif.

Loftness, R. L. 1978. *Energy Handbook*. Van Nostrand Reinhold Co., New York.

Lund, J. W. 1976. "The Utilization and Economics of Low Temperature Geothermal Water for Space Heating," Proceedings of 11th Intersociety Energy Conversion Engineering Conference, American Institute of Chemical Engineering, New York. pp. 822–827.

MacLachlan, A. November 28, 1979. "The Geysers: 15 Acres of Cheap But Malodorous Power," *The Energy Daily*. Vol. 7, No. 226, pp. 2-3.

Maloney, M. J., et al. June 1978. *End Use Energy Consumption Data Base: Series 1 Tables*, DOE/EIA-0014, U.S. Department of Energy.

Marlay, R. C. 1981. *Effects on Investment in Energy Conservation of DOE's Programs and of Market Forces*, U.S. Department of Energy.

Maulhardt, M., et al. October 1979. *Some Potentials for Energy and Peak Power Conservation in California*. LBL-5926 revised. Lawrence Berkeley Laboratory, Berkeley, Calif.

Mead, J. J. 1979. "The Performance of Government Energy Regulations," *American Economic Review*, Vol. 69, pp. 353-356.

McClelland L. and Cook, S. 1980. "Energy Conservation Effects of Continuous In-House Feedback in All Electric Homes," *J. Env. Sys.* Vol. 96, pp. 169-172.

McNutt, B. D., et al. October, 1979. *Consumption of EPA and In-use Fuel Economy of 1974-1978 Automobiles*, SAE-790932 U. S. Department of Energy.

Mullins, M. E. 1980. "Liquid Biomass Fuels," ORNL internal memorandum. Oak Ridge National Laboratory, Oak Ridge, Tenn.

National Geographic. February 1981, "Can We Live Better on Less." p25500pp. 52-53.

Nordhaus, W. D. September 1974. "The 1974 Report of the President's Council of Economic Advisers: Energy in the Economic Report," *American Economic Review*, LXIV(4), pp. 556-565.

Nordhaus, W. D. January 14, 1981. Personal communication to T. D. Anderson.

Norwood, C. H. 1980. *Wood Energy Consumption in the United States, 1973 to 1979*, U. S. Department of Energy, Washington, D.C.

Nuclear Fuel. March 19, 1979. "Reoriented 'NURE Puts Reserve Estimate Up, But Total Resource May Go Down." Vol. 4, No. 6.

Office of Technology Assessment March 1979. *Residential Energy Conservation*.

O'Hare, M. 1977. "Not on My Block, You Don't: Facility Siting and the Strategic Importance of Compensation," *Public Policy*, Vol. 25, No. 4.

Oil & Gas J. 1979a. "Carter Orders Decontrol of Heavy Crude." Vol. 77, No. 35, p. 38.

Oil & Gas J. 1979 *b*. "ERA Moves to Boost Enhanced Recovery." Vol. 77, No. 35, p. 35.
Slope System." Vol. 78, No. 19, p. 79.

Olszewski, M. January 1980. "U. S. Energy Reserves, Resources, and Production Capabilities." Overview Paper. Oak Ridge National Laboratory, Oak Ridge, Tenn.

Parikh, S. C. March 1979. *A Welfare Equilibrium Model (WEM) of Energy Supply, Energy Demand, and Economic Growth*, Systems Optimization Laboratory, Department of Operations Research, Stanford University. Stanford, Calif.

Pasini, J. May 1980 . "Unconventional Sources of Oil." Overview Paper. Science Applications, Inc. , Morgantown, W. Va.

Peele, R. W., et al. 1981. *An Evaluation of the Long-Term Energy Analysis Program Used for the 1978 EIA Administrator's Report to Congress*, ORNL-5741 Oak Ridge National Laboratory, Oak Ridge, Tenn.

Pimentel, D., and Terhune, E. C.1977. "Energy and Food," *Annual Review of Energy*. Vol. 2, pp. 174-195.

Pine, G., et al. "Rational Energy Use — A U.S. Perspective," Chapter 4 of D. J. Rose and W. Fulkerson's *Nuclear Policy Studies Project Report*. To be published. Oak Ridge National Laboratory, Oak Ridge, Tenn.

President's Commission on Coal. March 1980. "Recommendations and Summary Findings," Washington, D.C.

Ray, D. L. December 1973. *The Nation's Energy Future*, WASH-1281, U.S. Atomic Energy Commission.

Report to the President by the Interagency Review Group on Nuclear Waste Management. March 1979. TID 29442.

Reichle, L. F. C. October 30, 1979. "The Economics of Nuclear Versus Coal." Presented before the Richmond Society of Financial Analysts, Richmond, Virginia.

Resource Planning Associates December 1977. *The Potential for Co-generation Development in Six Major Industries by 1985: Executive Summary.*

Robel, R. J., et al. 1978. *Enhanced Oil Recovery Potential in the United States*. Office of Technology Asssessment.

Roberson, R. J., November 1979. "How Energy Was Used: 1978, by End Use, by Fuel Source." Internal memorandum. Oak Ridge National Laboratory, Oak Ridge, Tenn.

Roger Seasonwein Assoc. 1980. "1979/1980 National Probability Samples by Telephone, 1,000 Adults," conducted for Union Carbide Corp.

Ross, M. H., and Williams, H. July 1979. *Drilling for Oil and Gas in Our Buildings*. PU/CEES 87, Princeton University. Princeton, N.J.

Roy, R., et al 1978. *Solidification of High-Level Radioactive Wastes*. National Research Council.

Samuels, G. "Rational Energy Use—Transportation Sector." In *Nuclear Policy Studies Project Annual Progress Report*. To be published. Oak Ridge National Laboratory, Oak Ridge, Tenn.

Samuels, G. 1981. "Transportation Energy Requirements to the Year 2010." ORNL-5745, Oak Ridge National Laboratory, Oak Ridge, Tenn.

Samuels, G. December 1979. "Unconventional Sources of Gas." ONEP Overview Paper Number 16.

Schmitt, R. C., et al. 1976. "Direct Application of Geothermal Energy." Proceedings of the 11th Intersociety Energy Conversion Engineering Conference. American Institute of Chemical Engineers, New York. pp 815–821.

Schurr, S. H.,et al. 1979. *Energy in America's Future: The Choices Before Us*, Johns Hopkins University Press, Baltimore, Md.

Seamans, Jr., R. C. June 1975. *A National Plan for Energy Research, Development and Demonstration: Creating Energy Choices for the Future. Volume I: The Plan*, ERDA-48, U.S. Energy Research and Development Administration.

Segal, M. R. September 11, 1980. *Gasohol: The Alcohol Fuels*. Issue Brief Number IB-74087, Library of Congress, Congressional Research Service.

Solar Energy Research Institute. December 1979. *Heliostat Production Evaluation and Cost Analysis*. SERI/TR-8052-2.

Shackson, R. and Leach, H. J. 1980. Mellon Institute. Personal Communication with T. J. Wilbanks, Oak Ridge National Laboratory, Oak Ridge, Tenn.

Shonka, D. B. 1979. *Transportation Energy Conservation Data Book, Edition 3.* ORNL-5493. Oak Ridge National Laboratory, Oak Ridge, Tenn.

Simmons, M. K., et al. 1979. *Domestic Potential of Solar and Other Renewable Energy Sources.* National Research Council.

Sladek, T. A., et al. 1980. *An Assessment of Oil Shale Technologies.* Office of Technology Assessment.

Smock, R. August 1979. "The Top 100 Electric Utilities 1978 Operating Performance." *Electric Light and Power*, Vol. 57, pp. 11-15.

"Special Workshop on Radwaste," December 17, 1979. Oak Ridge National Laboratory. Oak Ridge, Tenn.

Spiewak, I. and Cope, D. F. February 1980. "Nuclear Power," Overview Paper. Oak Ridge National Laboratory, Oak Ridge, Tenn.

Stobaugh, R. and Yergin, D. eds. 1979. *Energy Future: Report of the Energy Project at the Harvard Business School.* Random House, New York.

Tepel, R. C. 1980. Personal communication.

Tolley, G. S. and Wilman, J. 1977. "The Foreign Dependence Question." *Journal of Political Economy* Vol. 85, No. 2, pp. 323–247.

Tyner, W. E. and Wright, A. W. 1978. "U.S. Energy Policy and Oil Independence: A Critique and a Proposal." *Materials and Society* Vol. 2, pp. 15-22.

U.S. Council of Economic Advisors. April 1981. *Economic Indicators.* Washington, D.C.

U.S. Department of Commerce. 1970. *Historical Statistics of the United States, Colonial Times to 1970, Part 2.* Bureau of the Census. Washington, D.C.

U.S. Department of Commerce. 1976. *Statistical Abstract of the United States 1976*: 97th ed. Bureau of the Census. Washington, D.C.

U.S. Department of Commerce. 1977. Bureau of the Census, Series II, *Current Population Reports*, Series P-25, No. 704. Washington, D.C.

U.S. Department of Commerce. 1978. *1977 Business Statistics 21st Biennial Edition*. Bureau of Economic Analysis. Washington, D.C.

U.S. Department of Energy. 1977. *Inventory of Power Plants in the United States*. DOE/RA-001. Washington, D.C.

U.S. Department of Energy. 1978. *Interim Report on the Performance of 400 Megawatt and Larger Nuclear and Coal-Fired Generating Units*. DOE/ERA-0007. Washington, D.C.

U.S. Department of Energy. 1979 *a. Additions to Generating Capacity, 1979-1988 for the Contiguous United States*. rev. 1. DOE/ERA-0020/1. Washington, D.C.

U.S. Department of Energy. 1979*b. Annual Report to Congress, 1978* Vol. 2. DOE/EIA-0173/2. Washington, D.C.

U.S. Department of Energy.1979 *c. Draft Environmental Impact Statement: Management of Commercially Generated Radioactive Waste*, Vol. 1. DOE/EIS-0046-D. Washington, D.C.

U.S. Department of Energy. 1979*d. Federal Energy Data System Statistical Summary Update*. DOE/EIA-0192. Washington, D.C.

U.S. Department of Energy. 1979*e. Industrial Sector Technology Use Model (ISTUM): Industrial Energy Use in the United States, 1974 = 2000, Vol. 1: Primary Model Documentation*. DOE/FE/2344-1. Washington, D.C.p.

U.S. Department of Energy. 1979*f. Monthly Energy Review*. DOE/EIA-0035/10(79). Washington, D.C.

U.S. Department of Energy. 1979*g. National Energy Plan II*. Washington, D.C.

U.S. Department of Energy. 1980*a. Annual Report to Congress, 1979, Volume Two: Data*. DOE/EIA-0173(79)/2. Washington, D.C.

U.S. Department of Energy. 1980*b. Annual Report to Congress, 1979, Volume Three Projections*. DOE/EIA173(79)3. Washington, D.C.

U.S. Department of Energy. 1980*c. Electric Utility Status Report*. OUS/PSR 50. Washington, D.C.

U.S. Department of Energy. 1980*d. Monthly Energy Review*. DOE/EIA-0035/04(80). Washington, D.C.

U.S. Department of Energy. 1980*e*. *Monthly Energy Review*. DOE/EIA-0035/05(80). Washington, D.C.

U.S. Department of Energy. 1980*f*. *Monthly Energy Review*. DOE/EIA-0035(80/08). Washington, D.C.

U.S. Department of Energy. 1980*g*. *Monthly Energy Review*. DOE/EIA-0035(80/11). Washington, D.C.

U.S. Department of Energy. 1980. *Solar Power Satellite Project Division Program Assessment Report*. Statement of Findings. DOE/ER-0085. Washington, D.C.

U.S. Department of Energy. 1980*j*. *Low Energy Futures for the United States*. DOE-2525568. Washington, D.C.

U.S. Department of Energy. 1981. *Monthly Energy Review*. DOE/EIA-0035 (81/07). Washington, D.C.

Vath, J. E. January 1980. "Unconventional Sources of Uranium." Overview Paper. Oak Ridge National Laboratory, Oak Ridge, Tenn.

Walsh, P. J. et al. January 1980. "Environmental/Health Implications of Unconventional Sources of Fossil Fuels." Overview Paper. Oak Ridge National Laboratory, Oak Ridge, Tenn.

Webb, M. March 1978. "Policy on Energy Pricing." *Energy Policy* pp. 53-65.

Weil, S. A. et al. November 1978. *The IGT HYTORT Process for Hydrogen Retorting of Devonian Oil Shales*. CONF-7811122-1. Institute of Gas Technology, Chicago.

Wertheim, M. May 1980. "Fusion Power." Overview Paper. Grummen Aerospace Corp., Beth Page, N.Y.

Wilbanks, T. J. May 1980. "Decentralized Energy Planning and Consensus in Energy Policy." Presented at the National Energy Policy Conference, Morgantown, W. Va.

Winett, R. and Neale, M. 1979. "Psychological Framework for Energy Conservation in Buildings." *Energy and Building*.

World Bank. 1980. *World Development Report, 1980*. Oxford University Press.

World Energy Resources 1985–2020. 1978. IPC Science and Technology Press. New York.

Yeoman, J. C. Jr. December 1978. *Wind Turbines*. ANL/CES/TE 78-9. Prepared by Oak Ridge National Laboratory. For Argonne National Laboratory, Argonne, Ill.

Zausner, E. et al. November 1974. *Project Independence*. Federal Energy Administration. Washington, D.C.

Zehr, F. and O'Neal, D. 1981. *The Performance and Economics of Residential Solar Space Heating*. In preparation. ORNL/CON-70, Oak Ridge National Laboratory, Oak Ridge, Tenn.

APPENDICES

APPENDICES

APPENDIX A
THE ROLE OF RESEARCH
AND DEVELOPMENT

R&D in Perspective

Earlier it was concluded that the United States can solve its imported oil problem with technologies that are either commercial or near-commercial. Furthermore, the demand/supply analysis of Chapter IV strongly suggests that the United States' long-term energy future, at least to 2020, could be very acceptable using relatively modest extrapolations of present technologies. Why, then, is there a need for energy research and development? There is not now, nor has there ever been, an *absolute* need for peacetime research and development; for the most part, it represents an opportunity, not a basic need. But history shows us that the opportunities created by scientific research and technological development can, and have, dramatically improved the lot of mankind. Advances in science and technology have extended life expectancy, increased food production, reduced disease, and broadened freedom of choice in life styles. It is this understanding that has been the traditional justification for R&D. Society's support for research and development is an expression of hopefulness for and confidence in the future, not of desperate need in the present.

The role of energy R&D is quite simply to create the opportunity to reduce the total social cost of energy or energy service. These cost reduction opportunities range from market costs of energy to environmental, health, and social impacts.

Supporting R&D Related to the Oil Problem

This study shows the desirability and feasibility of reducing oil imports to 20%, or less, of total oil use within the next twenty years. On this time scale, research and development cannot play a central role in reducing oil imports, but it can play an important supporting role. In general, R&D can:

- Improve the technology base and help remove bottlenecks to the implementation of existing technologies.
- Reduce impediments to action through better information on environmental, health, and policy-related matters.

The R&D areas believed to be related to the goal of reducing oil imports are shown in Tables 85 and 86. Table 85 covers national activities that are expected to be the main line efforts directed toward reducing oil imports within the next 20 years. Table 86 lists those activities that could make some contributions, but that are less important.

Table 85. Research and development on major factors in resolving the imported oil issue

National activity area	Example R&D topics	Comments
Energy supply technologies		
Conventional oil and gas exploration and production	Deep drilling techniques for onshore and offshore exploration and production Improved tools for exploration	Efforts to find more conventional oil and gas and to produce oil and gas from formations previously inaccessible could slow or halt the decline in U.S. production
Enhanced oil recovery	Development of improved EOR techniques	Because "exhausted" oil fields still retain two-thirds of the oil that was originally contained in the formation, EOR is an important component of domestic oil production
Unconventional gas	Improved fracturing techniques for tight sands and shale formations Coal-seam recovery methods	The potential resource base of natural gas in formations that are currently uneconomical to tap is large
Synfuels from coal—indirect liquefaction and intermediate-Btu gasification	Improvements and refinements in current and emerging technologies for producing intermediate-Btu and synthesis gas from coal. Methods for feeding coal into pressurized systems and for processing caking coals are examples of development needs Improvements and refinements in current and emerging technologies for producing liquid fuels through catalytic conversion of synthesis gas	Technologies for producing intermediate-Btu and synthesis gas from coal are fundamental in the quest for reducing oil imports; the products can be used as substitutes for oil and natural gas in utility boilers, in industrial boilers and process heaters, and as a feedstock to indirect liquefaction plants. Indirect liquefaction aimed primarily toward transportation fuels is also an important near-term component of increasing domestic production of oil

Table 85. (continued)

National activity area	Example R&D topics	Comments
Western oil shale	Improvements and refinements in known surface retorting technologies, including more efficient use of water and improved environmental control concepts Disposal of spent shale Land reclamation	The western shale resource is large and is destined to be a major source of energy for the U.S. The shale oil industry needs to start with available technologies. Some R&D support could make these technologies more acceptable
Coal combustion	Development of package pressurized fluidized bed boilers for industrial use Improved environmental control technologies for pulverized coal boilers for utilities and industry	The direct combustion of coal in utility and industrial boilers is a major element of the proposed fuel substitution program. Concepts that are economical in smaller sizes would hasten the use of coal in industry. Improvements in environmental control technologies would increase the acceptability of coal
Coal mining	Improved mining and reclamation methods and technology	The nation's drive to eliminate imported oil will put a heavy burden on coal. Improvements in productivity, safety, and environmental protection are important
Light-water reactors	Safety and reliability Away-from-reactor spent fuel storage Waste isolation	The LWR is probably the most important electric power technology. Any R&D that will speed implementation should be strongly supported

Table 85. (continued)

National activity area	Example R&D topics	Comments
Energy demand technologies		
Transportation refinements to existing technologies	Improved internal combustion (IC) engines, transmissions, tires, and lubricants	The best opportunity to reduce oil imports through conservation is in the transportation sector
	Lightweight automotive structural design and materials	
	Infinitely variable transmissions with lock-up coupling and other drive-chain improvements	
	Improved aerodynamics	
Buildings sector conservation retrofit	Advanced heat pump systems	The primary relationship between building conservation and oil imports is that oil substitutes can be released to displace oil elsewhere. The greatest conservation potential in the near term is in existing buildings
	Furnace efficiency improvements	
	Side wall insulation retrofit	
Industrial conservation	Improved processes	Industry uses more energy than any other sector. Roughly 70% of the energy used is either oil or gas. Energy-efficiency improvements in industry are, therefore, very important
	Efficiency improvements in fuel-burning installations	
	Heat recovery systems	
	Process and materials substitution	Chosen to reduce energy requirements and problems of imported material

Table 85. (continued)

National activity area	Example R&D topics	Comments
Supporting research and information		
Environmental and health effects research	Genetic and carcinogenic effects of synthetic fuels from oil shales and from indirect liquefaction of coal	Better environmental and health effects data are needed to provide a rational basis for emissions standards and other regulations. Emphasis should be on those technologies that will actually be used in the next twenty years
	Health effects of emissions from coal combustion and their relationship to wide-area environmental effects such as acid precipitation	
Combustion research	Parameters affecting emissions from combustion of coal	Better basic knowledge about the dynamics of combustion could allow more efficient uses of fuels with less emissions
	IC engine combustion chamber research	
Materials research	High-temperature materials	Improved materials for shale retorts, coal gasification, and fluidized bed combustion technologies would be beneficial
	Corrosion erosion resistant materials	
Energy information and analysis	Improved information about where and how oil and gas are used, especially in the industrial sector	Need to deemphasize tool making (i.e., data bases and model building) and to concentrate on issue analysis. Information that can be understood (and therefore used) by policymakers is the goal. Data bases and models are needed as tools to get answers, but tools are not the objective
	Intertie requirements to displace oil and gas use through interutility transfers	
	Impact of various conservation measures on oil and gas consumption. Cost benefit analyses to focus on most effective conservation measures	

Table 86. Research and development on less important (modest-to-minor) factors in resolving the imported oil issue

National activity area	Example R&D topics	Comments
Energy supply technologies		
Solar space and water heating	Low-cost collectors	Low-temperature solar installations for buildings could save oil and natural gas, but significant cost reductions are needed for wide acceptance
	Improved concepts to reduce installation labor	
	Reliability improvements	
Synfuels from coal-direct liquefaction, high-Btu gasification, coal pyrolysis, and coal-oil mixtures	Improved processes for producing light hydrocarbons from direct liquefaction and pyrolysis processes	Direct liquefaction, substitute natural gas production, and coal pyrolysis could make some contributions to reducing oil imports before the turn of the century
	Lower-cost SNG	If developed, this could be a major contributor
Eastern shales	Hydroretorting of shales to improve oil yield	The resource base of hydrocarbons, uranium, and strategic metals is large, but economic production on a large scale will require considerable development
	Co-production of oil, uranium, and other strategic metals from eastern shales	
Biomass	Effective uses of urban wastes	Cost-effective uses of biomass could make some contribution to reducing oil imports
	Alcohols from woody biomass	

Table 86. (continued)

National activity area	Example R&D topics	Comments
Cogeneration	Low-cost means of transporting thermal energy long distances from central plant to distributed users	Cogeneration is an efficient and thoroughly demonstrated means of producing electricity and steam. Cogeneration with oil and gas is generally not supportive of the goal to reduce oil imports. Coal- or nuclear-based cogeneration plants need to be large to be economical
District heating	Lower cost transmission and distribution systems	District heating, supplied by coal or nuclear cogeneration plants, could displace oil and gas for heating in some high-density metropolitan areas
Energy demand technologies		
Transportation electric vehicles and alternative fueled-engine concepts	Low-cost, high-power density batteries Alcohol and vegetable oil burning internal combustion engines for fleet or agricultural use	Electric vehicles for specialized uses may be able to displace some oil. Similarly, engines burning pure alcohol or vegetable oils could be used in special applications
Conservation in new buildings	Passive solar concepts Improved building envelopes	It is important that new buildings be energy efficient, but the old buildings will dominate energy use for the next 20 years

Highlights of R&D activities that could support the main line (most important) activities are as follows:

- Natural Oil and Gas
  - Improved technologies for exploration and production of conventional oil and gas.
  - Advanced techniques for enhanced oil recovery.
  - New methods for tapping unconventional gas resources.
- Synthetic Fuels
  - Improved intermediate-Btu gasification and indirect liquefaction technologies for producing synfuels from coal.
  - Refined surface retorts for producing oil from western shale.
  - Improved direct liquefaction technologies for producing desired fuels efficiently from coal.
- Coal
  - Improved combustion technologies.
  - Advanced mining and reclamation methods.
- Light Water Reactors
  - Increased understanding of safety related issues.
  - Implementation of waste storage and terminal waste isolation.
- Conservation
  - Refinements to existing highway transportation technologies.
  - Improved conservation measures for existing buildings.
  - Improved industrial processes.
- Supporting Research and Information
  - Increased understanding of environmental effects of energy technologies that will actually be used in the next 20 years.
  - Continued biological research to elucidate the mechanisms of cancer induction and the underlying bases of toxic effects of chemicals and radiation.
  - Supporting applied research related to near-term technologies.
  - Improved energy demand and supply data and analysis to guide policy-making.

The foregoing list represents national R&D topics, not just federally supported activities. The appropriate balance between private and government support is not clearly defined, but there are important roles for each sector. Health, safety, the environment, and high-risk technology areas, although not the exclusive responsibility of government, certainly need government support. The private sector's R&D role is primarily in those areas (e.g., oil exploration and production, transportation technologies) where strong industries, with an R&D tradition, exist.

R&D Activities Related to Longer-Term Issues

In general, the long-term goal of R&D is to provide options for delivering energy service at the lowest societal cost. Listed in Table 87 are those national activities that are believed to be most closely related to the long-term goal. It is emphasized that R&D efforts related to longer-term issues should not be delayed. Many decades are required to implement new technologies and to gain an understanding of their potential impacts; low R&D priority on long-term technologies and issues could doom us to perpetual energy crises in the future.

Table 87. Research and development related to long-term energy issues

National activity area	Example R&D topics	Comments
Energy supply technologies		
Breeder reactor	Completion of demonstration plant and development of fuel recycle	The breeder could supply the world's energy needs for centuries, and it has been shown to be technologically feasible. The United States needs to regain its leadership position in this area
	Improved designs for greater inherent safety and lower capital cost	
	Safeguards	
Advanced converter reactors	Fuel utilization improvements in LWRs	Converters could be a long-term (~50 year) energy option for the United States. To support this possible option, we need an R&D program aimed at (1) making more uranium available and (2) using available resources efficiently. The support for advanced converters (HTGR) is not, and should not be, considered a substitute for a breeder program. Rather, it should be viewed as a complementary program with the additional potential to supply process heat for shale oil recovery, for for coal liquefaction, and for industrial complexes
	Alternate converter concepts development high-temperature gas-cooled reactor, etc.	
	Uranium exploration methods	
	Recovery of uranium from low-grade resources	
	Advanced isotope separation	
Fusion energy	Demonstrate scientific, technical, and economic feasibility for either inertial or magnetic confinement, or both	Fusion, like the breeder, represents an "ultimate" energy source in that, for all practical purposes, it is inexhaustible. R&D at a reasonable level should be pursued
Solar energy	Combined heating and cooling systems for buildings	Because solar energy is inexhaustible and is distributed relatively uniformly over the populated regions of the world, economical means of harnessing this energy source could be of great value to mankind
	Photovoltaic conversion	

Table 87. (continued)

National activity area	Example R&D topics	Comments
	Biophotolysis	
	Improved crop yields for cultivated biomass. Conversion to liquid and gaseous fuels	
Conversion of thermal and electrical energy to chemical energy forms	Thermochemical water splitting	Several long-term energy sources fusion, breeders, and solar produce thermal energy or electricity. The economical conversion of these energy forms to chemical fuels and feedstock may eventually be necessary
	Advanced water electrolysis	
Synthetic fuels from shales and coal	Direct liquefaction of coal to light products	The shale and coal resources of the U.S. will probably be a major source of energy for a long time perhaps, for centuries. Continued research to improve processes and to reduce environmental and health risks is highly desirable
	In situ coal gasification and shales retorting	
Energy demand technologies		
Transportation	Batteries and fuel cells	Transportation will continue to be an important energy-consuming sector well into the future
	Advanced heat engines	
	Composite materials for lightweight structures	
Industrial conservation	Advanced production processes, especially in the chemical and primary metals industries	By 2010, the industrial sector will need greatly increased energy, more than all other sectors combined. Efficient use of energy is necessary to produce low-cost products and to compete in world markets

Table 87. (continued)

National activity area	Example R&D topics	Comments
Buildings sector conservation	Advanced concepts for energy-efficient buildings	
	Storage heat pumps and other advanced space conditioning technologies	
Agriculture	Genetic engineering to produce plants with higher yields and needing less fertilizer and other energy inputs	With fixed land resources, agricultural output will need to increase faster than population growth. Research in agriculture promises more food from the same land and from less energy.
	Improved tillage methods	
Supporting research		
Environmental and health effects research	Determination of effects of CO_2 release and the mechanisms and parameters governing rate of accumulation of CO_2 in the atmosphere. Effects of other emissions on global environment	With world energy production and consumption likely to increase severalfold in the next few decades, strong support for environmental and health research is needed to avoid unexpected, unpleasant effects
	Carcinogenic and genetic effects of products from direct coal liquefaction and other advanced synthetic fuels processes	

Table 87. (continued)

National activity area	Example R&D topics	Comments
Basic research	Extend the frontiers of our knowledge concerning the basic properties of the four states of matter: elementary particles, nuclear matter, atomic matter, and plasma matter	Continued inattention and weakening support for basic research would eventually leave engineers and applied scientists with a "bare cupboard"
Applied research	High-temperature, corrosion-resistant alloys and ceramics	Applied research applicable to a broad range of energy technologies can create opportunities for technological advances
	Geology and geochemistry	
	Energy-related social studies	
	Processes to ensure availability of strategic materials for energy production	For example, platinum group metals for catalysts and cobalt and chromium for construction materials

APPENDIX B

OVERVIEW PAPERS

The study group utilized the special experience and knowledge of Oak Ridge National Laboratory staff by commissioning a number of papers that summarized specified areas of energy or environmental technology and policy. In a few cases consultants outside the Laboratory also contributed. These papers provided much of the technical assessment and analysis used to accomplish the work of the study group.

"The Effects of Marginal Cost Pricing of Energy," S. Parmeshwaran, TRW Corporation (October 1979).

"Non-technical and Non-market Costs in U.S. Energy Prices," B. Y. Wilkes, ORNL (December 1979).

"U.S. Energy Reserves, Resources, and Production," M. Olszewski, ORNL (January 1980).

"U.S. Energy Requirements," B. E. Prince, UCC-ND (February 1980).

"Environmental and Health Implications of Present Energy Systems in the Future," R. B. Craig and M. S. Salk, ORNL (October 1979).

"Atmospheric CO_2 Concentration," A. M. Perry, ORNL, background notes for workshop.

"The Coal Fuel Cycle," W. L. Greentreet, R. L. Carmichael, and R. E. Kuhlman, ORNL (February 1980).

"The Outlook for Coal Combustion," E. C. Fox and R. L. Graves, ORNL, (January 1980).

"Liquid and Gaseous Fuels from Coal," H. D. Cochran, Jr., ORNL (January 1980).

"Nuclear Power," I. Spiewak and D. F. Cope, ORNL (February 1980).

"Nuclear Wastes Management," T. M. Besmann, ORNL, background notes for a workshop.

"Unconventional Sources of Oil," J. Pasini, SAI (May 1980).

"Unconventional Sources of Gas," G. Samuels, ORNL (December 1979).

"Unconventional Sources of Uranium," J. E. Vath, ORNL (January 1980).

"The Outlook for Biofuels," D. D. Lee, ORNL (May 1980).

"Energy Conservation Potentials," R. Carlsmith, ORNL (1980).

"Unconventional Mix of Energy Carriers," J. A. Carpenter, Jr., ORNL (January 1980).

"Environmental and Health Implications of Different Standards," R. M. Cushman and F. C. Kornegay, ORNL (January 1980).

"Environmental and Health Implications of Unconventional Sources of Fossil Fuels," P. J. Walsh, A. P. Watson, E. Etnier, and C. E. Easterly, ORNL (January 1980).

"Constraints by Non-Fuel Mineral Resources," H. E. Goeller, ORNL (December 1979).

"Fusion Power," M. Wertheim, Grumman Aerospace Corporation (May 1980).

APPENDIX C

DEFINITIONS, STANDARDS, ABBREVIATIONS, AND UNITS

Definitions and Standards

Time Frames

Short-term	1980 to 1990
Mid-term	1990 to 2010
Long-term	2010 to 2050

Dollars

1980 dollars are used. Fuel costs given below are based on current fuel prices and the escalation rates specified below. Capital equipment is similarly escalated.

Economics

The economic analyses are performed on a levelized cost basis with the following ground rules for Industrial, Utility, and Government (real resource or public good financing) projects.

	Industry	Utility
Fixed charge rate (%)	20.6	16.4
Project lifetime (year)	20	30
Depreciation lifetime (year)	16	18.5
Depreciation method	SYD[a]	SYD
Debt to equity	30:70	53:47
Federal income tax (%)	46	46
State income tax (%)	3	3
Property income tax (%)	2.5	2.5
Insurance (%)	1	1
Investment tax credit	10	10
Return on investment (after tax) (%)	15	12
Interest on bonds (%)	9	9
Interest during construction (%)	12	8
Inflation rate (%)	6	6

[a]Sum-of-years digits.

Definitions and Standards (cont.)

Real Resource (or Public Good) Financing: FCR = 11.75% (20 years), 10.6% (30 years) (this is the capital recovery factor using a discount rate of 10%)

Escalation Rates

	Percentage
Construction	7.0
Operating costs	6.0
Oil	8.5
Gas	8.0
Coal	7.0
Electricity	6.6
Uranium	7.5

Levelizing Factors for Operating and Fuel costs
(corresponding to escalation rates and fixed charge rate ground rules)

	Industry	Utility	Real Resources (20 years)	Real Resources (30 years)
Operating costs	1.51	1.77	1.63	1.89
Oil	1.83	2.36	2.04	2.59
Gas	1.76	2.23	1.95	2.42
Coal	1.63	1.98	1.78	2.13
Electricity	1.58	1.89	1.72	2.03

Fuel	Costs (1980)	Higher heat value
High-sulfur eastern coal (mine mouth)	$31.82 t ($28.90 short ton)	25,560 kJ/kg (11,000 Btu/lb)
Low-sulfur western coal (mine mouth)	$15.32 t ($13.90 short ton)	22,770 kJ/kg (9,800 Btu/lb)
Oil	$30 bbl; $4.90 GJ ($4.65 10^6 Btu)	
Gas	$116 10^3 m^3 ($3.24/Mcf); $3.07/GJ ($3.24 10^6 Btu)	
Uranium	$106 kg ($48 lb)	

Conversion Factors

1 short ton (2000 lb) = 0.9 metric tons (t)
1 long ton (2200 lb) = 1.002 metric tons (t)
1 quad = 10^{15} Btu = 1.055×10^{18} J = 1.055 EJ
1 million barrels/day = 0.159×10^6 m^3/day
1 trillion cubic ft = 28.3×10^9 m^3
1 billion barrels = 0.159×10^9 m^3

ABBREVIATIONS

A/C:	Air Conditioning
ACEEE:	American Council for an Energy Efficient Economy
AEC:	Atomic Energy Commission
AFBC:	Atmospheric Fluidized Bed Combustor
AGA:	American Gas Association
CAFE:	Corporate Average Fuel Economy
CONAES:	Committee on Nuclear and Alternative Energy Systems
DOE:	Department of Energy
EDS:	Exxon Donor Solvent
EER:	Energy Efficiency Rating
EIA:	Energy Information Administration
EIS:	Environmental Impact Statement
EOR:	Enhanced Oil Recovery
EPA:	Environmental Protection Administration
ERA:	Economic Regulatory Administration
ERDA:	Energy Research and Development Administration
FBC:	Fluidized Bed Combustor
GDP:	Gross Domestic Product
GNP:	Gross National Product
IBG:	Intermediate-Btu Gas
IC:	Internal Combustion (Engine)
IGT:	Institute for Gas Technology
LBG:	Low-Btu Gas
LDC:	Less-Developed Country
LEAP:	Long-Term Energy Analysis Program
LEG:	Low Energy Gas
LNG:	Liquefied Natural Gas
LPG:	Liquid Petroleum Gas
LWR:	Light Water Reactor
MIS:	Modified in situ
MTG:	Methanol-to-Gasoline
NEPA:	National Environmental Policy Act
NEP-II:	National Energy Plan-II
O&M:	Operation and Maintenance
OCS:	Outer Continental Shelf
OPEC:	Organization of Petroleum Exporting Countries
ORNL:	Oak Ridge National Laboratory
OTA:	Office of Technology Assessment
OTEC:	Ocean Thermal Energy Conversion
R&D:	Research and Development

REUS: Rational Energy Use Study
ROI: Return on Investment
SASOL: South Africa's Synfuels Process
SERI: Solar Energy Research Institute
SNG: Synthetic Natural Gas
SRC: Solvent Refined Coal
SYD: Sum-of-Years-Digits
TVA: Tennessee Valley Authority
WEM: Welfare Equilibrium Model

UNITS

atm: atmosphere
bbl: barrel (42 U.S. gallons)
bble: barrel of oil equivalent (5.8 million Btu)
Btu: British thermal unit (1,055 joules)
°C: degrees Celsius
d: day
EJ: exajoules (10^{18} joules or 0.9479 quad or 163.4 million bble)
°F: degrees Farenheit
ft: foot (0.3048 metre)
ft²: square foot (0.0929 m²)
ft³: cubic foot (0.02832 m³)
gal: U.S. gallon (3.785 L)
GJ: gigajoules (10^9 joules)
GW(e):   gigawatt-electric
h: hour
J: joule (9.479×10^{-4} Btu)
K: degrees Kelvin
kJ: kilojoule (10^3 joules or 0.9479 Btu)
km: kilometer (10^3 metres)
               (0.62137 miles)
kg: kilogram (10^3 grams)
               (2.2046 lbs.)
kW(e):   kilowatt-electric
kWh: kilowatt-hour (3.6 MJ)
L: litre (0.2642 gallon)
lb: pound (0.4536 kg)
m: metre (3.281 ft)
m²: square metre (10.76 ft²)
m³: cubic metre (35.31 ft³)

million Btu: million British thermal units
Mcf: million cubic feet (10^6 ft^3 or 28,320 m^3)
million bbl: million barrels
million bbl/d: million barrels/d (2.234 EJ/year)
million tonnes: teragram (10^{12} grams)
mill: $0.001
MJ: megajoule (10^6 joules)
MPa: megapascal (9.869 atmospheres)
mpg: miles-per-gallon (0.4252 km/L)
MW(e):   megawatt-electric
billion tonnes: petagram (10^{15} grams)
quad: quadrillion Btu (10^{15} Btu or 1.055 EJ)
s: seconds
Tcf: trillion cubic feet (10^{12} ft^3 or 28.32 × 10^9 m^3)
ton: 2000 lbs. (short ton)
t: tonne = metric ton (1000 kg or 2204 lbs.)
TWh: terawatt-hour (10^{12} watt-hours)
W: watt (1 J/s)
year: 8760 hours